Westerns: Aspects of a Movie Genre
and
Westerns Revisited

'Philip French's study *Westerns* must be the definitive so far on that endlessly productive cinema genre.'

Margaret Hinxman, *The Sunday Telegraph*

'Mr French has done a dazzling job on a cinematic genre I find antipathetic and outmoded... a generally brilliant and enterprising series of shots at rehabilitating and *respectabilising* the Western.'

John Coleman, *New Statesman*

'A book about themes and trends, devoted, full of faith in the genre, full of faith in the continuing value of the Western. A newcomer to horse opera might think he compression too great for comfort. The addict will enjoy every page. Anyway I did.'

Dilys Powell, *The Sunday Times*

'His informal tour of the West actually succeeds not only in re-defining for us the general topography of the genre but in pointing out a number of interesting landmarks we hadn't noticed before... it provokes the reader to think through or expand for himself on arguments tossed succinctly into the air by the author'.

Nigel Andrews, *Financial Times*

'...an entertaining book, written with his customary wit and erudition... He wears his learning lightly and isn't afraid to bring politics and history relevantly in. It is a pleasure to read an expert film book which doesn't seem to have been written by a man who thinks the world stops when the house lights go on again.'

Gavin Millar, *The Listener*

PHILIP FRENCH was born in Liverpool in 1933. After serving with the Parachute Regiment in the Middle East he read law at Oxford, where he edited *The Isis*, and studied journalism at Indiana University. He was a senior producer for BBC radio from 1959 to 1990, and has been *The Observer*'s film critic since 1978. He has written regularly for numerous papers and magazines including the *Financial Times*, *London Magazine*, *The Times*, the *New Statesman*, *The Spectator* and *Sight & Sound*. His books as author or editor include *Age of Austerity 1945-51* (1963), *The Movie Moguls* (1969), *Three Honest Men: Edmund Wilson, F.R. Leavis, Lionel Trilling* (1980), *Malle on Malle* (1992), *The Faber Book of Movie Verse* (1993), *Wild Strawberries* (1995) and *Cult Movies* (1999). Philip French was a member of the jury at the 1986 Cannes Film Festival and a Booker Prize judge in 1988.

PHILIP FRENCH

Westerns
Aspects of a Movie Genre

and

Westerns Revisited

CARCANET

Westerns first published in Great Britain in 1973 by Secker & Warburg for the
British Film Institute. Revised edition published 1977. This edition, expanded
to include *Westerns Revisited*, first published in Great Britain in 2005 by
Carcanet Press Limited
Alliance House
Cross Street
Manchester M2 7AQ

A CIP catalogue record for this book is available from the British Library
ISBN 1 85754 747 0

The publisher is grateful for the support of Peter Thompson for the publication
of this book and other titles in the Carcanet film series.
The publisher acknowledges financial assistance from Arts Council England

Typeset by XL Publishing Services, Tiverton
Printed and bound in England by SRP Ltd, Exeter

I think nowadays, while literary men seem to have neglected their epic duties, the epic has been saved for us, strangely enough, by the westerns … has been saved for the world by of all places, Hollywood.

Jorge Luis Borges, The Paris Review, 1967

One of the most vapid and infantile forms of art ever conceived by the brain of a Hollywood movie producer.

Dwight Macdonald, The Miscellany, 1929

The XXth Congress had taken place, but there wasn't a line about the speech. It wasn't in any of the papers either, and by and by I realised that it had not been meant for us. Well: there were newspapers on sale two hundred yards beyond the border, next to wooden booths with all the rubber bands in the world, and tomatoes, and Hollywoood westerns that don't exist on our side either; the text of the speech was still around.

Uwe Johnson, Speculations About Jakob, 1959

The western remains, I suppose, America's distinctive contribution to the film.

Arthur Schlesinger Jr., Show, April 1963

What recent films have you found particularly stimulating?

'*The Searchers, Moby Dick, The Red Balloon* – and almost every film in which the heroes are white, the villains red and the United States cavalry gets there in time.'

The Rt. Hon. Peter Rawlinson, MP, replying to a questionnaire
in Sight and Sound, 1957

Other people, so I have read, treasure memorable moments in their lives: the time one climbed the Parthenon at sunrise, the summer night one met a lonely girl in Central Park and achieved with her a sweet and natural relationship, as they say in books. I too once met a girl in Central Park, but it is not much to remember. What I remember is the time John Wayne killed three men with a carbine as he was falling to the dusty street in *Stagecoach*, and the time the kitten found Orson Welles in the doorway in *The Third Man*.

Walker Percy, The Movie-goer, 1961

Acknowledgements

I am grateful to Penelope Houston, Tom Milne, James Price and David Wilson for their encouragement, patience and advice on the first edition of *Westerns*, and to Kersti French and Peter Thompson for urging me to produce this revised version. I am greatly endebted to Marja Walldén for her unstinting and generous IT support.

Parts of this book, in somewhat different form, have appeared in *The Times*, *Art in America*, the *New Statesman* and *The Observer*, and are reprinted by permission of their editors.

This book is dedicated to my late father, Jack French, who took me to my first western, and to Sean, Patrick and Karl, who saw their first westerns with me.

Contents

Preface

This book first appeared at the end of 1973. I was in my late thirties when I finished writing it, and there was a mere handful of studies of the western around at the time, most of them in French. Now there are a couple of rows of books as well as chapters in the numerous works on cinematic genres designed for use in schools and universities. Re-reading *Westerns* right through for the first time in over a quarter of a century at the age of 70 seems to confirm the old adage that the child is father to the man. It now seems like the work of someone from an earlier generation with whom I recognise some shared tastes and affinities. Inasmuch as the book is still of some value – which I think it is – then part of that worth resides in the fact that it belongs to and reflects a particular time and historical situation. That time, and I refer to it occasionally, was from 1963, when I began thinking of the western for an essay I never completed, to early 1977 when the revised edition was published. This was the period generally described now as the 60s but actually covering sixteen years, from the abbreviated presidency of Jack Kennedy to the election of Jimmy Carter. It was a violent, tempestuous era that encompassed the assassinations of Jack Kennedy, his brother Bobby and Martin Luther King; the Vietnam War; the rise of the counterculture; the destruction of Lyndon Johnson; the Watergate scandal and the disgrace of President Nixon, his Vice-President Spiro Agnew and many of their political associates. It was a time of political unrest and social divisiveness that seemed to threaten the future of the Republic.

I began the 1960s as an unreserved admirer of Jack Kennedy, and though reservations set in with the Bay of Pigs disaster, I wept at the news of his death and like most members of my generation I can remember with extraordinary clarity what I was doing that terrible day in Dallas. I respected Lyndon Johnson and was persuaded that he would rise to the challenges he faced domestically and internationally. As a result I supported him (producing several BBC radio talks that made out the case for his potential as a statesman), and until early in 1965 I thought, as a liberal anti-Communist, that his prosecution of the war in Vietnam was both

wise and just. In the spring of that year doubts arose and well
before the end of 1965 I was a firm opponent of the war. My
allegiances switched from the Washington political establishment to
the radical opposition among American students that had begun on
the University of California's Berkeley campus. This new and
hopeful attitude seemed to be bringing together the dormant post-
war demands for social change re-awakened by Kennedy, the Civil
Rights Movement, the opposition to what Dwight Eisenhower in
one of his last presidential speeches had named, and cautioned
against, as 'the military–industrial complex', and a crudely con-
frontational approach to the Cold War. In the autumn of that year
I spent five weeks in America on a BBC assignment – in New York,
California and Texas – and, at a time when small-talk was in
abeyance, found people talking of nothing but politics and social
change.

My feelings about the United States became extremely confused
and I worked on this book for a couple of years thinking I wasn't
getting anywhere, unable to pin things down. Eventually in order
to fulfil an obligation to *The Times* on which I was about to renege,
I offered the chapter on politics and the western, which only existed
in draft form. It was published in 1971 as a 'work in progress' in *The
Times* and attracted some attention. In the following week the head
of the Department of Comparative Studies at the University of
Texas, Don Weissman, phoned me from Italy where he was
enjoying a sabbatical, and invited me to be a visiting professor at
Austin the next year (coals to Newcastle, steers to Texas). Two days
later the editor of *Art in America*, Brian Doherty, who had also read
the piece, asked me to write an article on the Indian in the western
for a special edition of his magazine on the culture of what we now
call Native Americans. I suddenly realised that what I was engaged
in was of interest on both sides of the Atlantic and that in writing
about the western I was clarifying my life-long feelings about the
United States.

For these reasons *Westerns* seems located in its time, and I've
decided to change nothing in the original text of 1973 or in the
Afterword that accompanied the revised edition in 1977. In a long,
appreciative and appreciated review of the augmented version in
Sydvenska Dagbladet, the paper's witty critic observed that if every
three years I added the same amount of new material, by the turn-
of-the-century a 170-page monograph would have swelled to 420
pages. However in the years immediately following his piece there

did not seem to be an urgent need for major additions, and indeed there was a widespread feeling that the box-office calamity and critical failure of *Heaven's Gate* in 1980 had dealt the genre the *coup de grâce* and dispatched it to Boot Hill for good. This has happily not proved to be the case, and the further reflections I've added as *Westerns Revisited* deal with some trends, changes and developments that continue into the new century.

The circumstances in which movies were seen and experienced have changed radically since I wrote *Westerns*, a matter I touch on in the penultimate paragraph of my 1973 text, though I had no idea just how profound this change would be. There were no VHS cassettes then or DVDs (I now get more than a dozen review copies a week, and several times these past couple of years I've received ten westerns in a single package). There was no colour television until 1970 and then only on BBC2 (I couldn't afford a colour set until 1978), relatively few movies on TV, and only one person of my acquaintance owned a 16mm projector. Until 1970 the National Film Theatre had a single auditorium, and it was extremely rare for westerns to be shown there. Except for some private screenings laid on for me by the British Film Institute in their small viewing theatre (most of which I attended with Jim Kitses, then working for the BFI and like me writing a book for the BFI's 'Cinema One' series), I saw the movies I wrote about in cinemas. At that time westerns were largely to be found in independent suburban movie houses that specialised in revivals or more recent movies that had either completed their major commercial distribution or been rejected by the major circuits. These places, often out of the way, insalubrious and poorly maintained, had three changes of programme a week (on Sunday, Monday and Thursday) and showed films in continuous performances, the general practice in those days at most cinemas except for the occasional blockbusters that were given separate, bookable screenings. This led to a more casual form of movie going and to the now historic expression 'this is where we came in'. At these small movie houses (and indeed in suburban cinemas generally) movies of average duration were customarily shown in double-bills. The western was most often found on the lower half, and the prints were frequently in indifferent or bad condition. It was necessary to take a close look each week at the guide *What's On?* in order to catch a rare Budd Boetticher film that might be showing just on Sunday at the Essoldo, East India Dock Road, or an Anthony Mann film at the Tolmer off the Euston Road near Warren Street

Station, which sadly closed in 1972 when still charging half-a-crown (i.e. 12½ new pence) for the best seats. The continuous performances meant that students could see a film twice in a day and the cheapness allowed them to make several visits.

But a movie could disappear for years or for good. For instance, I was driving out of Santa Fe one morning in 1972 and passed a cinema showing a Monte Hellman double bill of *The Shooting* and *Ride in the Whirlwind*. The former had finally been shown in Britain in 1971, but the latter never got into cinemas here, and nearly a decade passed before I got to see it. All we had to rely on then were our memories and a few notes made in the dark (which often excited the suspicions of other patrons in the way their forebears distrusted Professor Henry Higgins as a police spy). Memory, of course, could play strange tricks and movies shown and re-shown in the mind could grow and take on enlarged and distorted forms. Or, in the case of westerns, merge into one gigantic frontier picture. In writing the additional material for this new edition I did not have to walk down memory lane in retrieval mode. I just went into the room I have put aside for the thousands of VHS and DVD versions of movies that have accumulated these past twenty-odd years. It's sad really. Mr Memory in Hitchcock's *The 39 Steps* wouldn't have to die now for the vital information stored in his mind. It would have been sent abroad by email. Incidentally, I've mentioned Hitchcock only once in this book, for his visit to the West in *Saboteur*, where in crossing the continent the innocent fugitive played by Robert Cummings visits a ghost town. I should of course have mentioned his later excursion into the West in *North by Northwest* (1959) featuring Cary Grant's cliff-hanging scene in South Dakota, as well as the fact that Hitchcock's next movie, *Psycho* (1960), opens in Arizona, and that the Master's signature appearance has him wearing a Stetson in the streets of Phoenix.

Philip French
2005

PART ONE

Westerns
(1973; 1977)

Introduction (1973)

T his ruminative monograph is neither another defence of the western nor a further attack upon it. My aim, I suppose, is to share with the sympathetic reader some of the reflections on the genre that I've had after thirty-odd years of moviegoing. The brevity demanded by the format of the 'Cinema One' series, and my resolve to concentrate upon areas where I feel I have something moderately original to say, have resulted in some fields of possible inquiry being ignored.

My concern here is entirely with American theatrical westerns, mostly those made since 1950. The explanation for this decision is simple. First, I dislike TV horse operas (though a deal of what I say about screen westerns applies to them too). Westerns need a large screen and are best enjoyed in the company of a thoughtful and occasionally noisy audience. Secondly, I cannot abide European westerns, whether German, Italian or British, and I don't much like American westerns filmed in Spain.[1] Thirdly, while many of my favourite pictures were made before the coming of sound, I have never cared for silent westerns. Cowboy pictures need the pounding of hooves, the crack of Winchesters, the hiss of arrows, the stylised, laconic dialogue (which looks so terrible on paper, but is in fact the only consistently satisfactory period speech that the movies – or for that matter contemporary dramatic literature – have found), and the music, which if rightly used can give a picture the quality of a folk song. There are anyway several books – Fenin and Everson's, Charles Ford's, Jean-Louis Rieupeyrout's – which trace the genre's history from the turn of the century to the 1960s, and combine with it a quantity of frontier history (in the case of Rieupeyrout's book, a great deal).

---

1   There's a body of opinion which would argue that this disqualifies me as a true student of the genre. So be it. In fairness, therefore, I should direct the reader to the August 1970 double issue of *Cinema* (nos 6 and 7) which contains a concordance of the Italian western by Mike Wallington and a study of the Italian western by Chris Frayling. The July 1971 issue of *Films and Filming* has an article by David Austen on Continental westerns and a filmography of 155 of them, which to me reads like a brochure for a season in hell.

Partly through ignorance, partly through inclination, I do not belong to any particular school of criticism. Those versed in psycho-analysis could have, indeed have had, a field day with the western, but in considering the central significance of, say, gunplay, I am reminded of Freud's comment that 'sometimes a cigar is just a cigar'. There is, I am sure, a consistent Marxist interpretation of the western, and I am aware that a good many structuralists currently find it fruitful to operate at a point where the apparatus of Lévi-Strauss and company of Paris impinges upon the apparel of Levi Strauss and Co. of San Francisco. Readers will find little reflection of this here, nor will they be regaled with a Leavisian Great Tradition of the horse opera. My approach is largely a social, aesthetic and moral one.

For reasons of space, because I am dealing with general tenden-cies and characteristics of the genre, and as there already exist numerous studies in French and English of single movies and the leading filmmakers' oevres, there are no detailed discussions here of individual pictures and directors. Moreover, some indifferent films may seem to have been mentioned or given disproportionate atten-tion when far superior ones are ignored or scarcely touched on. So to indicate where I stand, let me say that I think the best western ever made is the 1939 version of *Stagecoach*; that my favourite direc-tors in the genre are John Ford (whose best movies perhaps are non-westerns) and Anthony Mann (none of whose works outside the genre is particularly distinguished); and that, to show the catholicity and orthodoxy of my taste, my favourite twenty post-war westerns (limiting myself to a single film per director) are, in chronological order: Howard Hawks' *Red River* (1948), John Ford's *Wagonmaster* (1950), Fred Zinnemann's *High Noon* (1952), George Stevens' *Shane* (1953), Robert Aldrich's *Vera Cruz* (1954), Charles Haas' *Star in the Dust* (1956), Samuel Fuller's *Run of the Arrow* (1956), Delmer Daves' *3.10 to Yuma* (1957), Anthony Mann's *Man of the West* (1958), John Sturges' *The Law and Jake Wade* (1958), Arthur Penn's *The Left Handed Gun* (1958), Budd Boetticher's *Ride Lonesome* (1959), Don Siegel's *Flaming Star* (1960), Marlon Brando's *One-Eyed Jacks* (1961), Sam Peckinpah's *Guns in the Afternoon* (1962), Gordon Douglas' *Rio Conchos* (1964), Henry Hathaway's *The Sons of Katie Elder* (1965), Martin Ritt's *Hombre* (1966), Robert Mulligan's *The Stalking Moon* (1968) and William Fraker's *Monte Walsh* (1970).

1 Politics, etc. and the Western

Hardly anyone alive can remember a time when there weren't western movies. One of those who could was G.M. 'Broncho Billy' Anderson, star of Edwin S. Porter's *The Great Train Robbery* in 1903, and founder (with George Spoor) of Porter's Essanay Company, pre-World War I specialists in cowboy pictures, and he died early in 1971 at the age of 88. Despite the temporary competition of gangster films, science fiction and spy movies, the western continues to thrive, the subject of abuse, sometimes justified, sometimes not, but increasingly a matter for serious critical attention, some of it useful, some of it exceedingly heavy-handed.

There are two things that every schoolboy knows about the genre. First, that the western is a commercial formula with rules as fixed and immutable as the Kabuki Theatre. Second, that the events depicted have little to do with the real nineteenth-century American frontier life, that the rituals are enacted in a timeless world where it is always high noon in some dusty cow town west of St. Louis. Rather like, in fact, the Never Land of Barrie's *Peter Pan*, populated by children who refuse to grow up, fugitives from the urban nursery, marauding Indians and menacing bands of pirates.

Like most things that schoolboys so confidently know, neither of these simple contentions is wholly true, and there is general agreement that for better or worse the western has changed significantly since World War II, becoming more varied, complex and self-conscious. We now have little difficulty in identifying the reasons for this change. There was the House Un-American Activities Committee's investigation of Hollywood in the 40s and 50s, which caused the film industry to lose its nerve and look for safe subjects or a framework in which controversial issues could be handled in less obviously contentious fashion. There were the two generations that had passed since the official closing of the frontier by the US Census Bureau, two generations reared on cowboy pictures. Television gradually siphoned off the routine B-feature western, compelling the makers of movies for theatrical distribution to innovate. The introduction of wide screen formats in the early 1950s immediately benefited the western movies while initially posing problems for other subjects. The increasing availability of better, cheaper colour processes also favoured the western. Then there was the steady decline of censorship until, with the replacement of the Hollywood production code by a series of guidelines in 1968, it virtually ceased to exist. All these factors have played their part.

In 1946, C.A. Lejeune in *The Observer* took the producers of *The Virginian* to task for attempting a more sophisticated approach to the genre: 'It is the greatest mistake to suppose that people want novelty in their cowboy pictures.' By 1950, Dilys Powell in the *Sunday Times* was able to write, with mild disapproval, of *The Gunfighter* as being made 'in the current intellectual, Western style'.

Of course there had been westerns before which had dealt in a serious, responsible and often fairly complex way with adult themes, tragic situations and important aspects of the frontier experience. These films were exceptional, however, and regarded as such, and very few of them can be viewed today without a good deal of indulgence. What I am talking about here is a major transformation which took place over a relatively short period, and which, in my view, revitalised the genre and opened up new possibilities which might be described as boundless were it not that one recognises certain inherent limitations in the form.

In retrospect we can see those post-war years, which gave us John Ford's *My Darling Clementine* (1946) and his so-called cavalry trilogy (*Fort Apache, She Wore a Yellow Ribbon, Rio Grande*), King Vidor's *Duel in the Sun* (1946) and Howard Hawks' *Red River* (1948), as leading to the watershed year of 1950 when, in a mere four months, Hollywood released Delmer Daves' first western, *Broken Arrow*, Anthony Mann's first two cowboy movies, *Devil's Doorway* and *Winchester '73*, Ford's thoughtful *Wagonmaster* and Henry King's *The Gunfighter*. One French critic has even referred to 1950 as being 'a little like the 1789 of the genre's history'. Shortly after, there came a stream of new-style westerns, including the two immediately acclaimed instant 'classics'; Fred Zinnemann's *High Noon* (1952) and George Stevens' *Shane* (1953), both by distinguished directors who were new to the genre and never returned to it.

In 1949 there was only a single important box-office star whose name was associated principally with the western and that was John Wayne, and only a single major director, John Ford, and he had only directed five westerns in the sound era, four of them starring Wayne. Up to the early 1950s there were separate industry polls for the 'Top Ten Box Office Stars' and the 'Top Ten Western Stars' (the latter reserved for low-budget performers), as if they were different sides of the business. All this was to change. Westerns began to attract the best acting talent, the most skilled writers and accomplished directors, not just for occasional forays but regularly and with decreasing condescension. Critical attitudes, however, did not change overnight. Individual westerns marked by a manifest seriousness or an obvious contempt for the routine were admired or attacked less on their merits than according to the critics' view of what a western should be. Meanwhile, in the English-speaking world at least, the two most notable bodies of work from the 1950s – the westerns of Anthony Mann and Budd Boetticher – went almost unnoticed, to be resurrected in the 1960s after Mann had turned his attention to epics and Boetticher had retired to Mexico to make a documentary about bullfighting.

The sense of unease in the presence of the western that still existed in the 1950s is well caught by Truman Capote in his *New Yorker* profile of Marlon Brando. Capote visited Brando in Kyoto, where he was filming *Sayonara*. Discussing his future the star observed:

> Movies do have a great potential. You can say important things to a lot of people. I want to make pictures that explore the themes current in the world today. That's why I've started my own independent company.

Capote asked about the company's first picture, on the script of which Brando was then labouring.

> And did *A Burst of Vermilion* satisfy him as a basis for the kind of lofty aims he proposed?
> He mumbled something. Then he mumbled something else. Asked to speak more clearly, he said 'It's a Western.'
> He was unable to restrain a smile, which expanded into laughter. He rolled on the floor and roared. 'Christ, the only thing is, will I ever be able to look my friends in the face again.' Sobering somewhat, he said, 'Seriously, though, the first picture *has* to make money. Otherwise there won't be another, I'm nearly broke…

A little later Brando returned to the subject.

> 'But seriously though,' said Brando, now excessively sober, '*Burst* isn't just cowboys-and-Indians stuff. It's about this Mexican boy

– hatred and discrimination. What happens to a community when
these things exist.'[2]

A Burst of Vermilion eventually reached the screen some five years
later as *One-Eyed Jacks*, directed by Brando himself when Stanley
Kubrick departed after a couple of days' shooting. The film was no
laughing matter, and Brando has less reason to be ashamed of it than
he has for many of his pictures since *On the Waterfront*.

In 1961, *One-Eyed Jacks* accorded with a new pattern which had
developed in the western. Some brooding, over-indulgent
sequences, a strong undertone of masochism – these could be, and
were, attributed to Brando's direction. But in viewing this study of
the relationship between two former friends – one who retained his
integrity as an outlaw, the other who revealed his weakness and
hypocrisy through taking a job as lawman in a settled community
– no one thought the elaborately detailed characterisation, the carefully worked out symbolism of cards and bullets, the loving creation
of mood and the situating of people in the landscape, the atmosphere of dark pessimism and the suggestion of homosexuality,
particularly new or remarkable. And anyway the film's considerable
length was punctuated by set-pieces – a bank robbery, two jail breaks
and several gunfights – which were exemplarily staged enactments
of familiar events.

Clearly a certain innocence had been lost: the children had got
hold of Dr Spock and the nursery would never be the same again.
A Catch-22 situation developed in which the charge of *fausse naïveté*
could be brought against those who attempted to recapture a lost
simplicity, while the too knowing or ambitious would be accused
– not always unjustly – of being pretentious, decadent over-reachers.
Nevertheless, moviegoers and filmmakers alike have continued to
carry in their minds a firm notion of the archetypal western where
everything goes according to a series of happily anticipated moral
and dramatic conventions – or clichés. Perhaps there was a time
when this was so, though it is certainly no longer true. What created
this feeling (and has sustained it) is the way in which westerns good,
bad and indifferent have always tended to coalesce in the memory
into one vast, repetitive movie with a succession of muddled brawls
in bar-rooms, tense and inscrutable poker games in smoky saloons,

2 'The Duke in His Domain', *Selected Writings of Truman Capote* (Hamish
Hamilton, London, 1963), pp. 417–18.

gunfights in empty streets, showdowns among the rocks with whining bullets, cavalry pursuits and Indian ambushes, mysterious strangers riding into town in search of vengeance or redemption, knights errant galloping to the relief of the oppressed. This simple image of the 'traditional western' provides the moviemaker with a model upon which to ring variations and the audience with a yard-stick by which to judge the latest product.

The late Frank Gruber, a prolific author of western screenplays and novels, is responsible for the widely quoted dictum that there are only seven basic westerns: the railway story, the ranch story, the cattle empire story (which is the ranch story epically rendered), the revenge story, the cavalry versus Indians story, the outlaw story, and the marshal or 'law and order' story. While it is true that the vast majority of cowboy movies can be accommodated within these pigeonholes, Gruber's Law would tell us little about the tone or character of any individual picture so deposited. For this reason a form of critical shorthand has grown up over the years which testi-fies to the problems writers have faced in indicating the kind of cowboy movie they are talking about. An incomplete list, which at least suggests some of the apparent variety within the genre, would include: epic western, sur-western (or super-western – a French coinage to describe large-scale works which betray the genre's essential simplicity), adult western, satirical western, comedy western, chamber western, liberal western, sociological western, realistic western, anti-western, psychological western, allegorical western and, most recently, spaghetti western (seized on by TV commercial makers to sell spaghetti hoops) and paella western.

These are epithets to pin down the character of a movie. A further set of terms exists to locate, in time and space, action movies that resemble cowboy pictures but cannot strictly be regarded as west-erns. At one end of the time scale there is the 'pre-western' which deals with the coonskin-capped frontiersman armed with a flintlock musket and travelling by foot in the late eighteenth-early nineteenth century, the Fenimore Cooper Leather-Stocking figure. At the end of the first half of *The Alamo* (1960), John Wayne as Davy Crockett abandons his coonskin cap and appears on the mission battlements wearing a black Stetson to join his fellow heroes in a monumental grouping and stare out stoically at Santa Anna's Mexican force. The siege of the Alamo was in 1836, and marking as it does the death of two of the last legendary frontiersmen and the beginning of Texan independence from Mexico, we can regard this as a reasonable starting date for the genre, though in fact there are relatively few westerns with pre-Civil War settings.

At the other end of the time scale is the 'modern western' or 'post-western', set in the present-day West where lawmen, rodeo riders and Cadillac-driving ranchers are still in thrall to the frontier myth. Halfway between them is the Civil War movie, essentially the product of an established society: the Eastern terrain with its carefully cultivated land and lovingly tended hedgerows, its Southern plantations and a sun casting a more tolerant or seemingly benevolent light, creates an ambience, a psychological landscape quite alien to the western proper.

The best Civil War pictures have been modestly conceived productions situated in the margin of the conflict, usually directing us away from the more divisive central issues raised somewhat ambivalently in Michael Curtiz's *Santa Fe Trail* (1940), which concludes with the hanging of John Brown, and most controversially by Griffith's *The Birth of a Nation*. One thinks of Ford's *The Horse Soldiers* (1959), Huston's *The Red Badge of Courage* (1951), the Sanders Brothers' *Time Out of War* (1954), Hugo Fregonese's *The Raid* (1954; a superb little movie about a group of escaped Southern PoWs who infiltrate a Vermont town from Canada, which inspired John Arden's *Serjeant Musgrave's Dance*), and Anthony Mann's *The Tall Target* (1951; a thriller concerning the frustration of a plot to assassinate Lincoln on a Washington-bound train on the eve of the war).

Several important westerns have the Civil War as a backdrop. A recurrent situation is the Western fort manned by misfits and commanded by martinets who can be spared from the war (*The Last Frontier, Company of Cowards*), or the conflict between Union soldiers and their Confederate prisoners in Western outposts (*Two Flags West, Major Dundee, Escape from Fort Bravo*, and most uncompromisingly *The Long Ride Home*, where unusually for this sub-species no possibility of reconciliation is suggested). Equally a great number of westerns, perhaps the majority, taking place in the unceasing ripples of the war's aftermath, turn to the war as a source of character definition and motivation: Southerners drifting West to work as cowhands, ex-members of Colonel Charles Quantrill's guerrilla band turning to civilian outlawry, wartime treacheries to be revenged (*The Deadly Companions, Rio Lobo*) and so on. Tensions in the West on the eve of the Civil War have attracted relatively few filmmakers, though 'bleeding Kansas' is dealt with gingerly in

Santa Fe Trail and in Melvin Frank's *The Jayhawkers* (a confused 1959 account of the Kansas insurrectionist movement).

Then there are the so-called 'easterns', Japanese or Russian movies which resemble horse operas, and what are sometimes called 'para-westerns' – tales of the Foreign Legion and medieval knights which are cowboy pictures in different garb – or stories set in Australia or South Africa which attempt to celebrate pioneer life there in a style clearly influenced by the American model.

The western is not merely a cinematic form, but relates to a much larger international set of attitudes and beliefs, ranging from the symbolic status conferred on 'the West' from the dawn of civilisation, through everyone's ambivalent feelings about American culture, to the need for American politicians to define their public posture in relation to a national mythology. The notion that America was uniquely shaped by the frontier experience, though common currency for two centuries, was given its most eloquent and compelling form in the essays and speeches of the Wisconsin historian Frederick Jackson Turner, beginning with his celebrated 1893 address to the American Historical Association on 'The Significance of the Frontier in American History'. The existence of an area of free land, its continual recession, and the advance of American settlement westward explain American development, Turner asserted. And he went on to claim:

> The result is that to the frontier the American intellect owes its striking characteristics. The coarseness and strength combined with acuteness and inquisitiveness; that practical, inventive turn of mind, quick to find expedients; that masterful grasp of material things, lacking in the artistic but powerful to effect great ends; that restless nervous energy; that dominant individualism, working for good and for evil, and withal that buoyancy and exuberance which comes from freedom – these are traits of the frontier or traits that are called out elsewhere because of the existence of the frontier.[3]

In highly charged language of a kind that has continued to be part

3 Reprinted in *Frontier and Section, Selected Essays by Frederick Jackson Turner* (Prentice-Hall, Spectrum Books, Englewood Cliffs, New Jersey, 1961), with introduction and notes by Turner's leading present-day follower Ray Allen Billington. There is an excellent account of Turner's life, ideas and influence in Richard Hofstadter's *The Progressive Historians* (Jonathan Cape, London, 1969).

of the obligatory rhetoric of America's politicians, though only rarely of her scholars, Turner put forward his heady thesis at the very time that the Western experience was coming to an end – three years after the Superintendent of the Census had announced that the frontier 'can not any longer have a place in the census reports', three years after the last desperate Indians – for whose fate Turner's address evinced little regret – were massacred at Wounded Knee.

There is no theme you cannot examine in terms of the western, no situation which cannot be transposed to the West, whether it be the Trojan War turned into a Texas range conflict (Harry Brown's novel *The Stars in Their Courses*, a pretentious work which has Philoctetes as Phil Tate, the ace gunslinger nursing an incurable wound down Mexico way, Odysseus as the rancher Oliver Swindon who heads out for the territory when the fighting is over, and so on) or *King Lear* as a prairie land baron (the late Anthony Mann's final, unrealised project). An Italian company has made a frontier version of *Hamlet* (*Johnny Amleto*), and Delmer Daves' *Jubal* (1956) appears to be based on *Othello*, with an Iago-like cowhand (Rod Steiger) arousing the jealousy of the ugly ranch boss (Ernest Borgnine) when the job of foreman goes to his younger rival (Glenn Ford).

The gangster movies *Kiss of Death* and *The Asphalt Jungle* become the cowboy pictures *The Fiend that Walked the West* and *The Badlanders*; the social melodrama *House of Strangers* (about a patriarchal Italian family in New York) becomes in *Broken Lance* a tale of a Texas rancher and his brood. Raoul Walsh's *Distant Drums* (1951) bears a striking resemblance to his war movie *Objective Burma* (1944), with Seminole Indians standing in for Japanese, boats for planes; rather more remotely, the William Holden western vehicle *Alvarez Kelly* (1967) looks like an attempt to extract the salient dramatic and thematic qualities from Holden's biggest success, *The Bridge on the River Kwai*, and relocate them in the American Civil War. A child could tell (and indeed a TV-watching child did tell me) that Kurt Neumann's *Cattle Drive* (1951) is virtually a dry-land version of Kipling's *Captains Courageous*, with Joel McCrea as a trail boss taming the spoilt upper-class brat Dean Stockwell, just as earlier Spencer Tracy's Grand Banks fisherman had performed a similar service for Freddie Bartholomew. Akira Kurosawa's two greatest international successes, *Rashomon* and *The Seven Samurai*, were both bought up by Hollywood as the bases for the westerns *The Outrage* (1964) and *The Magnificent Seven* (1960), while his later *Yojimbo*, which Kurosawa admits was influenced by *High Noon* and *Shane*, was plagiarised for the first spaghetti western to receive wide international distribution, Sergio Leone's *A Fistful of Dollars*.

The western is a great grab-bag, a hungry cuckoo of a genre, a voracious bastard of a form, open equally to visionaries and opportunists, ready to seize anything that's in the air from juvenile delinquency to ecology. Yet despite this, or in some ways because of it, one of the things the western is always about is America rewriting and reinterpreting her own past, however honestly or dishonestly it may be done. The inadequacy of the western is less my immediate concern here than its power or persuasiveness. Take any subject and drop it down west of the Mississippi, south of the 49th Parallel and north of the Rio Grande between 1840 and World War I, throw in a mandatory quantity of violent incidents, and you have not only a viable commercial product but a new and disarmingly fresh perspective on it. Such at least is the hope and intention.

Consequently I would like to propose a way of looking at the western over the past twenty years through a series of simple categories, which recognises the diverse factors working upon it. The system depends upon making connections between the style, tone and content of movies and the rhetoric, beliefs and public personae of four prominent politicians. So it might be useful to preface my thesis by pointing to the association between two American artists and a leading statesman which throws some light on this question.

They were three Ivy League friends: the Yale Art School dropout Frederic Remington, the Harvard graduate Theodore Roosevelt and the other Harvard alumnus, Owen Wister. They were all well-born Easterners who went West in the late nineteenth century – Wister for his health and Roosevelt and Remington as ranchers, an activity at which both failed. Having tasted the painful reality of prairie life, they proceeded to help shape the visual, ideological and literary myth of the West that has come down to us. In doing so the trio can be regarded as having exerted an influence quite as powerful as the dime novels and stage melodramas from which the western movie sprang at the turn of the century. Because people took their words and images seriously.

As painter and sculptor, Remington became the most popular non-photographic recorder of the vanishing West as well as a notable illustrator and war correspondent; his work adorned Lyndon Johnson's White House and he has influenced the visual style of numerous 'realistic' westerns of recent years – his paintings are used behind the credit titles of Richard Brooks' *The Last Hunt* (1956), and whole sequences of *The Culpepper Cattle Company* (1972) and *Monte Walsh* (1970) look like animated Remingtons. The latter has credit titles based on paintings by another closely associated Western artist, Charles B. Russell.[4] When Peter Bogdanovich[5] asked John Ford 'Which of your cavalry pictures are you most pleased with?' the director replied:

> I like *She Wore a Yellow Ribbon*. I tried to copy the Remington style there – you can't copy him one hundred per cent – but at least I tried to get his colour and movement, and I think I succeeded partly.

The politician-adventurer Theodore Roosevelt was in the American tradition of the intellectual as a man-of-action. He wrote widely and romantically of life on the plains, produced a four-volume, White Anglo-Saxon Protestant interpretation of America's continental expansion, *The Winning of the West*, became a military hero, President of the United States and played a significant part in taking American into World War I.

With *The Virginian*, Owen Wister, literary protégé of Henry James, rose above the dime novel fiction of the day and wrote what is, for all its shortcomings, the first major Western novel. It was illustrated by Remington in one edition, by Charles Russell in another, and dedicated to Roosevelt on first publication in 1902; in 1911 it was rededicated 'to the greatest benefactor we people have known since Lincoln', in a prefatory note which hits out at both Wall Street and the emerging trade unions.

The best-known phrase from *The Virginian* – now a western

---

4 There is a stimulating article, 'Painters of the Purple Sage', by Harris Rosenstein in *Art News* (Summer, 1968) on the association of Remington, Wister and Roosevelt. Reviewing an exhibition of work by Remington and Russell called 'How the West Was Won', Rosenstein takes a fairly charitable view of the latter and a very scathing one of the former: 'There is... about Remington, most especially in his deadpan skillfulness, and aura of depressive guilty knowledge, the sense of an inner life not bottled up but atrophied by involvements that looked real but never were. In a way, cinematic virtuosity in the Western owes something to Remington in that by such ultimately irrelevant commitments as he had, he managed to dehumanise and sterilise the iconography. What he does is to kill the man but leave the dapperness, and with dapper dummies we have the props for a ventriloqual act.'

5 *John Ford* (Studio Vista, London, 1967), p. 87.

cliché but one which long preceded the coming of sound – is the hero's tight-lipped, 'When you call me that, smile.' The fictional provenance of the phrase is less well known and worth noting. Early in the book, the Virginian is called a son-of-a-bitch (though Wister cannot bring himself to write the term) and takes it in good part as an affectionate remark by a friend. Later, during a poker game, the villainous Trampas uses the same words, but this time the Virginian, as becomes an eminent Victorian, is not amused. The naïve Eastern narrator observes:

> Something had been added to my knowledge also. Once again I had heard applied to the Virginian that epithet that Steve so freely used. The same words, identical to the letter. But this time they had produced a pistol. 'When you call me that, *smile!*' So I perceived a new example of the letter that means nothing until the spirit gives it life.

My thesis turns on the names of four numinous figures who emerged in the early 1950s. The first pair are John F. Kennedy and Barry Goldwater, respectively the spokesmen for the New Frontier and the Old Frontier, who were both freshman senators in 1953. The second pair are Lyndon Johnson, who became Senate majority leader during President Eisenhower's first term, and William Buckley, whose *God and Man at Yale* and *McCarthy and his Enemies* established him in the same period as the most articulate representative of the New Conservatism.

In the 1964 presidential election, America was faced with a choice between two self-conscious Westerners, both sons of pioneer families – Johnson from Texas and Goldwater from Arizona. One was a Democrat who originally entered politics in the populist tradition which his political grandfather and father adhered to (though his own career was to take him ever further away from this, with tragic results); the other is a right-wing Republican and proponent of rugged individualism. Campaigning for office, Johnson claimed that he would avoid the rash, violent courses of action which Goldwater's foreign policy threatened. A sadly depopulated Texas township is named after one of Johnson's forebears and a rather grand ranch carries his initials or brand; several Arizona department stores bear the anglicised name of Goldwater's grandfather. The Easterners Kennedy and Buckley were both educated at Ivy League universities, came from rich Catholic families dominated by determined patriarchs, and gained an early reputation for style and wit;

one was a liberal Democrat, the other is an extreme Conservative. Kennedy made his 1960 ticket secure by taking on LBJ as his vice-presidential running partner to get the Southern and Southwestern vote. Buckley once conducted an elegant losing campaign in 1965 for Mayor of New York against the progressive John Lindsay, and when asked what he would do if he were elected, answered quick as a flash, 'I'd demand a recount.'

The principal stylistic features of a typical Kennedy western might be defined thus: the overall treatment would be taut and fast-driving; its rhetoric would be elegant, ironic, laced with wit; pictorially the images would be carefully composed, bringing out the harsh challenge of the landscape; its moral tone would be sharp and penetrating; its mood would be cool with an underlying note of the absurd or tragic sense of life; the past would be rendered in a moderately realistic fashion, almost without regret, just a token elegiacism. The overall style of the typical Goldwater western would be slack and expansive; its rhetoric would be sententious, broadly humorous, woolly; its visual surface would involve a casual acceptance of the landscape; the moral tone would be generous but ultimately unforgiving, riding on a knife-edge between cruelty and sentimentality; its mood would be warmly nostalgic.

The content of the Kennedy western would tend to feature the following ingredients: a slightly diffident hero, capable of change and development, with a rather unostentatious professionalism, though prone to a sense of anguished failure; there would be an accent on the need for community activity; minorities and aliens would be viewed sympathetically, compassionately; opposition would be expressed to the notion that man is essentially or necessarily violent; there would be an implication that one should look to the past for guidance towards the creation of a new and better condition in the future; the underlying argument would favour a wry optimism about the future development of society.

The content of the Goldwater western on the other hand, in its extreme form, would tend to reflect almost the opposite of these elements: the hero would be resolute, unswerving, rocklike in his own virtue and image of himself; emphasis would fall on individualism, self-help, the inevitability of inequality; it would see aggression as a natural aspect of man, and violence as unavoidable and perhaps to be enjoyed, certainly to be anticipated; a suspicious or somewhat patronising attitude would be shown to aliens and minorities; the general feeling would be that one should look to the past to find an ideal of behaviour and to discover how society should be organised; the underlying emphasis would support a guarded pessimism with an opposition to change unless it meant a possibility of moving back and regaining a golden age in the past.

The interplay between the Kennedy content and the Kennedy style produces the Kennedy western; similarly for the Goldwater western. However, if you treat the Kennedy content with the Goldwater style you get the Johnson western, and if you apply the Kennedy style to the Goldwater content you get the Buckley western. Inevitably, style transforms content and content modifies style, and this indeed is part of my argument; one corollary of which is that a filmmaker is more likely to swing between Goldwater and Johnson westerns or between Kennedy and Buckley movies than between the alternative pairings, despite the obvious ideological affinities.

Thus John Ford's westerns since the late 1940s fall into the Goldwater or Johnson categories: *The Searchers* (1956) is clearly a Goldwater picture, while *Two Rode Together* (1961), which is virtually a reprise of the same subject (two men looking for pioneers captured by Indians), is probably a Johnson western, as more obviously is the later *Cheyenne Autumn* (1964). All of Anthony Mann's films of the 1950s are Kennedy westerns (except for his final masterpiece, *Man of the West*, written by the liberal television playwright Reginald Rose: a real Buckley movie, whereas Mann's Kennedy films were scripted by the ultra-right-wing Borden Chase). So are the films of Delmer Daves. But Budd Boetticher's films, with their close stylistic affinities, are Buckley movies. A striking example of a McCarthy-period Buckley western would be Charles Marquis Warren's *Arrowhead* of 1953.

On another level one would note that John Wayne's *The Alamo* (1960) was a Goldwater western, which under the guise of saying 'better Tex than Mex' was actually affirming 'better dead than Red', with rhetorical material about the Republic of Texas (as opposed to American democracy) seemingly drawn from the Blue Book of the John Birch Society. But *The Alamo* was a Goldwater western at the time when the junior senator from Arizona was in the wilderness. In 1964, when Goldwater was shaping up as the Republican Party's presidential candidate, Wayne came out with *McClintock!*, a carefully guarded defence of middle-American Goldwaterism. Setting aside the coonskin cap of Davy Crockett and the blood and steel of *The Alamo*, Wayne now appeared as a benevolent turn-of-the-century New Mexico cattle baron with the appropriate name of George Washington McClintock. He happily embraces hard-working poor whites, bureaucrat-harassed Indians, mid-Western university graduates and a Jewish storekeeper (numbered among his close friends and admirers, and clearly reminiscent to 1964 audiences of Goldwater's grandfather, 'Big Mike' Goldwasser) as equal partners in the free-enterprise, self-help system. On the other side are the butts of the movie's unconcealed animus and heavy-handed comedy – Eastern dilettantes, the unappreciative young (an Ivy League college boy even apologises to Wayne for calling him a reactionary!), government agents, do-gooders and everyone else who has since earned the alliterative animosity and sarcastic scorn of Spiro Agnew. This 'silent majority' western might be taken as an anticipation of the emergence of the former governor of Maryland on to the national scene in 1968 and into this scheme.

I worked out these loose categories in 1963. Since the death of John Kennedy they have become less clear-cut, though I believe they remain equally valid and more interesting. With the sympathy for Black Panthers at home and revolutionary movements abroad which has been growing on the left, and the support for the Vietnam war and 'law'n'order' on the right, America's orientation towards violence has reverted to more primitive patterns, while at the same time political lines have become confused in the centre, sharper on the fringes.

One can see the blurring of the lines in the career of Sam Peckinpah, whose social ideas and political attitudes are both more complex and less clearly articulated than Wayne's. Peckinpah made his name in 1962 with *Guns in the Afternoon* (as *Ride the High Country* was called in Britain), a Kennedy western in which a pair of ageing marshals realise that their world is coming to an end and prepare two youngsters for a transformed society. He ended the decade with *The Wild Bunch* (1969), a violent, apocalyptic movie which back in the early 1960s would have been an obvious Buckley western – in contrast to *The Magnificent Seven* (1960), where a less equivocal wild bunch intervene in the internal politics of Mexico almost as if they had anticipated the call of Kennedy's inaugural address. The difference is analogous to that between two creations of John Kennedy – the Peace Corps and the Green Berets. Now one views *The Wild Bunch* as a new style, soured Kennedy western and a rather obvious and bitter allegory about Vietnam, and one observes that the bunch's leader bears the name 'Pike Bishop', which may or may not be a conscious reference to that key figure of the American 60s, California's late Bishop James Pike, humanist mystic and ecclesiastical drop-out.

Another late 1960s variant of the Kennedy western is *Butch Cassidy and the Sundance Kid* (1969), which enjoyed a popularity similar to that of *The Magnificent Seven* ten years earlier. With its cute, knowing style borrowed from fashion magazines, Sunday supplements and Pop Art, its cultivation of the insouciant, anti-social hero who goes off to fight his final battles in the Bolivian mountains after the manner of Che Guevara, *Butch Cassidy* is a prime example of what Tom Wolfe has called 'radical chic'.

As an illustration of the way American life throws light on the western and the western illuminates American life, one could do no better than point to what ten years ago appeared to be the arche-typal Kennedy and Goldwater westerns – the Kennedy *High Noon* (1952) and the Goldwater *Rio Bravo* (1959). The latter, expressly made by Howard Hawks as a riposte to Fred Zinnemann's *High Noon*, features John Wayne as a sheriff doing precisely the opposite of what Gary Cooper did in the earlier picture: he never for a moment loses his cool or doubts himself; instead of going round soliciting aid from reluctant townsfolk, he actually turns down the offer of help from non-professionals. And as we know, Wayne was incensed by what he thought was a leftist plot to betray Cooper and was particularly offended by the parting shot of the Zinnemann picture when Cooper throws his badge of office in the dust. *High Noon* was carefully blue-printed before shooting and lasts an intense 84 minutes (roughly the time of the action); *Rio Bravo* was written as it went along and rambles on for around two and a half hours. Today, in the 1970s, these two pictures can be interpreted in a rather different fashion.

High Noon, initially an allegory about existential man standing alone in the McCarthy era (and scripted as his last Hollywood picture by a blacklist victim, Carl Foreman), now suggests an over-commitment to an abstract principle. Marshal Kane could have cleared out of town and escaped the four gunmen who were coming to get him when the noon train arrived. He had after all retired with all his previous obligations fulfilled. I still find *High Noon* moving, intelligent and gripping, but I am no longer able to accept it as the splendidly liberal statement which it seemed to so many of us in the 1950s; and I am less inclined to laugh at the interpretation made at that time by the Swedish critics who found in it a quite different 'politisk-allegorisk dubbelmening'. Both Gunnar Oldin,[6] in an analysis of Stanley Kramer's early productions, and Harry Schein, in his essay *The Olympian Cowboy*, read *High Noon* as an allegory about American foreign policy and the Korean War. The marshal (America) had wanted peace after clearing up the town five years before (i.e. World War II), and reluctantly must buckle on his gunbelt again in the face of new aggression (the Korean War), and eventually his pacifist wife (American isolationists) must see where her true duty lies and support him. 'The sum total,' wrote Schein, 'seems to be that of course pacifism can be a good thing but that war in certain given circumstances may be both moral and inevitable.' Given this interpretation, John Wayne might well have leapt at the opportunity to make a contemporary Vietnam version of *High Noon* which would reflect Julie Nixon Eisenhower's claim during the 1972 presidential campaign that she would be 'willing to die for the Thieu regime'.

Compared with the earlier picture, *Rio Bravo*, in which Wayne actually has a prisoner in the jailhouse to hold for a mere couple of days – an expressly limited commitment, essentially defensive in character – seems to rest on a more solid foundation. There is of course a totally different tone to each of these films which – and this is my point – makes it necessary to consult the prevailing political climate at the time they were made to reveal their conscious meanings. However, the in-built ironies and contradictions of the Kennedy western *and* of John Kennedy's political postures are to be found in *High Noon*. In a highly diverting documentary play called *John Ford's Cuban Missile Crisis* which Albert Hunt and his students at the Bradford College of Art produced a couple of years ago, the 1962 Kennedy–Khruschev confrontation over Cuba was presented as a western directed by John Ford in which the American president was seen as a Henry Fonda figure, talking like a dove and acting like a hawk.

Further thought perhaps must be given to Richard Nixon's position in this framework. For as we know, that impressionable moviegoer saw *Patton* the night before he sanctioned the invasion of Cambodia and had a private screening of John Wayne in *Chisum* the evening before addressing the American Bar Association conference in Denver, when he coyly expatiated on the perennial appeal

6 Oldin's 'En amerikansk tragedi' and Schein's 'Den olympiske cowboyen' are in *Skott I Mörkret* (Wahlström & Widstrand, Stockholm, 1956); Schein's essay is translated in *The American Scholar* (Summer, 1955).

of the western ('This may be a square observation, [but] the good guys come out ahead and the bad guys lose') and embarrassingly prejudged the then *sub judice* Manson trial. At the 1972 Republican Party Convention at Miami, John Wayne returned the compliment by presenting a series of film clips from the President's career, while James Stewart did the same for Mrs Nixon.[7]

Nixon's interest in the genre is oddly enough paralleled by Joseph Stalin's as vouchsafed to us in *Kruschev Remembers*, where we read that for film shows at the Kremlin, Stalin

> used to select the movies himself. The films were usually what you might call captured trophies: we got them from the West. Many of them were American pictures. He liked cowboy movies especially. He used to curse them and give them the proper ideological evaluation but then immediately order new ones.[8]

Cursing horse operas, giving them the proper ideological evaluation and then immediately ordering new ones – Stalin sounds like the universal western fan and critic. What a pity it was that this highly critical student of the genre never got an opportunity to see *Storm in the West*.[9] This was an interpretation of the events leading up to World War II written by Sinclair Lewis and Dore Schary in 1943 in the form of an allegorical, didactic western. Stalin figured in it as Joel Slavin, a Civil War veteran from Georgia (where else?) who takes over 'the old Nicholas place' and later joins Ulysses Saunders (America) and Walter Chancel (Churchill) in a popular front against the outlaws Hygatt, Gribble, Gerrett and Mullison, whose iniquities have included gunning down Chuck Slattery (Czechoslovakia). Fred Zinnemann was among the directors

---

7 Since completing this book I am happy to discover that Eric Bentley has been thinking along similar lines. His *Theatre of War* (Eyre Methuen, London, 1973) contains an essay called 'The Political Theatre of John Wayne' in which he observes: 'The most important American of our time is John Wayne. Granted that all good things come from California, Richard Nixon and Ronald Reagan are only camp followers of Wayne, supporting players in the biggest Western of them all, wagons hitched to Wayne's star. In an age when the image is the principal thing, Wayne is the principal image, and if the soul of this image is *machismo* (a topic for another essay, a topic for a book, for *the* book of our time), its body is the body politic, and its name is Anti-Communism.'

8 Trans. Strobe Talbott (André Deutsch, London, 1971), p. 297.

9 The screenplay, rendered in narrative form with Sol Baer Fielding's pre-production illustrations and an introduction by Dore Schary, was published twenty years later (Stein & Day, New York, 1963; Sidgwick & Jackson, London, 1964).

considered for the weighty undertaking, but the script was rejected by the reigning MGM moguls as being 'too political'. One of their objections was to a close-up of a hammer and sickle hanging on the back of Joel Slavin's covered wagon.

Dore Schary attached such importance to *Storm in the West* that he resigned from MGM when the project was aborted. Sinclair Lewis on the other hand, as his biographer Mark Schorer has suggested, was intrigued but rather less than totally committed. 'I still can't take the movies seriously,' he wrote to a friend. Yet in the mid-1930s Lewis had written an unsuccessful play with a Western theme, *Jayhawker* (the first major professional production to be directed by Joseph Losey), in which the activities of the then threatening 'native fascism' of Louisiana's Governor Huey Long were rendered in allegorical form as a drama about the Kansas insurrectionist movement. At the very least Lewis was engaged by the virtuoso aspects of the film – the resonant names, the sharp parallels of plot, and so on. Oddly enough – or perhaps not so oddly – George Orwell was working on a quite different kind of allegory on the same subject which also led to publication problems. Orwell's embattled, over-explicit preface to *Animal Farm* has only recently come to light and, had it accompanied his book, would clearly have changed our feelings about the novel and probably have limited its appeal and shortened its life. Schary wrote a reminder to himself aimed to keep the allegory on the tracks and the movie on the MGM conveyor belt:

> The one big point behind the entire production must be the fact that no one connected with it should be concerned too much with the symbols that they stand for. They must be concerned with the people and the characters that have been created for them. The direction must be related to a western motion picture, not a picture of significance. The whole thing must be done so that when it is finished and shown, a person who had never heard of Hitler and the second world war could look at it and enjoy it for what it is.

It was as natural perhaps for Orwell to have gone to English rural life as it was for Schary to have resorted to the western for their allegorical exercises. *Storm in the West* was never made and so we are unable to judge its effectiveness; *Animal Farm* is now a classic work of allegorical satire that wholly transcends the immediate conditions that produced it.

In the terminology of William Empson, both *Animal Farm* and *Storm in the West* are 'versions of Pastoral', a traditional source of allegory. Orwell went on to a different form and produced the science fiction novel *1984*. (So did Dore Schary with his appalling *The Next Voice You Hear* in 1949.) Science fiction and the western are at once complementary and antithetical forms. Both are concerned with teaching lessons to the present through a rewriting of the past or by extrapolations of current tendencies projected into the future. Science fiction, however, is able to create a new consciousness – its realm is that of ideas, of apocalypse – and can treat of population growth, mutants, time, galactic travel, theology, mental telepathy, etc. The western is earthbound and circumscribed; its province is the simpler traditional concerns of man, where moral problems are considered by locating them in a pared-down historical framework. The ultimate root of the western is man and the traditional concerns of character and community; science fiction at best involves the free play of intellect in a self-defining milieu where anything is possible and the terrain infinitely pliable.

Horace Gregory, in a masterly attack on the limitations and deceptions of the Western cult, concluded by suggesting that the western was doomed to give way to science fiction:

> It is probable that the cowboy cult will dwindle in favour of another plastic, easily malleable symbol of American hopes, hilarities and fears, and within another decade the noise of jet-propelled space rockets on TV sets will drown out the explosions sounding from the guns of the roaring West.[10]

Gregory has been proved wrong, and so has the German seer Robert Junck, who at the same time claimed to have seen the moment when young American TV audiences abandoned the West and Hopalong Cassidy in favour of galactic exploration:

> I saw the downfall of Hoppy and the rise of his rival foreshadowed on the evening I had to dine with my Boston hosts without the presence of Johnnie. To his father's astonishment the hostess returned from the living room, from which emerged the sound of Hoppy's gallop, not alone as we had expected, but accompanied by her offspring, a pale little boy who remarked by way of explanation: 'That guy is beginning to bore me.'

10 'Guns of the Roaring West', *Avon Book of Modern Writing No. 2* (Avon Publications, New York, 1954).

A month later his father had bought him a space suit ($24.50), an antidote against cosmic rays (sweets at 60 cents) and a pair of anti-gravity shoes ($7.20).[11]

Such has not come to pass – maybe science fiction became science fact sooner than Gregory and Junck foresaw. Anyway, Marshall McLuhan in *The Medium is the Massage* chose to present a silhouette of a stagecoach in a driving mirror as a double-page spread to illustrate his contention:

> The past went that-a-way. When faced with a totally new situation, we tend always to attach ourselves to the objects, to the flavor of the most recent past. We look at the present through a rear-view mirror. We march backwards into the future. Suburbia lives imaginatively in Bonanza-land.[12]

I have invoked *Animal Farm* not only because of the coincidence of its composition with that of *Storm in the West*, but also because it raises the whole question of allegory in our time. We don't read *Animal Farm* to understand the nature of totalitarian politics; it isn't an imaginative footnote that illuminates Orwell's life and thought or his sizeable body of political writing, which is undeniably more complex and far-reaching than this 120-page book. *Animal Farm* exists in its own right, independent of its easily definable political provenance, in the way that all satire does from Aristophanes through Dean Swift. By analogy and with certain reservations, the same is true of westerns. Unlike the authors of *Animal Farm* and *Gulliver's Travels*, however, the filmmaker is drawing on a body of established knowledge readily accessible to the audience – in the same way, though for different reasons, that playwrights in, say, German-occupied France of World War II resorted to themes from classical mythology, or Eastern European dramatists and movie directors have reworked historical subjects or used Aesopean language in handling ambiguous contemporary fables. An immediate judgement, often rendered between the lines rather than explicitly, might acknowledge the dangerousness and present value of the exercise, and this can be as true of Hollywood as of Hungary. But an enduring response and ultimate judgement will inevitably be based on less ephemeral criteria.

In proposing my categories of the Kennedy, Goldwater, Johnson

11 *Tomorrow Is Already Here* (Rupert Hart Davis, London, 1954), p. 212.
12 Allen Lane, The Penguin Press, London, 1967, p.73.

and Buckley western, therefore, I am not attempting to establish any
hierarchy of values but rather to suggest a link between contemporary pressures of various kinds and an existing body of material that
is constantly subjected to them. In the long run – when, as Keynes
observed, we are all dead – there are no prizes for daring or inno-
vation. It depends of course on whether we are making aesthetic
judgements or mining popular culture for its sociological value, the
latter being a fascinating if rather dangerous enterprise. *High Noon*
touched off a series of law'n'order westerns, and only the movie
historian will be aware that it did so; and two of them, *Star in the
Dust* and *Rio Bravo*, were clearly superior to the original. Likewise
with *Winchester '73*, the commercial success of which inspired a
cycle of 'weapon westerns', *Colt 45*, *Springfield Rifle*, *The Battle at
Apache Pass*, none of them equalling the original, and only a social
historian bent on arguing from effect to cause would claim that they
answered an existing public need. Indeed the ingenious and persua-
sive Lawrence Alloway has so argued, and in defining the subject
matter of the cycle as being 'not only about the power new weapons
gave their owners, but about the social impact and consequences of
new weapons', suggests (if I understand him rightly) that these westerns expressed the prevailing ethos of the pre- and early Eisenhower
years which focused on equality, on closing the gap in the Cold War
arms race; and in the late 1950s, anticipating the advent of Kennedy,
'interest shifted to operational lore and responsibility (*Gunman's
Walk*, *The Tin Star*, *The Young Guns*, *Saddle the Wind*): another
cycle.'[13]

The most notable cycle at the time of writing is that inspired by
Peckinpah's *The Wild Bunch* (1969), a series of imitative and grossly
inferior pictures including Don Medford's *The Hunting Party* (1971),
Daniel Mann's *The Revengers* (1972), Michael Winner's *Chato's Land*
(1971) and John Sturges' *Joe Kidd* (1972), all of which focus upon a
disparate band of utterly corrupt hunters accompanied (or led) by
some fairly decent character who is increasingly sickened by his
companions and the task in hand. These pursuers have the support,
more or less, of society and the law; their quarries are outlaws but
generally sympathetic ones, possessed of greater character and moral
strength than their trackers. The immediate political and allegorical
background to these ferociously brutal stories is almost certainly the
conditions of the Vietnam war and the moral confusion that conflict

13 'Iconography of the Movies', *Movie*, No. 7 (London, 1963).

has engendered. At a social level the movies are reflecting current concerns and anxieties; from a commercial point of view a profitable subject is being exploited that seems to go down well at the box-office; viewed aesthetically, the cycle offers a cumulative series of variations upon an established theme.

Westerns don't appear to date like most movies, though I fancy I could see a 10-minute sequence of any cowboy picture and place it within a year of its production and probably – such is the enduring tradition of studio styles and laboratory processing – assign it to the right studio. The real judgements are aesthetic, and as a result even Marxists and structuralist critics finish up celebrating the westerns of Howard Hawks, John Ford and Samuel Fuller and rejecting (or denouncing) liberal westerns such as *High Noon* or William Wyler's United Nations hymn to peaceful coexistence, *The Big Country*. This, I feel, is fair enough, though having lived through these years and being by inclination a social historian I necessarily view any movie both in its immediate context and *sub specie aeternitatis*.

This leads me on to three cardinal aspects of the western that I can only deal with briefly. First, the western is ill equipped to confront complex political ideas in a direct fashion. The genre belongs to the American populist tradition which sees all politics and politicians as corrupt and fraudulent – the political career of James Stewart in *The Man Who Shot Liberty Valance* (1961) is treated by Ford as pure burlesque (totally lacking the warmth he brought to corrupt Boston politics in *The Last Hurrah*); the local politicians in Don Siegel's *Death of a Gunfighter* and Burt Kennedy's *The Good Guys and the Bad Guys* are caricatures, fantasy figures denied any humanity. One has to admit that the genre apparently cannot accommodate the problems of on-going political life and the compromises it involves. The 'Free Silver' issue, for instance, was one of the major concerns of frontier history and the Populist Movement, but not surprisingly it is a hopelessly complex matter ignored by the western, except for *Silver River* (1947). Raoul Walsh's film begins interestingly and in suitably symbolic fashion with Errol Flynn being disgraced for destroying the paper money cargo of a Union Army payroll wagon to prevent it from falling into Confederate hands on the last day of the Civil War, and then it sends him out West to become rather tediously involved in silver mining and the obscure politics of the gold and silver controversy.

Secondly, the western is an occasion for various kinds of virtuosity, a much disparaged quality at the present time which I am inclined to view as a disinterested, self-justifying enterprise. Admirers of Sergio Leone see his four westerns and one post-western (*Giù la Testa*, 1971) in this way, as a kind of opera; less indulgently, I recognise odd individual sequences which stage a gunfight or a cattle drive in an interesting manner, or certain movies such as Monte Hellman's *The Shooting* which employ the conventions of the genre in a bizarre and individual way, as enlarging the vocabulary of the western. Nevertheless one must be cautious – virtuosity is not the same as creative imagination (Ford, for example, was continually extending his range while rarely indulging in obtrusive bravura sequences), and must be distinguished from gimmickry. Sterling Hayden as a Scandinavian seaman going down main street to meet his adversaries equipped with a lethal harpoon was a simple one-off, unrepeatable encounter in Joseph H. Lewis's *Terror in a Texas Town* (1958). At a very different level, the final showdown in Hawks's *Red River*, where no one was killed and a sort of reason prevailed, could not establish a new convention although it responded to the demands of a *bien-pensant* element of the audience; it was effective precisely because it worked against the true wishes of the spectators.

The form of virtuosity which has traditionally aroused the ire of many dedicated western fans has been what they consider the indulgent cultivation of the merely picturesque. In a 1964 review of Walsh's *A Distant Trumpet* in *The Observer*, Kingsley Amis complained of the way in which directors, instead of getting on with the action, allowed the camera to linger on the texture of Indians' head-dresses just as ten years before Robert Warshow had deplored the 'unhappy preoccupation with style' in Ford's *Stagecoach* and the same 'aestheticising tendency' in *My Darling Clementine*, though he found the latter 'a soft and beautiful movie'. Having been to Monument Valley, where Ford shot *Clementine*, I now appreciate that it is nothing like Tombstone and, more importantly, that there are no giant saguaro cacti in that part of Arizona. Consequently, in whatever scene this species of cactus figures as a component of an impressive composition, it must have been placed there by Ford and his designer. This is most striking at the opening party by the still uncompleted church, where Henry Fonda and Cathy Downs tentatively move towards each other across the floor and three saguaros stand in the background between them at the poignant moment when they look into each other's eyes and then start to dance.

As I say elsewhere in this book, I am as happy to see a camera play over the seductive Western landscape as I am being regaled with the destruction of a saloon bar. The terrain and the décor are as worthy of detailed contemplation as the fortunes of those who inhabit and exhibit them. In the western the *trompe l'oeil* tradition of nineteenth-century American art is wedded to the landscape painting tradition. A striking case in point is the conclusion of Robert Parrish's remarkable *The Wonderful Country* (1959), so beautifully photographed by Floyd Crosby. Scripted, appositely some might think, by Robert Ardrey, subsequently to be celebrated as the author of *The Territorial Imperative*, the film concerns the quest for a national identity of one Martin Brady (Robert Mitchum), a man troubled by the same problems of allegiance as his fellow Irish-Americans, O'Meara (Rod Steiger) in Fuller's *Run of the Arrow* and Captain Benjamin Tyreen (Richard Harris) in Peckinpah's *Major Dundee*.

When we first see Brady, he is almost a parody of a Mexican as he rides lethargically through a Texas border town clad in sombrero and poncho, oblivious to the dust-storm blowing around him, on the handsome black horse presented to him by his Mexican warlord employer and called, suitably, 'Lacrimas'. After the complex events through which he moves in Texas and Mexico, he emerges at the end in an early morning mist on the southern bank of the Rio Grande. An assassin shoots his horse and in turn is killed by Mitchum. He gives the *coup de grâce* to his dying horse, then in long, lingering close-ups he places his poncho, sombrero and gun belt beside the dead Lacrimas and in a high angle long-shot walks down to the Rio Grande – to cross it and become an American. The sequence achieves the ritual effect of a church service in which the priest seems to be painfully unfrocking himself to take on a new role. This is self-consciously virtuoso filmmaking, of course (and one notes that director Robert Parrish served Ford, first as a teenage actor in *The Informer*, and later as an editor), but the virtuosity works to unite into a single compelling image the terrain, the highly charged décor and the movie's central theme.

Thirdly, there is the problem of anachronism. Without being a humourless pedant or a stickler for historical verisimilitude, one must raise the question as to how far a filmmaker can disregard the known conditions of a period. That is to say the most worked-over period of history as far as popular art is concerned and a relatively brief period of time concerning which – through the activities of local archives, pioneer museums, diaries, oral history programmes and so on – we have a quite extraordinary, almost embarrassing accumulation of knowledge. The easy answer perhaps is that in the field of historical romance we have to regard the western as *sui generis*, that no laws can be laid down. On the one hand a filmmaker can attempt to produce a pristine work reflecting the genuine currents of pioneer life derived straight from the archives of a state historical institute; on the other hand he may, like Sergio Leone and his European confrères, produce variations on the conventions of an established movie genre without having any personal roots in the actual culture which produced it. One way or another, anachronisms will occur – the genre is itself a charming anachronism. Yet somewhere between the past and the present lies the disruptive point where the western no longer responds to our present needs or the too urgent demands made upon it, where the rituals and our understanding of them will destroy themselves. We do not appear to have reached that situation yet, but it would be foolhardy to believe that the genre is capable of such infinite renewal that such a time will not come.

2 Heroes and Villains, Women and Children

In that set of archetypes and expectations I have called the model western, the hero is the embodiment of good. He is upright, clean-living, sharp-shooting, a White Anglo-Saxon Protestant who respects the law, the flag, women and children; he dresses smartly in white clothes and rides a white horse that is his closest companion; he uses bullets and words with equal care, is a disinterested upholder of justice and uninterested in personal gain. He always wins. The villain, on the other hand, is the embodiment of evil; he dresses in black, rides a dark horse and is doomed to die. He is often a smooth talker and has lecherous designs on women; he is only concerned with advancing his own cause but beyond that has a positive commitment to destruction. The religious source of such a conflict is generally thought to be New England puritanism or American fundamentalism, its dramatic provenance taken as Victorian melodrama.

In the western and popular culture generally we note the persistence of dramatic modes and types which have long since passed out of serious literature and high culture. H.J. Chaytor could almost have been talking about early cowboy movies when he wrote:

> Mediaeval literature produced little formal criticism in our sense of the term. If an author wished to know whether his work was good or bad he tried it on an audience; if it was approved, he was soon followed by imitators. But authors were not constrained by models or systems, and independence or originality could enlarge and decorate any ground plan that had found general acceptance. Development proceeded by trial and error, the audience being the means of experiment. The audience wanted a story with plenty of action and movement; the story as a rule showed no great command of character drawing; this was left to the reciter for portrayal by change of voice and gesture. The story might contain or depend upon the most improbable coincidences or the wildest historical anachronisms; the audience would swallow them without demur. Unity of action could be provided by the

use of allegory... or by emphasis upon love-motive... So, to appreciate the mediaeval narrative poem, we have to bear in mind that the women are peerless beauties, and the men are heroes dauntless among perils arising from foes often more than human.[14]

But as tastes have changed so has the character of the western's *dramatis personae*. A certain complexity of motivation has marked occasional westerns since silent days, but in the 40s and early 50s the vogue for popular psychology and sociology swept Hollywood and came to challenge the simple moral basis of the western. A striking early example of the Freudian western was Raoul Walsh's *Pursued* (1947), where Robert Mitchum played a mentally disturbed cowboy torn by inner doubts caused by his status as an adopted child. Another was Henry Levin's *The Man from Colorado* (1948), in which Glenn Ford took the role of a psychotic judge. In a later, quite ludicrous movie, *The Fastest Gun Alive* (1956), the climax is a duel to determine who has the right to the film's title between a deranged outlaw (Broderick Crawford) whose wife has run off with a gunslinger, and a tormented storekeeper (Glenn Ford) who is haunted by childhood memories of failing to avenge the murder of his lawman father.

These are extreme but not atypical instances of the simpleminded attempts to make the genre more 'adult', to provide a substitute for a declining belief in good and evil, and they represent what is popularly and pejoratively understood as the 'psychological western'. Heroes and villains alike became victims of their childhood and environment, neither good nor bad and often just 'sick'. The genre has never entirely recovered from this discovery nor completely given in to it. *Shane*, for example, has two parallel stories. On the one hand there is the social conflict between the hardworking farmers and the not unsympathetic rancher who is anxious to hang on to his open range; on the other hand there is the mythic confrontation between the tight-lipped, black-clad hired gun, Wilson (Jack Palance), who is the very incarnation of evil, and Shane, the buckskinned knight errant of the plains.

Perhaps one inevitable form of anachronism in the western lies in attributing acceptable present-day motivations to these characters living in a historical context, however formalised. As Lionel Trilling has observed:

14 *From Script to Print: An Introduction to Medieval Vernacular Literature* (Sidgwick & Jackson, London, 1966), p. 3.

A characteristic of the literary culture of the post-Victorian age was the discovery that villains were not, as the phrase went, 'true to life', and that to believe in their existence was naïve. It became established doctrine that people were 'a mixture of good and bad' and that much of the bad could be accounted for by 'circumstances'. The diminished credibility of the villain, the opinion that he is appropriate only to the fantasy of melodrama, not to the truth of serious novels or plays, may in part be explained by the modern tendency to locate evil in social systems rather than in persons. But it is worth considering whether it might not have come about because the dissembling which defined the villain became less appropriate to new social circumstances than it had been to preceding ones. Perhaps it should not be taken for granted that the villain was nothing but a convention of the stage which for a time was also adopted by the novel. There is ground for believing that the villain was once truer to life than he later became.[15]

Of course the first person we think of in the western is the hero – the cowboy, the Westerner. Not surprisingly the two best-known studies of the genre focus on him, as their titles suggest – Robert Warshow's *The Gentleman with a Gun* and Harry Schein's *Den Olympiske Cowboyen*. And in his essay 'Cowboys, Movies, Myths and Cadillacs', Larry McMurtry, author of the novel filmed as *Hud*, has proposed that we might employ Northrop Frye's terminology for fictional modes and categorise westerns as 'high mimetic' or 'low mimetic' according to whether the hero is mythically apart from and superior to his fellow citizens or realistically on the same level as them.[16] I take McMurtry's point, but my own feeling is that to concentrate so much on the hero is misleading. First, because a western is defined by certain kinds of actions within a particular historical setting. Secondly, because a picture is no less obviously a western when the central character is an outlaw or an Indian, or when it has no definable hero at all, as is the case with Monte Hellman's *The Shooting* and Dick Richards' *The Culpepper Cattle Company*. Thirdly, because the principal character is usually involved dramatically or psychologically with some opponent who

15 *Sincerity and Authenticity* (Oxford University Press, London, 1972), p.14.
16 *Man and the Movies*, ed. W.R. Robinson (Louisiana University Press, Baton Rouge, 1967).

may, depending on the circumstances, possess greater charisma or social acceptance than himself.

Moreover, the western has come in recent years to challenge the very concept of heroism – not necessarily to destroy it, but to bring its traditional nature into question. Perhaps the most marked characteristic of the genre since the early 1950s has been its increasing emphasis not upon victory and success but upon losing – the suggestion that to remain true to oneself will almost invariably result in defeat. This in a society traditionally committed to success, to winning. Henry King's *The Gunfighter* and Brando's *One-Eyed Jacks* are notable instances. In the latter, a gunman suggests to the Mexican hero Rio that they should just go into town and kill their crooked opponent. 'That's not my style, Bob,' Rio replies. To which the gunman retorts, 'Then you better change your style, 'cos your style is a little slow.' Leaving aside the question that this might be a comment on the somewhat stately progress of the picture itself and the genre in general, we see here the notion of the hero becoming too good for this world. Instead of his triumph setting an example, his defeat and death become a rebuke to society. That is the message of most of Peckinpah's films. It is only in his superb study of a contemporary rodeo performer, *Junior Bonner* (1972), that he is able to treat the same theme unrestricted by the genre's demand for violent action; here he can let his victorious losers ride off into the sunset (the father onwards ever hopefully to a new frontier in Australia, the rueful, unembittered son driving his Cadillac and horse-trailer to yet another rodeo performance) instead of leaving them stretched out dead in the dust.

As winner or loser, as a mythic gunfighter like Shane or an accurately observed ageing cowhand like Will Penny, whether battling forces of existential evil or keeping the peace in the face of misunderstood delinquents, the western hero nevertheless meets certain needs that other kinds of films and aspects of our culture fail to recognise or to satisfy in the same way. And when those needs are deliberately not fulfilled, when our expectations are deliberately frustrated, we are both upset and intrigued. Robert Lowell touched on this in reflecting on the courage of John Kennedy:

> We have some sort of faith that the man who can draw most quickly is the real hero. He's proved himself. Yet that's a terribly artificial standard; the real hero might be someone who'd never got his pistol out of the holster and who'd be stumbling about

and near-sighted and so forth. But we don't want to admit that. It's deep in us that the man who draws first somehow has proved himself. Kennedy represents a side of America that is appealing to the artist in retrospect, a certain heroism. And you feel, in certain terms, he really was a martyr in his death. He was reckless, went further than the office called for; perhaps you'd say that he was fated to be killed. And that's an image one could treasure and it stirs one.[17]

Lowell's comments on Kennedy – delivered off the cuff in conversation – invoke the immense complexity, the many-layered resonance of the western hero's position. And as I have suggested, we cannot view him in isolation from his setting or his adversaries. It is not always easy to tell when western moviemakers are unconsciously drawing on traditional mythology and when they are consciously constructing their plots from what Orson Welles (apologising for the 'Rosebud' motif in *Citizen Kane*) called 'dollar-book Freud'. Ultimately it does not really matter. The recurrent conflicts between fathers and sons (a son hunting a killer who turns out to be his own father in John Sturges' *Backlash*, or a father shooting down his own son in Phil Karlson's *Gunman's Walk*), between brothers competing to be the true heir to their father (Mann's *Winchester '73* and numerous other films), between former comrades-in-arms, between outlaws-turned-sheriff and their onetime companions, between the upright man and the evil brood ruled over by a self-righteous patriarch (*My Darling Clementine*, *Will Penny*, etc.) – all of these relationships can be traced back to traditional mythological sources. Equally they can be derived quite consciously from them. The extent to which the deep-dyed villain (Lee Marvin), the gunslinger (John Wayne) who shot him down, and the fumbling greenhorn lawyer (James Stewart) who took the credit for his demise and went on to found a political career upon the deed in John Ford's *The Man Who Shot Liberty Valance*, are symbolic, symbiotic figures, is a matter of conjecture. As one of the crudest and at the same time most involved of Ford's westerns, *Liberty Valance* is a genuine puzzle – the surface in fact is so unattractive that many observers (including Budd Boetticher who has denounced it as a Ford misfire) have not been persuaded to penetrate this muddled masterpiece.

17 A. Alvarez, *Under Pressure* (Penguin Books, London, 1965), p. 101.

More easily accessible is *Cat Ballou*, featuring Marvin once again, but this time in the dual role of a deadly killer and a superannuated sheriff who may be twin brothers. As becomes a confident satirist, Elliot Silverstein fully understood the relationship between the two, and equips them – in lightly handled vein – with the crucial flaws of their callings. The upright Kid Shelleen is a helpless drunk, his sense of vocation and social purpose lost until he is briefly redeemed, carefully prepared again for the knightly lists, wins and returns once more to his drunken self-doubt. His evil alter ego Tim Strawn wears a tin cover to conceal his missing nose (the symbolic castration is pretty obvious) and can only express himself in violent action – he has no way of mediating his doubts. A companion of Cat Ballou refers to Tennyson ('Tennyson spins a good yarn, doesn't he?'). Cat herself carries a collected Tennyson concealing a Wild West dime novel, and Strawn's land-grabbing employer is an English nobleman (Reginald Denny) appropriately called Sir Harry Percival, suggesting none too subtly an element of Arthurian legend.

Less easy to pin down is Monte Hellman's *The Shooting*, where one cannot be sure within the exigencies of a chaotic, small-budget production what was calculated and what fortuitous. Names like Leland Drum and Willet Gashade hazily invoke ancient nursery rhymes and more recent mythology. ('Aiken Drum' was the surrealist figure who 'lived in the moon' – traditionally a figure beyond death – in the Scottish ballad to which he gives his name; the last verse of the anonymous Western ballad *Jesse James* tells us that 'This song was made by Billy Gashade, As soon as the news did arrive.') In Hellman's film the bemused Gashade (Warren Oates) is hired by a woman to accompany her (and later an inscrutable gunman) on a strange mission into the desert culminating in a fatal, ambiguous confrontation between himself and a man who may or may not be his brother Coigne (Gashade's dying shout), but is certainly his *doppelgänger*. One wonders if it is carrying exegesis too far to suggest that 'Coigne' is a contraction of 'Cockaigne', the fabulous mythical place of idleness and plenty which America and the uncharted West was known as before, and for some time after, the voyage of Columbus.

During the credit titles of *How the West Was Won*, the vast Cinerama screen is filled with the words 'The Civil War directed by John Ford'. The audience invariably laughs, I imagine. Yet at the same time they recognise a certain ironic truth. Of course Ford didn't do

it entirely alone: indeed, the publicity handout for the picture insists
that it would have been impossible 'for one director to carry the
entire burden', and so an 'unprecedented' solution was arrived at in
which 'three of Hollywood's most renowned directors, working in
close coordination, shared the tremendous task', with the assistance
of four top cinematographers and a cast of twenty-four stars. This
may have been a lot for a single movie, but when one steps back
from this epic production – and the shimmering lines that marked
the joins between the Cinerama triptych encouraged the spectator
to do so – one finds that a small, tight-knit group of familiar faces
won the West, for the genre employs only a relative handful of
directors, writers, cameramen and performers. One could draw up
a roster of about fifty actors – fewer than the number of players
under contract to the National Theatre and the Royal Shakespeare
Company – who constitute the western stock troupe, and between
them their credits would include virtually every western of any note
(and a great many of no distinction) made over the past quarter of
a century. A computer could reduce this to a much shorter list.
Heroes: John Wayne, James Stewart, Henry Fonda, Gary Cooper,
Randolph Scott, Joel McCrea, Glenn Ford as section one, followed
by Burt Lancaster, Richard Widmark, Robert Mitchum, Gregory
Peck, Charlton Heston, Kirk Douglas, Robert Taylor, Alan Ladd,
Van Heflin, William Holden, Clint Eastwood. Villains: Lee Marvin,
Richard Boone, Robert Ryan, Arthur Kennedy, Dan Duryea,
Edmond O'Brien, Neville Brand, John Dehner, Slim Pickens,
Robert Wilke, Ian Macdonald, Claude Akins, Lee Van Cleef, Jack
Elam, Royal Dano, Warren Oates, Anthony Quinn. Ranchers,
sheriffs, deputies, sidekicks, assorted citizenry: Charles Bickford,
Millard Mitchell, Edgar Buchanan, Ward Bond, Chill Wills, John
Ireland, Walter Brennan, Ben Johnson, Harry Carey Jr., Noah Berry
Jr., John McIntyre, Jay C, Flippen, Andy Devine, James Millican,
Elisha Cook Jr., R.G. Armstrong.

Taken along with the familiar plots and recurrent situations, these
well-known and increasingly well worn faces serve to give the
western its quality of *déjà-vu* and reinforce the sense of ritual. The
physical presence and established properties of these actors have
become part of the genre's iconography, to be accepted literally or
to be worked into new patterns or mined for fresh meanings. Alone
or in conflict with each other they determine the tone of a picture,
and most directors are intuitively aware of the way an actor's image
and attributes can be manipulated and within what limits. Few of

them are exactly protean performers, though some are more versatile than others.

John Wayne, for instance, could never figure in a movie which demands much interior complexity in its hero; the complexity therefore, if sought, must come from the film's structure, as in *The Searchers* or *The Man Who Shot Liberty Valance*. Randolph Scott is an even more rigid performer, whose course is unswerving if usually more concealed than Wayne's. Inevitably he will make any group of crooks who join up with him appear colourful, sometimes to the point of eccentricity (as in his Boetticher movies); still there's something not quite open about Scott's screen persona and in the right context, such as the Confederate agent he played in *Virginia City* (1940) or the corrupt ex-lawman of *Guns in the Afternoon* (1962), he can infuse colour into the essentially pallid performances of moral rectitude represented respectively in those films by Errol Flynn and Joel McCrea. Glenn Ford will impart a note of realism, intensity and ambiguity to the most simple moral tale; where these elements are already present he can heighten them to a rare degree, as in *3.10 to Yuma* (an apparently realistic western, though it is in fact a complex working out of the Grail legend in the West) or *Day of the Evil Gun*, or take them over the edge until the film can seem neurotic, cynical or absurd. Richard Boone's powerful villains threaten to overwhelm the forces of good; cast Boone on the side of society and you can almost dispense with a villain. Henry Fonda, a true Westerner born in Nebraska, was rushed into the genre in 1939 as the sympathetic outlaw Frank James in *Jesse James*, as a pioneer in the pre-western *Drums Along the Mohawk*, and as the future president in *Young Mr Lincoln*. He then repeated his outsider role in Fritz Lang's *Return of Frank James* (1940) and William Wellman's realistic, anti-lynch law *The Ox-Bow Incident* (1942), became confirmed as a key figure in the Ford pantheon as upright Marshal Earp in *My Darling Clementine*, and in the late 1960s was ripe to be cast again as a sympathetic ageing outlaw in *Firecreek* and a smiling, sadistic thug in the most ambitious of all spaghetti westerns, Sergio Leone's *Once Upon a Time in the West*. When Wayne is cast as a criminal there's usually a suggestion that something is wrong with the law in a local, easily resolved way; when Fonda is cast as an outlaw the implication is that there's something basically wrong with society. Outside the western, he fulfils this function in, for instance, *You Only Live Once*, *Grapes of Wrath* and *The Wrong Man*.

The use of Fonda and Wayne proposes fairly immediate social

readings of the genre. Alan Ladd's performance in *Shane* is rather different. Perhaps no other actor could have given the character quite that quality of blank, ethereal detachment which Ladd brought to the part. He is like an angel in an otherwise realistic medieval painting, and sets off the earthy realism of Van Heflin's father, Jean Arthur's unfulfilled pioneer mother and Brandon De Wilde's deprived, yearning child. An identical film starring Wayne, Cooper or Stewart would have quite a different feel to it. In hindsight, apart from being the archetypal, highly stylised western it seemed at the time (conceived of and accepted as 'classic'), *Shane* in many ways strikes one as a forerunner of *Theorem* (1968), though far richer and infinitely more congenial than Pasolini's disastrous little allegory. It is interesting to note that immediately before his appearance as the deliberately unidentifiable spirit of something or other in *Theorem*, Terence Stamp starred as a doomed outsider in a western called *Blue* and as an English actor cast in a spaghetti western in 'Toby Dammit', Fellini's episode of the Franco-Italian portmanteau picture *Histoires Extraordinaires* (1968).

This repertory of western players has been getting older over the years, and many of them were not in their first flush of youth two decades ago. In consequence their very endurance has given an increasing gravitas to the genre and has helped (or compelled) the writing into it of the subject of ageing. A by-product of this has been a curious shaping of the role of younger actors: excluding them, forcing them to adopt a more elderly mien, placing them in positions of tutelage, or sacrificing them on the altar of inexperience. At its most extreme we are regaled with 121-year-old Dustin Hoffman in *Little Big Man*, and Paul Newman's reappearance as a grizzled centenarian to give the twentieth-century world its richly deserved quietus at the end of John Huston's *The Life and Times of Judge Roy Bean*.

In the model traditional western there are two kinds of women. On the one hand there is the unsullied pioneer heroine: virtuous wife, rancher's virginal daughter, schoolteacher, etc.; on the other hand there is the saloon girl with her entourage of dancers. The former are in short supply, to be treated with respect and protected. The latter are reasonably plentiful, sexually available and community property. There is obviously a correspondence between these two groups and historical actuality in the West – and an even greater connection between them and the orthodox thinking of the late

Victorian world as enshrined in Lord Baden-Powell's *Rovering to Success* (1922), whose impressionable young readers were told that 'there are women and there are dolls'. The two classes of women also correspond, with the rewards and penalties their lives predict, to the demands of the Hollywood Production Code.

In archetypal form they appear as the cavalry officer's pregnant wife (Louise Platt) and the banished saloon girl (Claire Trevor) in Ford's *Stagecoach* (1939), whose passenger list is an almost perfect cross-section of western types – the two women, the chivalrous Southern gambler, the big-hearted alcoholic doctor, the snooty, larcenous banker, the 'good' outlaw, the comic, prissy salesman, the jolly, uncomplicated driver, the gruff, sterling sheriff, with the cavalry and the Indians lurking ready to appear when needed. As custom dictates, the officer's wife has the demure Wasp name Lucy Mallory, while the saloon girl bears the nickname 'Dallas'. (In *My Darling Clementine*, for instance, the Eastern heroine is named Clementine Carter, and the saloon girl 'Chihuahua', while in *Destry Rides Again*, *Johnny Guitar* and *Rio Bravo*, the worldly female leads played by Marlene Dietrich, Joan Crawford and Angie Dickinson are called, respectively if not respectably, 'Frenchy', 'Vienna' and 'Feathers'.)

Just as all the other *Stagecoach* archetypes have been constantly reworked, so too have the women's roles changed. This reflects both a relaxation in censorship and the changing status of women in society. Which is not to say that in the past every western was committed to these old conventions: the fact that Claire Trevor in *Stagecoach* is obviously a prostitute and gets to marry the hero suggests that they were never exactly mandatory. This is, however, a fairly rare instance of relative explicitness and an unusual case of a woman not having to pay heavily for her sins. Redemption in the western, and in Hollywood films generally, has largely been a male prerogative. William Wellman's otherwise unremarkable *Westward the Women* (1952) is the story of a wagon-train of girls, mostly of previous dubious virtue, being transported by an exasperated trail boss, Robert Taylor, to marry sex-starved miners in California, is a singular, somewhat unedifying case of women being redeemed by the harsh experience of crossing a hostile land.

Now of course we have brothels clearly marked as such, resorted to by hero and villain alike, and taking their place alongside the saloon, the sheriff's office and the livery stable as one of the essential amenities of any western town. By 1970 it was even possible to set a whole film in one, as was the case with Gene Kelly's *The Cheyenne Social Club*, the ultimate whores' opera, where James Stewart inherits a bawdy house in Wyoming to his, and also the audience's, embarrassment. The liberation here, if it be such, is not that of women but of filmmakers from old moral standards.

Just as one cannot any longer tell the good guys from the bad guys, one cannot with quite the same ease distinguish between the good girls and the bad girls. A striking instance is to be found in Ted Post's *Hang 'Em High* (1968), a stolid western with a fashionable line in bondage and necrophilia reminiscent of the same director's *Legend of Tom Dooley* (1957). The hero (Clint Eastwood), who spends a good deal of time consorting with whores, is rather surprised when the film's store-keeping heroine (Inger Stevens) constantly rebuffs his advances. It transpires that she isn't an old-fashioned girl protecting her virtue but is suffering from frigidity as the consequence of a traumatic group rape. From this affliction the hero cures her one suitably stormy night.

These changes – made possible, in some cases insisted upon, by Hollywood's increasing permissiveness – have occasionally led to the depiction of more mature relations between the sexes and the appearance of many an anachronistically liberated woman on the range; but the western remains a man's world. Yet it is no longer possible merely to accept the solitariness and implied misogyny of the Westerner: questions of sex and the single cowboy must be explained or demonstrated. In the Randolph Scott-Budd Boetticher movies, for example, Scott was almost invariably presented as a widower, and in three cases (*Seven Men From Now*, *Decision at Sundown* and *Ride Lonesome*) he was actually seeking revenge on the men who killed his wife. In Sam Peckinpah's movies the heroes rarely meet any women except whores, and one cannot escape the implication that in the director's view prostitutes have a greater honesty than other women. Beneath the surface of fashion and the veneer of realism in so many recent films, we could be seeing confirmation of what has long been thought about one shared aspect of most western heroes, which is to say that while not necessarily a latent homosexual, the hero secretly fears women and the civilisation, compromise and settled life they represent; he sees them as sources of corruption and betrayal, luring him away from independence and a sure sense of himself as well as from the more comforting company of men.

If the western is the supremely male Hollywood genre, the

musical is its feminine counterpart or complement. While rather pallid males like Gene Autry and Roy Rogers dominated that now thankfully defunct form, the 'singing western', the 'western musical', altogether a more *ad hoc*, less run-of-the-production-line thing, was largely the province of female stars. On stage (Ethel Merman) and screen (Betty Hutton) it was the sharp-shooting Miss Oakley who drew first in *Annie Get Your Gun* (1950), even if she was subsequently forced to conceal her talents to get her man; and in what is virtually a pastiche of Irving Berlin's Broadway triumph, David Butler's likeable *Calamity Jane* (1953), Doris Day not only took centre stage but rode shotgun as well.

She was soon followed by Rosemary Clooney in George Marshall's mildly satirical *Red Garters* (1954), and a few years later by Debbie Reynolds in Vincent Sherman's *The Second Time Around* (1961). She was long preceded, however, by Judy Garland in what is possibly the best western musical, George Sidney's *The Harvey Girls* (1946), a tribute to those intrepid New England ladies who went West in the late nineteenth century to provide miners and cowboys with an infinitely superior service and cuisine to that to which they had become accustomed. The Fred Harvey Company, as a sub-division of the Amtrak Organisation, is still a part of the living West, having a monopoly of hospitality around the Grand Canyon and on the edges of the Navajo reservation. *The Harvey Girls* contains the finest musical tribute to the technological pioneers of the West in the bravura presentation of Johnny Mercer's number 'On the Atchison, Topeka and the Santa Fe'.

Westerns of course have to feature women if only because commercial movies must offer some so-called romantic interest. When women take the centre of the stage in this most masculine of genres, the result is less likely to be a blow in favour of sexual equality than a strong whiff of erotic perversity. I don't refer here to actresses who have given major and memorable performances in traditional roles: Marlene Dietrich's saloon girls in *Destry Rides Again* (1939) and *Rancho Notorious* (1952), Jean Arthur's farm-wife in *Shane*, Angie Dickinson's singer in *Rio Bravo* (1959), Diane Cilento's tough hotel proprietress in *Hombre* (1967), Maureen O'Hara in half a dozen movies, to name but a few examples of the opportunities which, contrary to accepted opinion, the western has afforded to actresses over the years. What I mean are those movies which cast women in essentially masculine roles as outlaw leaders or as ranch bosses: Barbara Stanwyck, leading exponent of the all-American bitch, in several films, most notably Samuel Fuller's *Forty Guns* (1957); her close rival Joan Crawford doing battle with Mercedes McCambridge in Arizona in Nicholas Ray's much admired *Johnny Guitar* (1953); Jeanne Crain as a ruthless cattle queen in King Vidor's *Man Without a Star* (1955). The effect of such casting is invariably to produce a quality of savagery, heartlessness, heavy-handed eroticism and extravagant sexual symbolism and innuendo, bordering on the risible. Some might think this outcome only too predictable, since it is indeed a literal travesty of the western. In addition, it diverts women from their principal dramatic role in cowboy movies – as well as in most male action movies for that matter – which is to be the voice of reason speaking out against violence, its character-building function, and the idea that human affairs can be settled by force.

Perhaps this view is an unrealistic and sentimental one, and it could be argued that my criticisms of these films – particularly *Man Without a Star* – are in fact the very points they are actually making. That this is the case with the eponymous heroine played by Jane Fonda in *Cat Ballou* (1965) is certain, but that film is perhaps the only comedy western worth taking seriously as a genuine, well-observed satire on the genre. The ugly, role-reversing phenomenon of the belligerent, gun-happy woman is given a good deal of conscious critical attention in Burt Kennedy's stark allegorical fable *Welcome to Hard Times* (1966), where a likeable, hard-hearted Irish whore (Janice Rule) despises her lover, the town's pacifist mayor (Henry Fonda), and ensures that her adopted son is instructed in the use of guns so that he will be able to kill the madman who has raped her. The result is that when the rapist eventually returns, not only is the boy's instructor shot dead, but she herself is accidentally killed when the boy takes his rifle to protect her. So much, the film implies, for women who step outside their appointed role; and so much too, one senses, for the American housewives (so vividly depicted at small-arms classes in Haskell Wexler's *Medium Cool*) who assiduously take shooting lessons and turn their suburban homes into arsenals.

Whatever may be happening in other branches of the cinema, the western remains a place dominated by men, and mostly men of fairly mature years. The juvenile delinquent doesn't last long. If he pulls a gun, for instance, as the wild youngster played by Russ Tamblyn does in *Cimarron* (1960), he'll soon be stretched out in the morgue instead of going to reform school or, like Skip Homeier (the arche-typal Hitler Youth in the wartime propaganda movie *Tomorrow the World*, who graduated to being the West's archetypal Peter Pan thug) who shot Johnny Ringo in the back in *The Gunfighter*, he'll briefly inherit a doomed reputation. If he joins a gang of fellow tear-aways, he may well find himself up against not only an unbeatable sheriff but an ageing outlaw as well, as in *The Good Guys and the Bad Guys*.

In a rather old-fashioned way, the western assumes that young people have a lot to learn from their elders and very little to teach them, and that the process of learning is long and painful, that a man must prove himself in a variety of rituals before he can take his place in adult society. The western is in fact a highly didactic form, and so prominent is this pedagogic strain that it seems to disprove Keats' assertion that we hate that which 'has a palpable design upon us'. As the fleeing judge in *High Noon* hastily packs his belongings, he tells Marshal Kane that this is 'no time for a lesson in civics, boy'. In this he is mistaken. Whatever else may have to be set aside in the western, there is always time for a little instruction. Not surprisingly, one of the few harbingers of civilisation that the Westerner tradi-tionally respects is the schoolteacher: in *The Gunfighter*, Ringo's estranged wife is a schoolmarm; in *Man of the West*, the interrupted journey which brings Gary Cooper back to his old gang has as its object the hiring of a teacher; in *The Big Country* the voice of reason, courted by both sides in a range war, is schoolmarm Jean Simmons. Unquestionably the nastiest character in Charles Haas' highly stylised little western *Star in the Dust* (1956) is the local school-teacher, a man of some intelligence and organising ability who throws himself into a range war on the side of the farmers against the ranchers to further his political ambitions. 'I'm not cut out to be an underpaid schoolteacher all my life,' he says, setting aside the disinterested attitude expected of him. (Close students of Hollywood casting methods will note that he is played by the same slightly sinister actor, Robert Osterloh, who was shot dead in his classroom by a home-made zip-gun wielded by a pupil of his in *City Across the River*, made in 1949, one of Hollywood's earliest and most sensational juvenile delinquency pictures.)

Normally, when his actions are questioned, the western hero will answer with a laconic 'There are some things a man can't ride around,' or 'A man's gotta do what a man's gotta do,' or 'Well, if you don't know, I can't tell you.' Faced with a child or an adolescent, however, he feels obliged to pass on what he knows about life, which frequently comes down to matters of handling guns, women, cattle and drink – and especially guns. For every Showdown at Wichita there's a little Teach-In in Dodge City.

In *Shane*, the eponymous hero (Alan Ladd) explains to the little boy Joey how to use a pistol. 'Some like to have two guns, but one's all you need if you know how to use it,' he says, and in a burst of furious shooting he reveals how close the honourable gunman is to the killer. In *Man Without a Star*, the hero takes an inexperienced Easterner under his wing to show him the ropes, and the film's subplot turns on the way this young man initially goes astray by only aping his master's external style before attaining self-mastery. Similarly, in Peckinpah's *Guns in the Afternoon*, a cocky young gunman who has learned his skills from one master, discovers how to use them responsibly from another. (He is also upbraided for littering the countryside, and under the stern eye of his mentor retrieves a piece of paper and pockets it.) One of the most remarkable instances of the handing on of gun lore is to be found in Phil Karlson's *Gunman's Walk* (1958). Here a prosperous, middle-aged rancher (Van Heflin, combining his own stolid farmer role from *Shane* with Alan Ladd's panache) has two sons, one of whom is dull, decent and pacific, the other strident, attractive and tough. The first has his father's stability and integrity but none of the skill and ruthlessness which enabled him to establish himself in the pioneer West. The second son has the father's drive and style, but none of the inner balance. The father tends to view one with guarded contempt and love the other, but an early scene of shooting practice explosively demonstrates that the weak boy who loathes shooting is best equipped for life now that the frontier has closed, and that the apparently strong boy, who revels in guns, has inherited a dangerously outmoded style and outlook. This early realisation is amply confirmed by the boy's anti-social conduct, and finally in a climactic gunfight the father is forced to kill his own son – which in symbolic terms involves killing part of himself.

One of the more likeable aspects of the sadistic *Nevada Smith* (1966) is the emphasis on the hero's education. He learns to shoot from a travelling gunsmith who tells him that 'handling the things is only part of it – the other part is learning to know human nature.' Subsequently the wild young Smith (Steve McQueen) discovers how to drink, play poker, handle whores and bide his time. He even takes up reading and there is a nice touch when his life is preserved by a copy of a reading primer he carries in his pocket. '*The McGuffey Reader* saved your heart,' the doctor tells him.

Such instruction has a clearly symbolic purpose – to teach judgement, self-restraint, self-sufficiency, a code of conduct and morality which goes with the acquiring of character. In the case of a picture like *Nevada Smith*, though, the purpose to which the education is put is only too literally an extension of the very nature of the instruction itself – killing, revenge, the assertion of character in terms of primitive machismo. The hero's inevitable satiation and disgust with killing is hardly a substitute for genuine irony. Nor is much irony to be found in Mark Rydell's *The Cowboys* (1972), where John Wayne is forced to recruit a team of innocent adolescents to conduct his cattle drive and introduces them to guns, whores, drinking and killing. Somehow they have become men, and when Wayne is gunned down they can carry on his task and dispose of his murderers in exultant fashion.

A much sharper, more critical account of the situation in *The Cowboys* is to be found in Dick Richards' excellent *The Culpepper Cattle Company*, which appeared around the same time. Here we see a 16-year-old Texan (Gary Grimes) joining an arduous cattle drive out of a romantic desire to live the cowboy's life. He too becomes a man, but the film's authors – and to a lesser extent the boy himself – show real awareness of the kind of man he is becoming as he is initiated into the squalid pleasures, the self-seeking, the random violence around him. Without ever making it too explicit, Richards seems to be implying that the Culpepper Cattle Company is America – a business ploughing relentlessly on, totally amoral, fighting when it must, compromising when it can, a few deranged or misguided members galloping off from time to time to pursue 'idealistic' Vietnam-like missions on the side which neither adversary nor apparent beneficiary justifies.

Apart from their presence *in statu pupillari*, and to afford their elders the opportunity of passing on the bruised fruits of their experience, children fulfil other roles in the western. One, naturally, is a decorative function in contributing to the sense of community. Another more dramatic role is to act as an ironic comment upon the action. In *High Noon*, as Marshal Kane goes about his vain attempt to enlist the aid of his fellow citizens, the kids in the street anticipate the climax by playing a little game called, 'Bang, bang, you're dead, Kane'. In *The Gunfighter*, the children are full of dime novel talk about Western heroes, and stare through the window at the legendary Johnny Ringo as he sits in the saloon under a steel engraving of Custer's Last Stand. When Ringo sees his own son, from whom he has been long absent, he discovers that the boy's hero is Wyatt Earp. In a pre-credit sequence to Allen Miner's *The Ride Back* (1957), a child playing in an empty street with a toy gun seems to have fired a real shot, until the sudden revelation that the noise came from the pistol of bandit Anthony Quinn running for his life.

There is thus a triple role for children: being trained to take their place in society; being caught up in, and possibly corrupted by, the Western myth and the mystique of frontier violence; reminding us that the aggressive instinct and a fascination with violence are things we are born with. In no moviemaker's work is this given more prominence than in that of Sam Peckinpah, who was himself brought up in the West as the descendant of pioneer grandparents. In his first movie, *The Deadly Companions*, the hero accidentally shoots a little boy who has come out to get a better view of a bank robbery; the journey which forms the dramatic spine of the picture is made by his mother to bury him in a remote town beside his father. In the opening sequence of *Guns in the Afternoon*, emphasis is given to the mollycoddling attention of mothers to their over-dressed children in a turn-of-the-century Californian town on which civilisation has imposed its baleful hand in the form of street lamps, horse-less carriages, uniformed cops; and by implication their conformism is contrasted with the opportunities a young gunman and a farm girl have of learning about life from two old marshals with whom they ride into the mountains away from the town. In *Major Dundee*, the first thing children do after being released from their Apache captors is to play with bows and arrows, and it is real guns they look at with wide-eyed fascination in *The Wild Bunch*; at the end one of them shoots William Holden in the back.

3 Indians and Blacks

I have spoken earlier of 1950 being the watershed year in which the western took on a new depth, seriousness and resonance. This change was most marked in the treatment of the Indian, whose predicament was at the centre of the first westerns directed by Anthony Mann and Delmer Daves. I use the word 'Indian' here and elsewhere with the embarrassed knowledge that the term is considered offensive by present-day descendants of the original Americans, though they have yet to agree among themselves upon an acceptable description. However, Leslie Fiedler has suggested in *The Return of the Vanishing American* that all American literature can be divided into Northerns, Southerns, Easterns and Westerns, and that stories set in the West which do not involve Indians are 'unfulfilled occasions for myth rather than myth itself':

> The heart of the Western is not the confrontation with the alien landscape (by itself this produces only the Northern), but the encounter with the Indian, that utter stranger for whom our New World is an Old Home, that descendant of neither Shem nor Japheth, nor even like the Negro imported to subdue the wild land, Ham.[18]

In Fiedler's analysis the hero of the New England-set Northern is transformed into a Yankee; the hero of the Southern, through his confrontation with the Negro or the spirit of blackness, is turned into 'Whitey'; in the Eastern he becomes a *déraciné* cosmopolitan or a tourist who heads home. In the Western, however,

> the tensions of the encounter are resolved by eliminating one of the mythological partners – by ritual or symbolic means in the first instance, by physical force in the second. When the first method is used possibilities are opened up for another kind of Western, a secondary Western dealing with that New Man, the American *tertium quid*; but when the second is employed – our home grown Final Solution – the Western disappears as a living form, for the West has, in effect, been made into an East.

18 Jonathan Cape, London, 1969, p. 16.

To return to the less heady world of Hollywood in 1950, Anthony Mann's film was *Devil's Doorway*, in which a Shoshone brave, symbolically named Broken Lance (Robert Taylor), returns from distinguished service in the Civil War to find himself an alien in his own Wyoming home. 'Under the law you're not classed as an American citizen – you're a ward of the American government,' he is told, and at the climax of the film he dons his old army uniform to die a defeated man, though saying to a sympathetic woman lawyer with whom a tentative romance has been suggested, 'Don't worry, Anne – a hundred years from now it might have worked.'

Throughout the film Taylor is presented as an unblemished hero and is always photographed in such a manner (for example, low angle shots against the sky or lit from behind) as to make him dominate the scene. The same is true of Jeff Chandler's appearance as Cochise, the peace-loving Apache leader in Daves' *Broken Arrow*, which also made a serious if self-conscious attempt to present Indian life with sympathy and some authenticity. In this case, however, the film ends with the suggestion of permanent peace, but only after the death of Cochise's daughter. No doubt she had to die as punishment for the crime of miscegenation: she had married a cavalry scout (James Stewart), the movie's instrument of racial reconciliation.

The considerable impact of these pictures (*Broken Arrow* proved one of the year's most successful and widely discussed films) has to be seen against the then established role of the Indian in the western. Conventionally the redskin has been one of the hazards facing those bent on taming a continent and winning the West. At best he was the noble savage of Fenimore Cooper, sharing the same qualities of primitive grandeur which resided in the challenge of the wild terrain and harsh climate, At worst he followed a tradition established by early Victorian melodrama: he was treacherous, bloodthirsty, uncompromising, threatening rape, mutilation and death.

The depiction of Indians before 1950 was not always unsympathetic. Back in 1912, D.W. Griffith's *The Massacre* showed them as hapless victims of an unprovoked cavalry raid; James Cruze's *Covered Wagon* (1923) made clear that they were motivated by a reasonable desire to protect their hunting grounds; *The Vanishing American* (1925) sketched a history of the American Indian from early cliff-dwelling days up to the ignominious death of a World War I Indian hero (Richard Dix) back on his neglected reservation. Indeed the historians of the genre, George N. Fenin and William K. Everson, in their book *The Western*, argue that in the early days of the silent era 'the Indian was seen as a hero almost as frequently as the white man, but already there was a difference. He seemed more of a symbol, less an individual than the cowboy.'

This faceless symbol became a stereotype: historically a figure to be confronted and defeated in the name of civilisation, dramatically a terrifying all-purpose enemy ready at the drop of a tomahawk to spring from the rocks and attack wagon trains, cavalry patrols and isolated pioneer settlements. Unlike other racial minorities or foreigners, the Indian was unprotected by the Hays Office Code, box-office caution, or political influence. There has of course never been a shortage of crooked traders or Indian-hating officers to provoke conflict and also serve as scapegoats for the white race. But this, I think, is also part of the filmmakers' approach to their subject, for the Indian could not even serve as an individually realised villain.

The liberal, anti-racist cycle that followed *Devil's Doorway* and *Broken Arrow* has continued unabated up to the present. But if Hollywood made token amends to the Apache, the Sioux, the Cheyenne and a dozen other tribes well before Edmund Wilson made his celebrated *Apologies to the Iroquois* in 1960, the Indian stereotype has not so much been shattered as reshaped. The immediate successors to *Broken Arrow* were mostly content to repeat that apparent breakthrough, trading in an easy optimism that blithely rewrites history in terms of reconciliation and peaceful coexistence, like *Sitting Bull* (1954), *The White Feather* (1955) and *The Indian Fighter* (1955), or giving a perfunctory elegiac shrug as in *Hondo* (1954). A few pictures attempted to go rather deeper. Particularly memorable are the opening sequences of Robert Aldrich's *Apache* (1954), where a garish white civilisation is seen through the eyes of a fugitive Indian (Burt Lancaster) making his way back West after escaping from a deportation train taking him with Geronimo's followers to exile in Florida. A tragic ending was planned for this picture, but the front office insisted on optimism and this is what the makers delivered in a hopelessly unconvincing way.

So, for all the fine liberal sentiments, the Indian remained one of the pawns in the western game, to be cast in whatever role the film-maker chose. Commercially this was inevitable, and an aesthetic case can be made out (indeed, frequently has been) against too drastic a change in the genre's established conventions. Clearly, from around 1950 the Indian in the contemporary allegory can stand for the Negro when the implications are social or for the Communist when the implications are political, though generally the identification is

somewhat woolly. *Broken Arrow* obviously could be viewed as a plea
for racial tolerance on a domestic level and for peaceful coexistence
on an international one. The same is true of numerous other movies
which followed it: during the McCarthy era Hollywood artists were
often forced to turn to allegory to handle themes which the studio
bosses would have rejected as too controversial in a modern setting.

The natural tendency of the western is 'hawkish', whatever
the pacific intention of its individual exponents. Consequently a
movie like Charles Marquis Warren's *Arrowhead* (1953), however
distasteful it may seem beside its liberal contemporaries, had a charge
which was largely lacking in many well-meaning pictures of its time,
as well as not appearing to impose worthy latter day sentiments on
to earlier situations. The central character, an Indian-hating cavalry
scout called Ed Bannon (Charlton Heston), was apparently based
on a real-life scout, Al Sieber, and it is with astonishment that we
realise that he is the film's authentic hero, leading a drive to put
down the ghost-dancing heresy as it sweeps through Texas. For
neither the first nor the last time in a western the ghost-dance movement, contrary to all historical evidence, is presented as a violent
insurrectionist activity instead of the largely pacifist one that it was.
The leader of the uprising is the Apache chief Toriano (Jack
Palance), who returns from an Eastern college to arouse his people.
There is a striking image as Toriano arrives home in immaculate
white man's clothing and removes his Stetson to shake down a mane
of black hair, a good dozen years before such a hairstyle became the
badge of the disaffected young. Virtually his next act is to kill his
blood brother, a Wells Fargo agent.

Arrowhead ends with a terrifying hand-to-hand fight in which
Bannon breaks Toriano's neck and with it his influence. 'There's
your inviolable one,' he says to the Indian's distraught followers.
While I have no idea what the conscious motivations of the writer-
director were, the picture strikes me as an ultra right-wing allegory
of the McCarthy period in which the Indians – and especially the
college-educated Toriano bringing his heresy from the East – do
service for Communists, and the whites, with their unwavering
leader Bannon, for those red-blooded American patriots bent on
rooting out the Communist conspiracy at home and standing up to
its menace abroad.

There are relatively few westerns of the past twenty years that
take such an overtly hostile attitude towards the Indians as
Arrowhead. It is generally the role of a white villain to echo the 1869

sentiment of General Sheridan that 'the only good Indian is a dead Indian'. On the other hand many people might agree with the opinion expressed in a 1971 *Playboy* interview by John Wayne, who has spent much of his life fighting Indians on the screen:

> I don't feel we did wrong in taking this great country away from them. There were great numbers of people who needed new land, and the Indians were selfishly trying to keep it for them-selves.

The movies are after all an expression of the dominant culture. Consequently the Indians are invariably seen, whether sympathet-ically of not, from the point of view of the victorious pioneers and their White Anglo-Saxon Protestant society. When serious doubts arise about this culture, however, the Indian will be viewed in a different light. I shall be touching later on the gradual movement in this direction.

But in passing one should perhaps say something about the neglect in the American cinema of the plight of the contemporary Indian. There have been touching if evasive accounts of the sad lives of the 1912 Olympic champion Jim Thorpe, the Sac-Fox Indian from Oklahoma who was stripped of his athletic honours after being charged with infringing his amateur status by accepting money for summer baseball games in college (*Jim Thorpe – All American* in 1951 with Burt Lancaster as Thorpe), and of the World War II hero Ira Hayes, the Pima Indian from Arizona who took to drink back on his neglected Arizona reservation (*The Outsider*, 1961, starring Tony Curtis). In the years of his pathetic decline Thorpe appeared in several low-grade westerns of the 1930s, and in 1950 Ira Hayes was called to Hollywood to re-create the famous flag-raising tableau in the John Wayne movie *The Sands of Iwo Jima*.[19]

A number of TV documentaries have exposed the Indians' situ-ation, and in 1962 there was Kent McKenzie's *The Exiles*, an unsatisfactory study of the pathetic, *déraciné* Indian poor in Los Angeles, which had its moments but suffered from the director's inability to get his non-professional cast to act out their lives in a convincing fashion. More recently there has been Carol Reed's *The*

19 A much better version of the Ira Hayes story is, I'm told, John Frankenheimer's TV film *The American* (with Lee Marvin as Hayes), in which the doomed hero's life is unfolded in flashback as he staggers drunkenly around the set during the filming of *The Sands of Iwo Jima*. A description of this film is to be found in *Only You Dick Daring* by Merle Miller, who wrote the teleplay.

Last Warrior (1970), a well-intentioned film about Indian resistance on a present-day reservation which went disastrously astray through the unbridled performance of Anthony Quinn doing another of his boozy, outsize, life-force figures, in this case a sort of Arizona Zorba the Navajo. And the equally well intentioned, and only slightly more successful *Billy Jack* (1971), written and directed (under the pseudonym T.C. Frank) by Tom Laughlin, who also plays the eponymous hero, a half-Indian Vietnam War veteran wandering around Arizona and becoming idealistically involved in a melodramatic fashion with reservation Indian radicals and white counterculturists. The subject is promising, but despite some pungent satire provided by the San Francisco Committee company, the execution is unsatisfactory.

On an altogether higher plane from *The Last Warrior* and *Billy Jack* stands *When the Legends Die* (1972), the first movie to be directed by Stuart Millar, producer of Arthur Penn's *Little Big Man.* Millar's film, which belongs to the current cycle of rodeo movies, in some ways resembles Robert Rossen's *The Hustler* in its story of an ageing alcoholic cowboy (Richard Widmark) who trains a 19-year-old Southern Ute Indian, Thomas Black Bull (Frederick Forrest), in bronco-busting and takes him round small-town rodeos to cheat the local gamblers. But what the picture is really about is the rejection of contemporary America and the success ethic by Tom Black, who has gained a reputation as a 'killer' for the ferocious way he rides and punishes the animals he was raised to love and care for. Through his eyes we experience the disfigured Western landscape, the phoney patriotic charades of the rodeo circuit, and the lurking prejudice and meanness surrounding him. In one of the film's highpoints we see him crouching with his hat on at a garish indoor rodeo as the band strikes up the national anthem. Slowly, reluctantly, he rises among his fellow competitors, eventually removes his Stetson and brings it to his heart with a contemptuous slap. At the beginning of the film he had been unwillingly brought to a coldly sterile boarding school for Indian reservation orphans, and his elderly guardian-translator was informed, 'Tell him that we will listen to what he has to say about the old ways when he has learnt the new ways.' At the end he quits the rodeo business and returns 'to be with the horses'. 'I've learned the new ways,' he says wearily – a 23-year-old veteran who wants nothing more than to drop not out but back into his counterculture.

This should be a growth area in the western genre, and the material for a potential masterpiece is lurking there waiting for the right artist to shape it. However, the fact that Indian tribes in New Mexico are now financing movies does not necessarily mean that the pictures they back will be revolutionary in character. On the contrary, current projects suggest that they are putting their money into conventionally conservative western fare like Lamont Johnson's *A Gunfight* (1970). Still, my real concern here is with the treatment of the Indians in western movies, which is a complex enough subject in itself, if admittedly trivial when set alongside what is happening in the slums and reservations of contemporary America.

Two dominant traits during the 50s and early 60s were on the one hand the role of the Indians as an external force in uniting Americans and, on the other, the cultural clash between pioneer and redskin. In pictures as crude as John Sturges' *Escape from Fort Bravo* (1953) and as subtle as Sam Peckinpah's *Major Dundee* (1965), we have seen murderously divided parties of Northern soldiers and their Confederate prisoners drawn together in a new sense of national solidarity in the face of an Indian attack. This has become almost a cliché. The other category is more interesting: those movies which deal with whites living among Indians and Indians (usually, but not always, half-breeds) attempting to get along in white society. The major examples of this species are John Huston's *The Unforgiven* (1960) and Don Siegel's *Flaming Star* (1960), where white families stand together to protect an adopted Indian sister (Audrey Hepburn in *The Unforgiven*) or half-breed brother (Elvis Presley in *Flaming Star*) from rejection by white society or reclamation by their tribes. Thematically these movies are declarations in favour of the American melting pot; dramatically they are a recognition of the profound difficulties and personal tragedies involved in the process of assimilation.

A more complex approach to similar issues is to be found in Robert Mulligan's *The Stalking Moon* (1968), a ferocious metaphysical western with a strong Lawrentian undertow, in which a retired cavalry scout (Gregory Peck) and an unseen Indian chief struggle for the allegiance and cultural identity of the Indian's mute half-breed son. I mention Lawrence here because few films so directly bring up the issues he raised in *Studies in Classic American Literature*, and few pictures have so consciously exploited the naked power of the symbolic Indian.

A rather different emphasis from *The Unforgiven* and *Flaming Star* is revealed in films about white settlers embarking on expeditions to regain members of their families captured by Indians, which are testimony to the fragility of white civilisation. These pictures raise the questions: can these prisoners, even if located, be rehabilitated? And will the seekers themselves remain the same? In the last couple of years more robust and optimistic answers have been given to these questions, or rather the nature of the questions themselves has been challenged. But in the 1950s there was an underlying anxiety about them, and they are to be found at the centre of John Ford's *The Searchers* (1956), a film of great charm and much crudity dominated by the cultural assurance of John Wayne, and the same director's *Two Rode Together* (1961), where Ford took a more pessimistic view of the effects of captivity but at the same time showed greater sympathy for the captors and the culture into which the white women and children had fallen. I don't think one is reading too much into these films in seeing them as expressing a fear about the possible breakdown of American society in the face of an under-lying drive towards anarchy and disintegration, a feeling that the inhabitants of America have a tenuous grasp upon their continent.

One dominant direction of the western during the post-war period, and increasingly in the 1960s, lay in setting movies at the very end of the frontier period, and thus confronting the old virtues of the West with the corrupt values of the burgeoning twentieth-century commercial civilisation. This was taken to its extreme in William Fraker's *Monte Walsh* (1970), in which the ageing cowhands are presented quite explicitly as victims of anonymous corporations ultimately controlled from Wall Street. In most of these films Indians in their post-Wounded Knee subjugation are notable by their absence. The only major western dealing centrally with the Indian during this post-frontier period is Abraham Polonsky's *Tell Them Willie Boy Is Here* (1969), which tells the true story of a Paiute outcast who in 1909 was hounded to death in a chase across Southern California by a posse of vindictive whites after the accidental killing of his girlfriend's father. It is played out against a background of unyielding racial intolerance and social indifference, as well as the concurrent visit to the West by President Taft, which led to insane rumours of assassination threats and a massive Indian uprising.

The Indian as perennial outsider – as represented by Willie Boy – is not a new theme in the western. One can go back to a picture which appeared in the same year as *Broken Arrow* to find the Indian presented in terms of parity with Mormons, fugitive gunfighters and travelling entertainers, as social outcasts within the implied framework of an intolerant American conformity. This movie is John Ford's *Wagonmaster*. In a sense, Indians have always been outsiders in Ford's films, though his treatment of them, except in *Wagonmaster* and his last western, *Cheyenne Autumn*, has always been an embarrassing subject for his admirers, despite the increasing sympathy which parallels his decreasingly sanguine attitude to the contemporary world. Peculiarly offensive now, if little remarked on at the time, and fairly reflecting his earlier attitude, is the sequence in *My Darling Clementine* (1946) where Wyatt Earp (Henry Fonda) asserts his claim to the moral and civic leadership of Tombstone by going into a saloon, from which the frightened patrons have fled, to arrest a drunken gun-toting Indian. 'What kind of town is this – selling whisky to Indians?' he demands scornfully. Moreover he doesn't bother to put his pathetic prisoner in jail, but casually kicks him in the rump, saying, 'Indian – get out of town and stay out.' The Indian in effect has no place in the community that Earp is shaping.

This is the way that villains are established today, not heroes. Fourteen years after *My Darling Clementine* and a decade after *Wagonmaster*, John Sturges' *The Magnificent Seven* establishes the liberal credentials and nonconformity of the Seven's leaders (Yul Brynner and Steve McQueen) through an opening scene in which they take over a hearse carrying the body of a dead Indian, drive it up to the white cemetery and force a hostile racist community to accept the Indian for burial there. More recently we have seen Martin Ritt's *Hombre* (1967), whose eponymous white hero (Paul Newman) has been reared as a child by Indians, grown to manhood in white society and subsequently elected to live as an Indian. Nothing is vouchsafed to us about his Indian background; its honesty and superiority are assumed and considered to be beyond question. When eventually he finds himself a lonely, brooding figure in a decaying pioneer community, he serves dramatically as an unimpeachable moral centre from which the film judges, and ultimately condemns, his white companions. In some ways he embodies Norman Mailer's concept of the 'White Negro' and inevitably has to die.

Hombre is an extraordinary landmark in the development of the western. An equally pronounced example, and a rather comic one, of the way attitudes towards Indians have changed over the past couple of decades is found in comparing Shelley Winters' response to the same situation in Mann's *Winchester '73* (1950) and Sidney Pollack's *The Scalphunters* (1968). In the earlier film she is a young pioneer wife trapped with a cavalry patrol by an Indian war party. As the Indians prepare for their final assault, James Stewart slips her a gun. Contemplating a fate worse than death, she nods in stoic recognition, and referring to the final bullet, she says, 'I understand about the last one.' As a blousy, big-hearted whore in *The Scalphunters*, she quite happily quits the company of uncouth, ill-smelling outlaws with whom she has been travelling, to go off with her handsome Kiowa captors. 'What the hell, they're only men,' she shrugs and reflects that the Indian chief is going to get 'the damnedest white squaw in the Kiowa nation'.

Implicit in many of these pictures is a rejection of the view that Indians are a deadly menace and that their culture is too alien to live with. From this position it is a relatively short move towards seeing what can be learned from them, and only another step to seeing them as an alternative, or counter, culture. This was proposed back in 1956 in Samuel Fuller's didactic *Run of the Arrow*, which centres upon an Irish-Southerner (Rod Steiger) who fires the last shot at Appomattox and, refusing to be accommodated to post-Civil War life, goes West to undergo the painful initiation which will make him a full member of the Sioux nation. Reluctantly he is won back to white civilisation by a Northern cavalry officer who gives him a glib lesson in American history, and the picture concludes with the admonitory title (replacing 'The End'), 'The end of this story can only be written by you.' It is characteristic of Fuller, incidentally, that at one stage he identifies the troublesome young Sioux braves with present-day American juvenile delinquents.

Run of the Arrow anticipated by a decade several of the most ambitious works of the past few years and a social trend among the young which has led to books on Indian history flooding the avant-garde bookshops from San Francisco to St Germain-des-Prés. In the theatre we have seen Arthur Kopits' play *Indians* (1968), and in the cinema Elliot Silverstein's *A Man Called Horse* (1970), Ralph Nelson's *Soldier Blue* (1970) and Arthur Penn's *Little Big Man* (1970). All these films, in their varying ways, present Indian life as a valid counterculture, a more organic, life-enhancing existence than white society, from which the central character in each film gains a new perspective on society and a new humanity. In *A Man Called Horse*, he is an English nobleman (Richard Harris), revitalised by a peculiarly gruelling sojourn among the Sioux; in *Soldier Blue*, an American girl (Candice Bergen) becomes an incredibly articulate critic of her culture (as well as an unbelievably foul-mouthed one) after her period of captivity among the Cheyenne; in *Little Big Man*, a picaresque hero (Dustin Hoffman) drifts back and forth between his adoptive Cheyenne family and a corrupt white frontier society. All three films are less inhibited in their acknowledgement of the brutal aspects of Indian life than the earlier liberal movies that argued a case for mutual respect, tolerance and peaceable relations.

Indicative of their closeness to contemporary concerns is the fact that both *Soldier Blue* and *Little Big Man* offer direct parallels with the Vietnam situation, and perhaps even with My Lai, in their presentation of cavalry massacres and the deliberate policy of exterminating Indians. The climax of *Soldier Blue* is a reconstruction of the Sand Creek Massacre, which is updated from 1864 to 1877 to place it the year after Custer's defeat at Little Big Horn. *Little Big Man* has at its centre a quite dazzling re-creation of the Washita River Massacre of 1868. Both are unsparing in their fashionable attacks on white 'civilisation', which they see as hypocritical, barbarous and death-seeking. There are token 'good whites', to be sure, but the central thrust is directed against the ideology and behaviour of a whole society. (*Soldier Blue* handles the material with bludgeoning crudity, *Little Big Man* with feeling and subtlety, but the general drift is much the same.) In the introductory sequence to *Little Big Man*, in which the 121-year-old narrator is encouraged to reminisce by a present-day historian, the term 'genocide' is openly used to characterise the nineteenth-century treatment of the Indians.

This contemporary framework makes possible what a few previous pictures have only been able to imply. In Richard Brooks' forceful *The Last Hunt* (1955), for example, we had a pathological Indian-hater (Robert Taylor) bent on exterminating the remaining herds of bison. 'One less buffalo,' he says, 'means one less Indian.' *The Last Hunt*, a box-office disaster in its day, would no doubt be welcomed now as a significant ecological western.[20] Again, in John Ford's *Cheyenne Autumn* (1964), there is a clear comparison made between the persecution of the Indians and the German extermination camps in the performance of Karl Malden as Captain Wessels,

---

20 Long before the state of the environment became an international preoccupation, the western took up the cause. The low-budget *Back in the Saddle* (1941) is a pure ecological western with Gene Autry fighting against an evil mill-owner who is poisoning cattle by dumping copper sulphate into a river running through the valley and refuses to desist from his anti-social activities.

a rigid Teuton just doing his duty as commandant of a grisly prison in which the remnant of a decimated Cheyenne tribe is briefly incarcerated. But *Little Big Man* presents the issue directly as the shame of a whole society and its almost conscious policy.

Little Big Man also manages for the first time to give a major role in a big budget movie to an Indian actor in casting Chief Dan George as Dustin Hoffman's Indian 'father', Old Lodge Skins. Previously, star Indian roles and even minor speaking parts of any importance have regularly been assigned to white actors; indeed it was only a chance last-minute decision to cast Chief Dan George. The film also goes some way towards finding a satisfactory dramatic language for the Indians, and Dan George manages to avoid that unctuous solemnity of movie Indians. The result is not entirely satisfactory, but a move in the right direction. The alternative, I suppose, is subtitles. In Raoul Walsh's *A Distant Trumpet* (1964) and in Stuart Millar's *When the Legends Die* (1972), subtitles were used and they at least gave the Indians the dignity and respect which attaches to foreigners and the prestige of subtitled European movies; no one else has resorted to this except the makers of *Texas Across the River* (1967), a feeble comedy western, one of the better touches of which was to have the Indians speak in their native tongue and provide unintelligible subtitles in Indian sign language.

Little Big Man, with its beautifully realised evocation of Cheyenne life, is perhaps the present high-water mark in the treatment of Indians in the movies, as well as being a major satirical comment on the values and appeal of the western genre. Nevertheless, it is still open to the accusation of manipulating the Indians according to the political ideas and unconscious cultural predilections of its makers. The charge has been made that the Cheyenne in *Little Big Man* are less Indians than New York Jews, and there is a good deal to be said for this view. Indeed at the end, when Old Lodge Skins fails to bring about his ritual, ceremonial death on a hilltop outside his village, he stands up, dusts himself down, and stoically observes: 'Well, sometimes the magic works and sometimes it doesn't.' We should of course remember that it was the belief of Joseph Smith and the Mormons that the Indians were in fact Jewish, the descendants of the lost Hebrew tribes.

Considering that probably 25 to 30 per cent of working cowboys in the nineteenth-century West were Negroes, the absence of black faces during the seventy years of the western's history is another case of Hollywood's failure to accord the country's black minority an adequate, or even token, representation in the American cinema, beyond acknowledging their presence as house servants. Not only has the western traditionally been devoted to upholding White Anglo-Saxon Protestant supremacy – which has involved virtually all minorities, not just blacks, appearing in supporting and frequently comic roles – but it has also tended to favour Southerners. Admittedly a large part of the transient labour force in the West was made up of ex-Confederate soldiers, yet to an unusual degree, both in Civil War movies (from *Birth of a Nation* through *Gone With the Wind*) and in post-Civil War westerns, Hollywood has tended to be an apologist for the South and to locate in the dispossessed Southerner the ideal of the chivalrous cowboy.

In the 30s and 40s, according to Fenin and Everson, there were apparently a number of low-budget horse operas featuring black actors made strictly for ghetto audiences in America and never shown abroad. Predictably, in the 1970s the sudden realisation that a profitable black audience exists again for rather more elaborate specialist fare has led to something of a revival, with such black westerns as Sidney Poitier's *Buck and the Preacher* (1972) and *The Legend of Nigger Charley* (1972). Where this unpromising start will lead remains to be seen.

As I have previously remarked, the Indian has often been a surrogate Negro in numerous liberal westerns of the 1950s, at a time when Hollywood was soft-pedalling in the area of contemporary social conscience movies, immediately following the brief rash of pictures about black–white relations (*Pinky, Lost Boundaries* and *Home of the Brave* all appeared in 1949); and this may have been of some slight consolation to Negro audiences, who are said to have identified in the past with Indians.

One of the obvious explanations for the presence of isolated black characters in recent westerns has been the need to provide roles in the most enduringly popular of genres for prominent black actors, such as Sidney Poitier as the cool, cynical cavalry horse-breaker in Ralph Nelson's *Duel at Diablo* (1965) and Sammy Davis Jr. in the feeble Sinatra Clan romp *Sergeants Three* (1962), a western remake of *Gunga Din* which gave Davis the opportunity to play Kipling's regimental bisti as a cavalry bugler.

A rather more rewarding role went to Ossie Davis in *The Scalphunters* (1968), a robust semi-comedy of impeccably liberal attitudes, where he plays an escaped slave of great social sophistication who puts to shame the uncouth, illiterate Westerners among whom he unhappily lands on his way to freedom in Mexico in the 1850s. He insists that he is a Comanche who has learned his fine ways through an association with an educated family in the South, but he becomes an object of trade and bargaining between both whites and Indians. Typical of the film's somewhat embarrassing good intentions is a fight in a pool between Davis and Burt Lancaster which leaves both so caked in mud as to be racially indistinguishable.

Several films have presented units of black cavalrymen. The best of them is Robert Parrish's *The Wonderful Country* (1959), where their role is marginal; the most significant is John Ford's *Sergeant Rutledge* (1960). Unfortunately Ford's film is gravely weakened by having as its dramatic structure an indifferent Perry Mason-style courtroom drama in which the almost saintly eponymous hero (Woody Strode) is wrongly standing trial for rape and murder. In handling this court-martial aspect, Ford is at his most embarrassingly self-indulgent, and one suspects that it held little interest for him. What he is interested in doing, and does well, is to present his black cavalrymen in precisely the same heroic manner that he earlier used for their white counterparts – silhouetted against the horizon, trekking through the desert, making dignified compositions of the statuesque Strode against sharply rising buttes. 'It's all right for Mr Lincoln to say we're free, but we're not free yet,' is the theme, and Ford wishes to give his black soldiers their due place in American history. 'The Ninth Cavalry was my home, my freedom,' says Rutledge, and addressing his men he insists that 'the Ninth's record is going to speak for us all one day and it's going to speak clean.' Sadly the film does not rank high in the great director's work, but it is touching to see him, after so many years of patronising black performers, confer on them one of the greatest gifts at his disposal, which is to make them full citizens of his beloved Monument Valley.

Woody Strode has also made other less celebrated excursions into the West – as an Indian in Ford's *Two Rode Together* and the lamentable British western *Shalako*, and as a tough bounty hunter and ace bow-man, hired as one of *The Professionals* (1966) to join Robert Ryan, Lee Marvin and Burt Lancaster on their expedition into revolutionary Mexico. Nothing is made of his colour here; everything focuses on his practical skills. Both of these elements, however, are central to the appearance of another top black athlete-turned-actor, Jim Brown, in the two westerns which take him into Mexico – *Rio Conchos* (1964) and *100 Rifles* (1968). The first is a compelling picture which inexorably builds to an apocalyptic climax in which

Brown, as a cavalry sergeant, and Richard Boone, as a surly Indian-hating racist Southerner, perish together in destroying a consignment of stolen weapons which has fallen into the hands of renegade Indians and their ex-Confederate allies. In *100 Rifles*, Brown figures as an American mercenary assisting Mexican revolutionaries (his political involvement has obvious contemporary parallels), and enjoys the sexual favours of Raquel Welch. It could be argued that the acceptance of the once taboo subject of miscegenation has been gradually prepared for through the relationships between white frontiersmen and Indian women, though the latter (e.g. Debra Paget in *Broken Arrow*, Dolores Del Rio in *Flaming Star*, Elsa Martinelli in *The Indian Fighter*, Audrey Hepburn in *The Unforgiven*) were all played by white actresses.

Western examples are naturally to be found of that favourite American and Hollywood activity – the lifting of the lid from a seemingly ordinary community to expose the seething vice, nastiness and racism underneath. The pursuit is a laudable one, but as often in the western the result can prove disturbingly anachronistic, making the audience only too well aware that attitudes widely accepted in their time are being exposed as egregious excesses. In *Invitation to a Gunfighter* the task of exposure falls to a sophisticated octoroon from New Orleans played by Yul Brynner, who gives the community a lesson in tolerance, as well as teaching the ignorant townsfolk how to pronounce his distinguished French name (Jules Gaspard d'Estaing), before perishing rather than kill the man they have hired him to eliminate, who ironically is a Confederate soldier lately returned from losing the Civil War. In *Death of a Gunfighter* (1969) the task of instruction falls to an ageing unwanted sheriff (Richard Widmark), and before dying at the hands of his anti-Semitic, anti-Mexican, antipathetic employers, his last act is to marry his mistress, the proprietress of the local saloon and brothel, played by the black singer Lena Horne. The part of the town's leading bigot and organiser of the sheriff's downfall is taken by Carroll O'Connor, later to make his name as Archie Bunker in *All in the Family*, the American television version of *Till Death Us Do Part*.

4 Landscape, Violence, Poker

If not from the start, when *Cripple Creek Bar-Room* (1898) was shot in the Edison Studio and *The Great Train Robbery* filmed on location in New Jersey, at least from quite early days the landscape has been an integral part of the western both as an ingredient in the genre's popular appeal and for its role in shaping the dramatic action. Frequently the landscape is simply there to be admired, which is not unacceptable. The American West has an intrinsic beauty worth recording for its own sake, as witness the work of painters, and later photographers, from colonial times to the present.

And the land is not only beautiful and awe-inspiring but possessed of strange surrealist qualities: Max Ernst was struck by the close resemblance between the imaginary landscape he dreamt up for his study of the destruction and renewal of life, *Europe After the Rain*, when he began his large CinemaScope-shaped canvas in 1940, and the real landscape of Arizona which he first saw during his American exile when he was halfway towards completing it. One of the most haunting Western scenes I know is to be found in Gordon Douglas' *Rio Conchos* (1964), where a deranged ex-Confederate colonel has established the headquarters of his band of marauders on a hill above a Mexican river in a half-built mansion; through the windows of the Palladian façade one can see the sky – and it looks like and has the same disturbing qualities as a Magritte.

The two most important native-born artists of the Abstract Expressionist school, Adolph Gottlieb (born New York, 1903) and Jackson Pollock (born on a ranch near Cody, Wyoming, in 1912) were deeply influenced by the West. A turning point in Gottlieb's development came in 1937 when he spent a year in the desert outside Tucson, Arizona, during which time he assimilated aspects of the local landscape and Indian art while casting off the European shackles he had so happily taken on in his youth. Look at, say, Boetticher's *Ride Lonesome* or Hellman's *The Shooting* – the burning sand, the oppressive sky, the fractured enigmatic shards of civilisation which litter the desolate terrain – look at them abstractly and you see and *feel* the world which helped shape the mature Gottlieb style and provided him with a personal iconography.

Pollock spent his formative years drifting around Arizona in the 1920s, from the Mexican border to the southern rim of the Grand Canyon, in the company of rough itinerant labourers. His biographer B.H. Friedman writes of the popular European image of Pollock as 'a hard-riding, hard-drinking cowboy from the Wild West who came roaring, maybe even shooting, his way into New York where he took the art galleries by storm.'[21] This is an expression of that conventional rhetoric of American life and the foreign response to it I have spoken of earlier, by which Henry Kissinger went into the last stages of the Vietnam peace talks in Paris introducing (ingratiating?) himself to the press as a wary gunfighter coming into town, to clear up the mess created by Lyndon Johnson, who once provoked Charles de Gaulle to say (according to his biographer Pierre Galante): 'He's a cowboy... born in the land of the ranch and the Colt, who shot his way up to sheriff.' Pollock was of course influenced by the frontier company he kept in his youth, but his art is more closely related to the West than Friedman's jocular gloss on his life-style conveys. Like Gottlieb, he too was immensely affected, as Friedman goes on to suggest, by the overwhelming landscape, the strange qualities of light, the Indian pictographs, and by, I think one can fairly say, the tragic sense and desperate challenge of the West.

The Western movie, like the best Western art, is naturally most effective when it goes beyond the merely picturesque. Certain directors have established their personal landscape in the West. The most notable and best known is John Ford's Monument Valley, straddling Arizona and Utah on the Navajo Reservation, with its cathedral-like buttes and mesas rising out of the flat red desert, where eight of Ford's thirteen sound westerns have been made. The terrain

---

21 *Jackson Pollock* (Weidenfeld and Nicolson, London, 1973), p. 3. I find it interesting that three notable American artists of the post-Abstract Expressionist period – Jasper Johns, Kenneth Noland and Frank Stella, each representing quite different schools – should have lent Navajo blankets from their personal collections to the celebrated exhibition which toured America and Europe in 1972–3. There is no suggestion that North American Indian art significantly influenced their work – on the contrary it was their paintings that helped fellow-countrymen to recognise the aesthetic value, admittedly divorced from the complex culture that produced them, of these extraordinary artefacts. But Navajo blankets and rugs – as well as the deliberately ephemeral art of sand-painting – arise from the Western terrain and light, and are part of the shared experience discussed here.

may not always have been suitable to the stated geographical location of the subjects, for Monument Valley is a unique and relatively
small area; but it provided him with what is universally regarded as
his own moral universe, which he has rendered so powerfully that
a visitor to Monument Valley is overwhelmed by recollection of
Ford movies. Other directors too have created their own worlds –
especially Budd Boetticher and Anthony Mann. Boetticher's arid
corner of the Southwest, with its smooth clusters of rocks like Easter
Island statues which have had their features rubbed away, is the
perfect setting for his series of severe little fables starring Randolph
Scott; verdant oases occur in his films as interludes for contemplation and sometimes (most notably the showdown in *Ride Lonesome*)
for thematic resolution. The reverse is the case with Anthony Mann,
who for the most part favours lush prairie and beautiful hill country
and tends to reserve denuded or snow-covered settings for his most
sombre dramatic statements.

In his study of the formative years of American culture, *O Strange
New World*, Howard Mumford Jones lists five 'significant compo-
nents in the delineation of the Western landscape in paint and
words': astonishment, plenitude, vastness, incongruity and melancholy.[22] All these are present in varying degrees whenever a camera
is turned upon the American landscape. And they play a part in
producing, as well as helping to characterise, what John W.
McCoubrey, in a fascinating and provocative book, has called *The
American Tradition in Painting*.[23] What Dr McCoubrey has to say
about American art from colonial days to the present has a great
bearing on the American cinema in general and the western in
particular:

> Our art is possessed by the spaciousness and emptiness of the land
> itself. No American painter can ignore it; to make its presence
> felt in his work, he has consciously avoided, or never needed,
> these skills which traditionally bottle up, control or make habit-
> able pictorial space... Thus figures in American paintings – like
> their viewers – are not given an easy mastery of the space they
> occupy. Rather, they stand in tentative relation to it, without any
> illusion of command over it.

22 *O Strange New World: American Culture: The Formative Years* (Chatto & Windus,
   London, 1965), p. 379.
23 George Braziller, New York, 1963.

And in comparing a European abstract painting by Soulages, which is tightly constructed and wholly contained within the canvas, with a superficially similar one by the American Franz Kline, he observed that the violent brush strokes in the latter, 'as they reach to the very edges of the canvas – and seemingly beyond – imply the continuation of vast distances, the presence of an enormous void, of which the area of the painting is but a fragment.'

The location of the Westerner in his landscape is a matter of paramount importance, and there are relatively few movies which do not begin with the single man or group of men riding through the countryside. This is even true of those pictures largely set in towns where the sense of space is implied – as in the Kline painting *Crosstown* referred to by McCoubrey – by the dusty streets reaching out to the limitless surrounding tracts, a feeling evoked by shots down the main street in *Rio Bravo* and by the railroad disappearing in the heat haze in *High Noon*. Both *Rio Bravo* and *High Noon* are prefaced by people riding into town – in each case these are visitors and not the marshals, for were it to be otherwise, the resident lawmen played by Wayne and Cooper would be detached from the communities which they embody. In another town-centred western, *The Gunfighter*, the person we see crossing the desert at the beginning, indeed almost the only person we see riding alone in the countryside at any time, is Gregory Peck as the doomed gunslinger, the man on the move whose arrival is a sure sign of disruption in the community.

This contrast between open land and the town, between the illusion of freedom and the necessity of compromise, between a relaxed association with nature and a tense accommodation to society, lies at the roots of the genre. Certainly the mood of a western is established at the outset by the way directors place their protagonists in relationship to the surroundings, and over the past twenty-odd years the approach to the question has become increasingly self-conscious. The way the detached buckskin-clad Alan Ladd almost floats down out of the mountains in *Shane* could scarcely be more calculated. The same is true of the opening of Don Siegel's *Two Mules for Sister Sara* (1969), a succession of panning shots from various animals (an owl, a fish, a rabbit, a mountain lion, a snake, a tarantula) over to Clint Eastwood as he rides confidently through the beautiful, unspoilt Mexican terrain. We take the filmmaker's point that the man is himself a wild animal very much at home in the country; but after a few shots we begin to become conscious of their calculation, full of the same kind of admiration for the cameraman's skill and patience that we feel when seeing a clever nature film like Disney's *Living Desert.*

Admittedly the aestheticised mood is built up only to be deliberately broken by Eastwood's horse crushing the last example of the local fauna, the tarantula. Nothing, we are made to feel, can stop this arrogant man – and we are right. How superficially similar and yet how different is the opening of *The Wild Bunch.* Here the outlaw band, their immaculate military disguise and steady riding pace placing them in such a confidently superior position to the demented pedestrians involved in a revival meeting, enter a Texas border town to stage their hold-up. Far from treading on tarantulas, the group's fate is prefigured by their identification with a couple of poisonous scorpions fed into a tray of ants and burnt by a crowd of callous children: 'As flies to wanton boys are we to the Gods, they kill us for their sport.'

A contrast of another kind would be with the openings of Arthur Penn's *The Left Handed Gun* (1958), Henry Hathaway's *From Hell to Texas* (1958) and Peckinpah's *The Ballad of Cable Hogue* (1970), which stress the vulnerability of their heroes by presenting them without, or rapidly dispossessed of, their horses, and facing a remorseless land, a situation which prepares us for the moral and dramatic evolution of their heroes in a very different way from Siegel's.

The allegorical journey where the land itself seems to determine and reflect the film's dramatic development is a common enough phenomenon and never more perfectly realised than in Anthony Mann's last important western, *Man of the West* (1958) – perhaps his finest and certainly his most pessimistic movie. The film begins with a reformed outlaw, Link Jones (Gary Cooper), warily entering an unfamiliar town to make a train journey, the object of which is to hire a schoolteacher for the remote Texas community in which he lives. He is thus a man already redeemed and accommodated to settled ways, unlike the heroes of earlier Mann westerns. But the implication of the movie is that he has merely broken with the past, set it aside, but not exorcised it. The train is attacked by bandits and he is stranded with a saloon singer and an unsuccessful gambler. Suspecting that his old gang was responsible for the hold-up, he leads his two companions to the only shelter he knows in the vicinity, an abandoned farmhouse where, sure enough, the gang is waiting, led by the insane Dock Tobin (Lee J. Cobb) and his sons, who are in effect the only family the younger Link had ever known.

Returning to this parody of a homestead and caricature of a family, standing amid hospitable green countryside which no one farms and where no cattle graze, Link is forced to accompany the Tobin gang on their last big job – the robbery of the bulging bank at the mining town of Lasso – before they head across the border into Mexican exile. As they progress, the atmosphere becomes increasingly tense, Tobin's behaviour ever more erratic; habitable land gives way to desert as they move further away from civilisation, culminating in the discovery that Lasso is now an arid, decaying ghost town. ('Lasso' suggests a trap and a noose, just as 'Link' has the obvious dual significance of a name drawn from Abe Lincoln and the implication of a figure standing between the settled and primitively atavistic.) Here Link must make his final settlement with his 'brothers' and his mad surrogate father, whose last destructive act is to rape the captive saloon girl. *Man of the West* has its longueurs, but few westerns can match its integration of setting, dramatic development and moral progress.

Mann's use of the ghost town was of course by no means new, and indeed it is among the western's most compelling settings. The genre seems happier with it than with an established community. Most western towns bigger than a handful of isolated buildings lack a sense of on-going life. They seem populated by extras shuffling uneasily around on purposeless errands, waiting to take their place as spectators in some imminent dramatic confrontation. This unease is employed to good effect in *Monte Walsh*, when a pair of old cowhands, newly arrived in town, ask a ranch foreman the question everyone has been dying to ask for years – why are all these people hanging around doing nothing? 'They're out of work,' is the laconic reply.

At any rate the ghost town as the objective correlative of the impermanence of American life, a pessimistic feeling about the fragility of American civilisation and its problems in putting down roots, is a forceful image. Like *Man of the West*, numerous westerns involve an inexorable journey towards a ghost town where the central characters are doomed to die or emerge shriven. At a conventional level we see this in Andrew McLaglen's *Bandolero!* (1968), where two brothers, reunited in crime, perish together and are buried side by side in a deserted Mexican adobe village, when they might have used the proceeds of a robbery to buy a ranch in Montana. In a more complex vein, the journey of self-discovery in Peckinpah's first movie, *The Deadly Companions*, is to a ghost town

where the heroine can bury her dead son by her late husband, and
those accompanying her can dispense with an unseen Apache
dogging their trail and settle a blood feud left over from the Civil
War. Likewise in John Sturges' best western, *The Law and Jake Wade*
(1958), the last third of the picture is set in an abandoned mining
town, where buried in the graveyard is the loot which binds a
reformed outlaw to his old gang. Oddly enough, Alfred Hitchcock's
first thriller with an American setting, *Saboteur* (1942), took him
briefly into a ghost town. And less oddly Joseph Losey, whose
American career was cut short before he had the opportunity to
make the western he planned, chose a ghost town as the location
for the final sequence of *The Prowler* (1950), using it as the ultimate
place of retreat for his pathetic, fugitive cop as his dreams of success
and social acceptance crumble to dust.

The ghost town inevitably imposes certain attitudes upon the
viewer. The open country on the other hand, as I have implied, is
subject to being manipulated to suit the filmmaker's purpose. The
magnificence of the landscape can be used to aggrandise the action
– to elevate the activities of the Westerner into Olympian encounters which derive a heroic purity and detachment from the
surroundings. This is the way the showdown between the one-eyed
bounty-hunter (John Wayne) and a band of ugly desperadoes works
in *True Grit* – as they ride towards each other across a clearing in
the forest, the scene takes on the aspect of a joust between medieval
knights. Whereas in Dick Richards' *Culpepper Cattle Company* we
are constantly aware of the discrepancy between the magnificent
scenery and the squalid events enacted within it and the sordid little
communities encamped upon it.

If I have given the impression that the visual aspect of the western
is largely a matter of the direct confrontation between the filmmaker
and the landscape, I must qualify this in several ways. No one today
can easily bring a totally fresh, primitive eye to the land. The traditions of American art, of photography, of the western genre itself,
interpose themselves. On occasion these traditions are consciously
present, as when a cinematographer bases his style on Western artists
like Remington and Russell, or on pioneer photographers. That
'authentic' Civil War look of John Huston's *The Red Badge of
Courage* derives from a close study of Matthew Brady's pictures, and
films like *High Noon* and Delmer Daves' *3.10 to Yuma* seem clearly
to have aimed at a gritty, grainy quality intended to evoke nineteenth-century photographs. *Butch Cassidy and the Sundance Kid* also

uses the style of contemporary photographers, but in an altogether
more showy way. *A Man Called Horse* would seem to have drawn
upon earlier Western painters of Indian life such as George Catlin,
Alfred Miller and Karl Bodmer for its compositions and colour
values. In several pictures set in Mexico one can detect the influence of Mexican paintings, particularly those of Diego Rivera and
José Clemente Orozco, with their stylised groupings of peasants and
revolutionaries. One sees this in the hieratic arrangement of the
importunate peons in the face of their American saviours in *The
Magnificent Seven*. Here their position is subservient. More often it
is heroic, as in the endless lines of identical, white-clad, sombrero-
topped Juaristas who appear on the skylines or the battlements to
look down on the American mercenaries in Robert Aldrich's
equally studied *Vera Cruz* (1954). In both cases the contrast is
between the individualised Americans and the anonymous, collective mass of the Mexicans.

'Violence,' said the Black Power ideologue Rap Brown, 'is as
American as cherry pie', and a non-violent western is as odd, as
unthinkable, as a vegetarian steakhouse. In the past twenty years,
however, a good many westerns have tended to be exceedingly self-
conscious about the way they earn their bread and butter. They have
preached sermons against violence, while benefiting from, or
exulting in, violence. Depending upon the direction from which
one approaches the subject, this could be called a central contradiction of the genre or simple hypocrisy. Apologists for the western's
traditionally healthy cathartic qualities have been troubled by the
discomforting violence in movies which – this disturbing element
aside – they would tend to approve of. Yet the simple fact is that
the more seriously violence is taken by the filmmaker, the more
likely its expression will be to break the accepted entertainment
conventions – shocking the audience and offending the susceptibil-
ities of liberal critics.

Consequently, the traditional approach adopted by the
Goldwater school will seem controlled, ritualised, acceptable, while
the sharper, more realistic depiction of similar events in the Kennedy
western might seem disturbing and, on superficial examination,
morbid or even sadistic.[24] In what I must call the more serious west-

24 I have written elsewhere on the history and the social and aesthetic problems
   of violence in the cinema, and I am here restricting myself to violence in the
   western. My essay 'Violence in the Movies', written originally for *Twentieth*

erns, the quantity of violence has diminished and its quality become altogether more intense. In Martin Ritt's *Hombre*, for example, there is a single violent incident in the first half-hour, when the hero employs a rifle butt to strike the face of a cowboy who has been taunting some Indians in an all-white saloon. The effect is literally shattering, for the victim is holding a glass to his lips, but the duration is about two seconds. In Boetticher's *Tall T* there is a mood of incipient violence throughout, carefully cued by social and domestic events, which wells up and quickly subsides as Randolph Scott despatches his three captors one by one, using methods which relate existential circumstance to individual comeuppance and calculated (morally and aesthetically) to give them their just deserts. Incipient violence, too, determines the structure of *High Noon*. As the clock ticks inexorably towards the final encounter, the actual scenes of physical confrontation – one fistfight, one shoot-out – occupy about five minutes of the picture. This very sparing use of action is dramatically admirable, and possibly socially responsible, yet it has the e ffect perhaps – as does the dull forty minutes of initial scene-setting in Hitchcock's *The Birds* – of almost making the audience *will* the violence upon the characters involved. It can also lead to over-emphasis on the purely aesthetic, virtuoso aspects of staging gunfights.

The tone of fistfights is usually a key to a film's approach to violence. In the Johnson and Goldwater-style films of John Ford and his natural successor Andrew V. McLaglen, these fights are hardly ever taken seriously. They are usually conducted between comrades and friendly rivals. Davy Crockett's followers engage in fisticuffs for fun in *The Alamo*; John Wayne and his brothers bust up the family home in *The Sons of Katie Elder*. Often a fight involves dozens of people, like the punch-up in *McLintock!* or the vast post-Civil War brawl between Northerners and Southerners on the Fourth of July in McLaglen's *The Undefeated*. The result of a hundred punches, shattered chairs, broken saloon mirrors, fractured banisters and falling chandeliers will at the most be a few bruises, a couple of black eyes and the odd piece of sticking plaster. The bartender has ducked and the pianist has gone into a frenzied rendition of 'Buffalo Girls' to accompany a playful ritual which can often be as stylised, graceful and artfully choreographed as a ballet.

Century (Winter, 1964–5), is reprinted in *Sight, Sound and Society*, ed. David Manning White and Richard Averson (Beacon Press, Boston, 1968) and *Violence in the Mass Media*, ed. Otto Larsen (Harper & Row, New York, 1969).

There is something here which reflects the rough-and-tumble of frontier life: this is actually framed within William Fraker's *Monte Walsh*, when some old cowhands nearly wreck their bunkhouse in a tough, friendly brawl and and end up laughing, sensing that they've caught a little of the old departed spirit, declaring that they haven't enjoyed themselves so much in months. They have, of course, been behaving like children, getting something out of their system, as a knowing glance from the ranch boss (representing the new, anonymous commercial 'system' itself) indicates. An observer of the scene in another attempt at a realistic depiction of Western life, *Will Penny*, looks at the irresponsible behaviour of cowboys and notes just that: 'Children – dangerous children.'

At the far end of the spectrum from the expansive brawling of John Wayne in Goldwater and Johnson movies, there are the westerns of Anthony Mann, where fistfights have even greater intensity than shoot-outs. In *Winchester '73* and *The Man from Laramie*, James Stewart and his opponents sweat, grunt, get really battered, and the camera edges in close on their brutal contests. The fights invariably end with someone getting badly hurt, and in the case of Gary Cooper taking on a ruthless opponent in *Man of the West*, two people get killed, one of them an innocent bystander. Here the dialectic of the western is at work, forming a bond within a society or destroying it, and both themes have their validity. Somewhere between the extremes of the Mann approach to fistfights and that of the John Ford school is the partly satirical marathon scrap between Eastern seafarer Gregory Peck and ranch foreman Charlton Heston in *The Big Country*, which is presented in long shot in the moonlight and continues until both men are down on their knees exhausted. The complex brawl in the present-day Prescott bar at rodeo time in Peckinpah's *Junior Bonner* draws on these established conventions – as understood both by the participants and a suitably conditioned worldwide audience – and enables Steve McQueen to provoke the disturbance and yet maintain his heroic stance while sensibly withdrawing from the subsequent mêlée.

If it is true that westerns most opposed to violence turn out to be the most violent, it is perhaps also true that they are likely to evidence a strong vein of masochism. Mann's heroes are frequently wounded in painful ways which go far beyond the obvious purpose of providing a revenge motive. In his two westerns (and in several of his other films) Marlon Brando undergoes extreme degradation at the hands of sadistic enemies. In each case the emphasis falls on his pain rather than his tormentors' pleasure. These symbolic wounds of course place the Westerner in a much older tradition of the mythic hero. And the recurrent ritual of removing bullets or arrows from the hero's body (a process drawn out to inordinate lengths in Don Siegel's *Two Mules for Sister Sara*) suggests that the aim is principally a test of manhood, of the ability to endure pain without flinching, rather than simply the punishment of the protagonist.

Having said all this, I must nevertheless reiterate that for film-makers and moviegoers alike the staging and viewing of violent spectacles are among the genre's prime attractions. Where this is the only motive – as it seems to be in most Italian westerns – there is perhaps cause for censure. Yet such moral judgements are not easily arrived at. A case in point is a recent preoccupation with the gallows and the business of hanging.

Certain crude movies of the 1950s which most critics roundly condemned – *The Hangman* (1959) and *Good Day for a Hanging* (1959) – led to the multiple legal executions shown in *Hang 'Em High*, *Bandolero!* and *True Grit*. The executions in *True Grit* might be explained away as the presentation of the true facts of frontier life and even their brutalising effects on the young, and intermittently in that picture there is a vein of black humour which informs the opening section of *Bandolero!*, in which James Stewart poses as a public hangman to free his brother's gang, and turns the notion of gallows humour into rope-and-timber reality. There is, however, in both films a morbid streak which colours the whole of *Hang 'Em High*, where the central relationship is between a law enforcement officer and a self-righteous 'hanging judge' based on the celebrated Isaac Charles Parker of Arkansas Territory, a personal appointee of President Grant. John Huston's *The Life and Times of Judge Roy Bean* (1972) also exploits the darkly comic aspects of hanging, to dubious effect. There are undoubtedly reflections of the time here, but whatever way one cares to look at the matter, the western – for all its constant preaching against lynch law – remains firmly committed to capital punishment. One could argue that for it to be otherwise would be a gross falsification of history. It is at such moments that one recalls a western of a more conventionally liberal cast, Raoul Walsh's *The Tall Men* (1955), which opens with Clark Gable and Cameron Mitchell riding towards a corpse hanging from a tree: 'Looks like we're near civilisation,' says Gable.

The trouble with western violence lies not with the inflexibility of the genre's metaphor or the audience's ability to interpret it, but with its immutability. At the end of Preminger's *River of No Return*, a little boy shoots his father's would-be killer in the back, thereby learning from experience how his father could once have done the same thing, been dubbed a coward and sent to jail. *Day of the Evil Gun* concludes with Glenn Ford exchanging his pistols for clothes and having his life saved when the storekeeper uses the gun against Ford's treacherous partner. Johnny Ringo in *The Gunfighter* lies dying, aware that his young killer will now carry the deadly curse of being the fastest gun around. The doomed outlaws in *The Wild Bunch* know that their way of life has come to an end, that they cannot change, and join together in a final confrontation that they cannot possibly survive. These are general and intelligible statements about life, of varying degrees of validity and complexity. One can duplicate them endlessly in a hundred other westerns. But in each case a man, or several men, will lie dead in the street. This is the murderous algebra of the western and its ultimate limitation. The same argument on the other hand could be levelled against dramatic tragedy.

The most immediate and continuously topical accusation against the western is the role it plays in sustaining an outdated and dangerous pattern of behaviour which not only encourages violence but, in lending assistance to the American gun lobby in its battle against legislation to control firearms, makes available the weapons which give lethal expression to that violent urge. 'The frontier myth is nonsense, literally bloody nonsense, because it can still excuse and glorify personal violence,' wrote Louis Heren, Washington correspondent of *The Times*, in the wake of the Robert Kennedy and Martin Luther King assassinations. And on the failure to enact effective laws to regulate arms, he remarked:

> The common excuse is the powerful lobby of the National Rifle Association, but I am not convinced. The main reason is the frontier myth, with its lonely hero triumphant in a hostile world, perpetuated not only by films and television but by authors ranging from Fenimore Cooper and Ernest Hemingway to Mickey Spillane. It is about time Americans grew up.

Mr Heren undoubtedly has a general point, but frankly I cannot see the frontier myth as a particularly significant factor in determining the actions of Sirhan Sirhan and James Earl Ray – or for that matter Lee Harvey Oswald and Arthur Bremer.

I do not think it right to deal with violence in the western without also mentioning the treatment of death. Death in cowboy movies is not the euphemistic embalming process of Forest Lawn, a matter to be avoided and disguised. Death is confronted directly as a fact of existence, possibly the ultimate fact, not to be taken lightly nor to be viewed without perspective. It is the great leveller uniting hunter and prey, part of a pattern which completes a life but at the same time implies a sense of the continuity of generations within families and societies.

To me the attitude towards ageing and death is one of the most impressive characteristics of the western, and sets apart the best examples of the genre, and many mediocre ones as well, from gangster films or spy movies. The gangster dies young and unmourned; his victims are fellow criminals or innocent bystanders. In spy pictures death is perfunctory, absurd and often comic; nobody bothers to pick up the corpses and we are not invited to remember them. The fact that westerns have taken to depicting violent death in all its pain and horror in no way alters my view. Good or bad, a Westerner is entitled to a Christian burial and his passing is marked. That life may be easily taken does not mean that it is cheap and of no significance.

Scenes of dying and the rituals of burial on the plains or in frontier cemeteries abound and constitute some of the most poignant sequences in the genre. This may well be a Victorian hangover, and while the presentation of these scenes cannot always be defended against the charge of sentimentality, they are usually far from being morbid. Moreover, there can be little commercial pressure to include them; they arise naturally from what is best in the morality of the form. The burial of Torrey, the murdered Southerner in *Shane*, of the stammering cowboy killed in the cattle stampede of *Red River*, of the old Mexican shepherd in *The Appaloosa*, are deeply moving in their unaffected simplicity. There is a feeling in these fairly typical examples of the price paid for settling the land. Not surprisingly, many westerns end on elegiac scenes of burial or in cemeteries – *True Grit*, *Bandolero!*, *The Magnificent Seven*. In Mann's *The Naked Spur*, a bounty hunter (James Stewart) acknowledges the futility of his revenge quest and renounces the reward his dead quarry will bring him by unstrapping the body from a horse and burying it before riding off to start a new life.

The corollary to this is a deep contempt for those who fail to respect the ritual. The opening scene of *Rio Conchos*, in which a deranged Indian-hating Texan (Richard Boone) cold-bloodedly shoots at distant Indians conducting a burial service during a dust storm, immediately establishes that he is beyond the moral pale; the end of *The Wild Bunch*, where the sordid band of singing bounty-hunters head back to the Texas border with the valuable bodies of their outlawed prey strapped to mules, is the film's ultimate image of cosmic disgust. By contrast, Peckinpah's next film, *The Ballad of Cable Hogue*, concludes rather laboriously on the most elaborately photographed and edited funeral sequence in the genre, signifying not just the death of a man but of a way of life.

There is, I think, nothing inconsistent between this respect for the correct rituals of burial and the mostly comic role assigned to the undertaker. The mortician is after all the man who profits from the business, and his dual function is that of grimly humorous *memento mori* and cynical commercial counterpoint to the central figures' tragic or disinterested activities. The hammering of coffin nails is a premonition of someone's death: when the dishevelled Gary Cooper in *High Noon* drops into the barber's shop to be cleaned up, the barber tells the coffin-maker in the back room to keep quiet, and Cooper informs him on leaving that he can get back to the job. One of the bleak jokes in *Welcome to Hard Times* is to have the vicious symbolic killer murder the undertaker, as if to prove that he can banish death itself, and to dispatch the hearse out of town carrying the dead mortician. The stranger who retrieves the elegant vehicle is then forced by the sheriff to become the town's new undertaker.

There are some notable death scenes that are not attended with the usual obsequies – these are private affairs signifying an individual rounding out his own life. One thinks here of Joel McCrea in *Guns in the Afternoon* sending his friends away as he prepares to die; in a memorably composed shot he looks up to the distant sierras for the last time before leaning back and slumping dead, his head just outside the frame of the wide-screen. And we remember his earlier state-ment: 'All I want is to enter my house justified.' One thinks, too, of Elvis Presley in Don Siegel's fine *Flaming Star*, riding off to die alone in the mountains as his Indian mother (Dolores Del Rio) had done earlier when, having seen the 'flaming star' of death, she had walked off into the night.

The cultural poverty of American life outside the great urban centres is a matter of fact and concern. The cultural poverty of the old fron-tier life, on the other hand, is rarely a matter that worries western filmmakers. If anything they have tended, by omission, to exaggerate it. At times, some of the Western mining towns of the nineteenth century could offer as wide a variety and a higher quality of entertainment than is currently provided in Las Vegas. Only a few pictures have suggested this: the actress Lily Langtry visiting Texas, for instance, in William Wyler's *The Westerner* (1940) and John Huston's *The Life and Times of Judge Roy Bean* (1972), or the Booth family touring their relatively high-quality Shakespeare productions in Philip Dunne's *Prince of Players* (1955). Mostly the movies have concentrated on more picturesque third-rate companies, like the one which makes a brief appearance in Ford's *My Darling Clementine*, a troupe so bad that its leader (Alan Mowbray) needs a prompt from Doc Holliday in Hamlet's soliloquy; or the Great Healy and Co.'s travelling theatre, starring Anthony Quinn and Sophia Loren, whose vicissitudes out West are charmingly recorded in George Cukor's *Heller in Pink Tights* (1960).

At a domestic level, culture tends to be frowned upon, regarded as a women's concern and an Eastern frippery, which is not altogether misleading as a reflection of American attitudes. Some tentative approaches have been made towards examining cultural activities as a status-seeking pursuit, but for the most part this aspect of life has been ignored. Occasionally we might come across an opera-loving Westerner like the trail-boss Reece (Glenn Ford) in Delmer Daves' *Cowboy* (1958), who looks with amused contempt on city-dwellers who do not share his passion: 'You live in Chicago, you call yourself civilised and you don't know about the opera season?' The purpose of *Cowboy* was iconoclastic – to take the known conventions of the genre and the articles of the cowboy code and turn them on their heads in the name of realism.[25]

Lately we have been regaled with a couple of tired lawmen, in *Pistolero of Red River* (1967) and *Death of a Gunfighter* (1969), who escape from their offices and the towns they despise for a little quiet fishing. Home-made entertainments in the form of singing and informal parties are a feature of numerous pictures, rarely more

25 It is ironic, though by no means inappropriate, that as the source for *Cowboy*, a film which sought to tell the unvarnished truth about Western life, director Daves should have gone to *My Reminiscences as a Cowboy*, an account of his few months on a cattle drive by the literary adventurer Frank Harris, the most notorious liar of his time. When asked if he'd ever known Harris to tell the truth, Max Beerbohm replied: 'Sometimes, don't you know – when his invention flagged.'

touchingly presented than the Fourth of July gathering in *Shane*, and never more eloquently than in the dance on the foundations of the half-built Tombstone church in *My Darling Clementine*, though comparable instances abound in Ford's work. Nevertheless, the overwhelming impression westerns give, and it is by no means a misleading one, is that the leisure time of cowboys was devoted to drinking, whoring, fighting and playing poker. The inevitable main street saloon, in varying degrees of opulence, is generally the focus for all these activities, frequently simultaneously. All of them are essentially male pursuits, and the only one that does not more or less correspond to some specific physical need is poker.

Now poker, to those who are not obsessed by it, is a rather tedious business which in the scale of card games stands in terms of simplicity and chance at a middling position – some way above faro but a long way below the top marked by bridge. Like the other Western game, blackjack, it is a contest of individuals and, in the many forms now popular, an indigenous American game. Yet despite the simple rules, I would guess that a minority of moviegoers understand how to play it. Consequently poker must be seen as in some way central to the western mystique – for surely an intrinsic interest in the game cannot have sustained it over the years as such an important part of the genre.

Poker in the western is at once a deeply serious activity and a marginal one. Success is defined as much by character as by skill, and personalities are determined by their attitude to the game and the way they play it. Those who devote themselves solely to poker as professionals, whether they be winners or losers, can never be accorded the centre of the stage, though they may have a certain superficial attraction for the audience and for women within the film.

Harking back to my Kennedy–Goldwater thesis, it is interesting to note that John F. Kennedy was a naval war hero (Goldwater too has a distinguished record in the air force), while Richard Nixon, also a naval officer in the Pacific, apparently spent much of his off-duty time with a supply unit playing poker – a fitting occupation for a fashionable anti-hero of the absurdist *Catch-22–M*A*S*H* school. (As suggested earlier, there does seem to be a place for the Nixon western.)

Returning to myth and the western (and almost reversing roles), in the various films about the Wyatt Earp–Doc Holliday relationship, Holliday is usually the more colourful figure, but his role is invariably secondary to the dour marshal. The hero on the other hand must be capable of acquitting himself well at the gambling table as proof of his manhood. Yet he should view the game philosophically and with detachment, as does Henry Fonda's Earp in *My Darling Clementine*. 'Sir, I really like poker – every hand has its different problems,' he says, while establishing his necessary ability to spot and outwit a cheat. Naturally no one can ever hope to base his career on an ability to cheat, and the cardsharp is inexorably doomed to finish up dead. A deliberately ironic exception to this is the open, unchallenged cheating by the octoroon gunslinger (Yul Brynner) in *Invitation to a Gunfighter* (1964), where his object is not profit but to expose the pusillanimity of the townspeople who have hired him to carry out their dirty work. The general public acceptance of this convention and the ethic it proposes is only too obviously the inspiration which led three directors almost simultaneously to make their eponymous heroes professional gamblers: Frank Perry's *Doc* (1971), looking at 1881 Tombstone from the tubercular dentist's point of view; Robert Altman's *McCabe and Mrs Miller* (1971); and John Huston's *The Life and Times of Judge Roy Bean* (1972), in which the commentary tells us that poker played as great a part in the winning of the West as the Colt revolver or the covered wagon – a contention not so much true or false as meaningless.

There is perhaps an analogy between poker and the western movie: one could say that it forms a microcosm or more accurately a paradigm of the form. In addition to the aspects already mentioned, the game might be seen as a steady progression, in which courses of action are undisclosed, towards a final confrontation between two men, the more circumspect and fainthearted (usually identified as the married, the marginally secure and the weak) having dropped out on the way and thrown in their hand. Even when not playing poker, Westerners (and now people generally) resort to its terminology: the showdown, the four-flusher, calling someone's bluff, keeping a poker face. Andrew Sarris has made out a case for regarding the Budd Boetticher–Randolph Scott westerns as metaphorical poker games, though to the best of my recollection no actual games are ever played in them. They are, he says, 'constructed partly as allegorical odysseys and partly as floating poker games where every character takes turns at bluffing about his hand until the final showdown.'[26]

26 *The American Cinema* (E.P. Dutton, New York, 1964), p. 124.

There is, however, so far as I know, only one horse opera, the 'chamber western' *A Big Hand for the Little Lady* (1966, British title: *Big Deal at Dodge City*), devoted exclusively to poker. In it a pioneering husband-and-wife team of cardsharpers shakes down a poker school made up of prosperous and gullible leading citizens of Laredo. The wife, affecting ignorance of the game, takes over the poor hand of her 'ailing' husband to raise the ante and deliver the *coup de grâce*. A lot depends upon the con man husband being played by Henry Fonda, whose presence serves to disarm both audience and fellow players before the gimmick ending, which would no doubt have been more effective in the short television play from which the overextended movie was derived. Another equally tedious western, *5 Card Stud* (1968), the poorest exercise in the genre by the usually reliable Henry Hathaway, turns upon a single poker game. Here a mad preacher (Robert Mitchum), who carries his gun in a Bible, kills off one by one the other players in a game that had resulted in the lynching of his cardsharp brother. A highly obtrusive device in the film is the repetition of overhead shots re-creating the position of the participants in the game.

Pursuing his debatable contention that the western hero is pre-eminently a man of leisure, Robert Warshow saw poker as 'a game which perfectly expresses his talent for remaining relaxed in the midst of tension.' His point is well taken if one emphasises that incipient violence is always present in that tension, that a false move or accusation can bring it on. It is not without good reason that, in that most calculated of recent entertainments, *Butch Cassidy and the Sundance Kid*, when we first see the eponymous heroes together they are forcing a gambler to back down. In fact, after the sweaty, heavy-breathing, laconic challenges, shot in an elegantly lit sepia-tone, all that is eventually needed to make the vexatious challenger with-draw is to hear his opponent's name. The ethical basis for this conflict is by no means clear; whereas in *Invitation to a Gunfighter* a man of probity deliberately cheats, the Sundance Kid is a figure of dubious credentials merely claiming that he has played a straight game. Perhaps one is splitting hairs, but the proud hired gun in the former seems to be engaged in a serious moral challenge, while Butch Cassidy and his sidekick are merely asserting the superiority of their style.

The moral judgement proposed by the code of poker provides the central motif for Brando's *One-Eyed Jacks*, and the striking opening image of Peckinpah's *The Deadly Companions*, both of which draw on the traditional symbolic power and visual beauty of playing cards – qualities seized on outside the western in gambling pictures like the marathon poker movie *The Cincinnati Kid* (1965), which began as a Peckinpah project, though he was subsequently fired, and the fortune-telling scene shot in colour as a prelude to Agnès Varda's otherwise black-and-white picture *Cléo de Cinq à Sept* (1961). In Brando's film, a distant reworking of the Pat Garrett–Billy the Kid story, his central characters are one-eyed jacks. The treacherous hypocrite Dad Longworth (Karl Malden), the essentially evil man, shows a good face to society; Rio (Brando), the misunderstood outlaw, shows a bad one. Their real faces are the concealed ones.[27] Again in the opening of *The Deadly Companions*, we are confronted with a close-up of a body suspended from the ceiling with its feet on a barrel and five aces pinned to the shirt. We thus have imposed upon us an overwhelming judgement on the man before we even see his sly features and register the mysterious, equivocal relationship between him and the withdrawn, poker-faced man who cuts him down.

Setting aside the internal moral significance of poker, there is a further use to which the game has been put as a criticism of a way of life. In Penn's *Little Big Man*, Wild Bill Hickok is ignominiously shot down at a poker table and dies unheroically, his neck bizarrely cradled by the boot of a fellow gambler. In *The Stalking Moon*, a half-breed scout, who acts as the film's chorus and commentator, suggests with cheerful irony that he should teach the rules of poker to anyone seeking to be assimilated into white 'civilisation': 'You gonna be white – you better learn the white man's game,' he tells the uncomprehending halfbreed boy at the centre of the film's metaphorical tug-of-war.

Far more emphatic than either of these is the insertion into the middle of John Ford's last western, *Cheyenne Autumn*, of a Dodge City interlude which worried many critics and puzzled audiences so much that it was wholly or partially removed from some copies

27 In gambling argot the movie's title refers to wild cards in poker – the jacks of spades and hearts – and the film clearly implies a symbiotic relationship between the film's two knaves of a kind I have mentioned earlier. Card-playing experts, I believe, have noted other possible elements in the film's symbolism, both in relation to poker and to the variations of the game 'Seven Up', and so have students of the more arcane aspects of playing-card iconography. Critics interested in the sexual symbolism of the genre have suggested that the title slyly invokes a slang expression for the penis.

of the film. This sequence is shot in an entirely different style from the sombre, near-tragic mood which informs the rest of the film. Here we see a lazy, cynical, unscrupulous Wyatt Earp (James Stewart) and Doc Holliday (Arthur Kennedy), as different from their counterparts in *My Darling Clementine* as the treatment of the Cheyenne is from Ford's approach to the Indians in his earlier films. Opulently dressed and sitting in the Dodge City saloon-cum-whorehouse from which they so obviously derive their good fortune, they drink and play poker totally unmoved by the suffering and depravity around them. The tone of this scene is farcical and indulgent, reeking of corruption, self-interest and indifference. By the indirection of caricature, irony and artifice Ford came eventually to a possibly more authentic depiction of Holliday and Earp than he did through the apparently 'realistic' surface of *My Darling Clementine*. From the gambling tables of Dodge City, by way of a burlesque chase of a single, starving Indian accidentally strayed into the vicinity which came to be known as 'The Battle of Dodge City', we return to the Cheyenne continuing their bitter journey from a desolate exile back to the tribe's confiscated hunting grounds.

5 The Post-Western

The history of the American West has been the story of the accelerating intrusion of civilisation into virgin territory. There came first the trapper and fur trader and the disinterested explorer travelling on foot or by canoe. Then the transient miner (usually a dubious character in westerns), the rancher and the farmer on horseback and with wagon trains, accompanied by the establishment of military bases. Primitive forms of communication like the stagecoach and the pony express are gradually supplemented, then replaced, by the train and the telegraph. With a suitable degree of nostalgia each of these phases has been dealt with in the western, and we must remember that the elegiac strain in a notably bitter and reactionary form is to be found as early as Fenimore Cooper, writing in the 1830s, which is to say well before the period of Western development that the cowboy movie treats. The wonders of nineteenth-century technology, the idea of inevitable and beneficial progress, have been celebrated in movies dedicated to singing the praises of *The Iron Horse* (1924), *Union Pacific* (1939), *Western Union* (1941) and the engineering feats attendant upon linking America coast-to-coast.

As the locomotive has declined in significance, its already considerable appeal has increased: the steam train is kept alive today partly by a few devoted railway buffs but mainly by the movie industry. One might look upon it as the great creator of community, as opposed to the car which is a private vehicle disruptive of community feeling. Only in the last fifteen years has the horseless carriage seriously entered the western, and it has done so not as a harbinger of the brave new world but as a symbol of a deadening mass society and a dehumanised technology.

I put it this way because its deployment is something more than a simple-minded Luddism; it reflects in fact not an attitude contemporary to the turn of the century, but current feelings about the shortcomings and blindnesses of our over-mechanised, polluted, unbalanced, disintegrating environment. Just take the progressively lethal use of the car by Sam Peckinpah. *Guns in the Afternoon* (1962) opens with an old marshal nearly being knocked down by a horseless carriage, possibly the first he has seen. In *The Wild Bunch*, the degenerate Mexican local dictator Mapache (a man, like post-World War II American technology, under the tutelage of German experts) is fascinated both by his new machine gun and his little red Tin Lizzie, and eventually uses the latter to drag the Mexican member of the bunch around town in the dust. In *The Ballad of Cable Hogue*, the eponymous hero, whose stagecoach watering post will shortly be made redundant by the internal combustion engine, is killed when the brake slips on the first car he has ever touched.

A major preoccupation of the western in the 60s and 70s has been the ugly intrusion of the modern world – the anonymous, rationalising conglomerate corporations which in *Monte Walsh* run the ranches from Wall Street and bring unemployment to the cowboys; the civil servants and bureaucrats in *McClintock!*; the politicians in *The Man Who Shot Liberty Valance*; the businessmen and civic boosters in *Death of a Gunfighter* and *The Good Guys and the Bad Guys*. There is, however, a gulf in fact and myth between the western and modern society which the cinema cannot bridge. A movie like Anthony Mann's last and only disappointing western, *Cimarron* (1960), based on Edna Ferber's epic novel, attempts the task with uneven results, by tracing the hero's career up to his death in World War I and showing developments in the community he has helped found after the Oklahoma land rush of 1889, but has deserted for other last frontiers, gold rushes and the Cuban War. The picture has a great void at its centre.

Even more so has *How the West Was Won* (1962), the first feature film using the Cinerama process, which spends three hours synopsising every known western situation in the tale of three generations of a pioneer family between 1840 and 1890, before making a breathtaking jump to present-day America. At one moment the screen is showing a retired sheriff and his family heading towards a new home in an unspoilt landscape after the last bandit has been shot down; the next moment we are regaled with a vertiginous montage of aerial shots of car-choked Los Angeles freeways. There is no suggestion elsewhere in the movie that its producers are doing anything but celebrating America, and in consequence we are expected to accept this coda as the marvellous visionary future which the pioneers struggled for and which has now been realised by their proud successors. A black humorist could scarcely have come up with a bleaker, more satirical ending.

Jumping with the makers of *How the West Was Won* from the

winning of the West to the problems of coping with the present, we come to a group of movies I have referred to earlier as modern or post-westerns. These are films about the West today, and draw upon the western itself or more generally on 'the cowboy cult'. A few movies, like Burt Kennedy's engaging *The Rounders* (1965) and Stuart Rosenberg's aimless *Pocket Money* (1972), deal in a fairly realistic manner with the hardships of working on the range today, in similar fashion to the way such movies as *Cowboy* and *Will Penny* present an unromantic view of the nineteenth-century cowpuncher's life. Quite a number of films look at the less glamorous underside of the cowboy's role as professional rodeo entertainer, where his traditional skills are divorced from day-to-day utility and placed at the service of a public spectacle nearly as dangerous as bullfighting. In the early 1950s there were several films of this type – most notably Nicholas Ray's *The Lusty Men* (1952), but also Boetticher's low-budget *Bronco Buster* (1952). Recently there has been a crop of such films – Cliff Robertson's *J.W.Coop*, the late Steve Ihnat's *The Honkers*, and Sam Peckinpah's *Junior Bonner*, all released in 1972 and taking an equally disenchanted view of present-day America.

Seen out of his time and place, the western hero seems an incongruous figure. Depending on the dramatic use to which he may be put, he can be variously seen as vulnerable and pathetic or dangerous and anarchic, an upholder of cherished traditional values or the embodiment of outmoded ways which linger menacingly on, a challenge to modern conformity or the incarnation of a past that must be rejected. There are many examples of this outside the western. In American fiction there is Earle Shoop in Nathanael West's *The Day of the Locust*, Joe Buck in James Leo Herlihy's *Midnight Cowboy*, Buck Loner in Gore Vidal's *Myra Breckinridge*, all three of which have been filmed. In scripting Carol Reed's *The Third Man* (1949), Graham Greene cast around for the most fitting occupation for Holly Martins, the naïve American thrown among the cynical sophisticates of corrupt post-war Vienna, and decided to make him an author of pulp western fiction who had never set foot in the West; the only person who genuinely befriends Martins is an English NCO who has read his novels. (One wonders if Greene had seen Jean Renoir's 1935 film *Le Crime de Monsieur Lange*, in which the eponymous hero, a sad though resilient employee of a shoddy Parisian publishing house, realises his dreams through stories about his imaginary western hero 'Arizona Jim', the popular success of whose adventures is seized upon by his unscrupulous boss and becomes the centre of the film's dramatic and moral structure.) Then there are the contrasting performances by Andy Griffiths in two movies of the 50s: the illiterate backwoods buffoon disrupting air force life in the comedy *No Time for Sergeants* (1958), and the guitar-twanging demagogue who threatens America with a home-grown totalitarianism in Elia Kazan's overwrought *A Face in the Crowd* (1956). Perhaps most striking of all is Major King Kong (played by Slim Pickens in one of his rare non-western appearances), the Texan pilot in *Dr Strangelove* who puts on his Stetson when the red alert comes, and rides the hydrogen bomb which will destroy the world as if it were a bucking bronco in a rodeo show.

In marked contrast to these figures is Sam the Lion (Ben Johnson), the retired rancher who keeps the conscience of the decaying Texas township in Peter Bogdanovich's *The Last Picture Show* (1971). And oddly enough, in Antonioni's curiously callow and unfeeling *Zabriskie Point* (1970), the one genuinely affecting image is in his single reference to the cowboy cult. This occurs in the desert café after his tiresome heroine has departed. Sitting at the bar is a leathery old cowboy, impassive, silent and perfectly still. He has been quite indifferent to the girl's presence, and now the camera lingers on him, viewing him through a window and giving the impression that what we are seeing is a combination of a portrait by Andrew Wyeth or Edward Hopper and a sentimental Norman Rockwell cover for *Saturday Evening Post*.

The most striking post-westerns are John Sturges' *Bad Day at Black Rock* (1954), John Huston's *The Misfits* (1960), David Miller's *Lonely Are the Brave* (1962), Martin Ritt's *Hud* (1963) and Don Siegel's *Coogan's Bluff* (1968). Central to them all is the way in which the characters are influenced by, or are victims of, the cowboy cult; they intensify and play on the audience's feelings about, and knowledge of, western movies.

Bad Day at Black Rock has something resembling a western plot. A one-armed stranger (Spencer Tracy) gets off the train one morning in a small desert town to be greeted with suspicion and hostility, which turns into a series of attempts to scare him away and then kill him when it transpires that he is seeking to meet a local Japanese farmer called Komoko. The year is 1945, just after the end of the war, and the stranger is an ex-army officer who wants to give the farmer the posthumously awarded medal his son had won in Italy while saving Tracy's life. The intruder is at first fobbed off with the story that Komoko had been interned along with other Nisei after Pearl Harbor; he later discovers that the man has been murdered after a patriotic drunken orgy marking the coming of the war, and that moreover he had already built up local resentment by finding water on a tract of apparently worthless land sold him by the local boss (Robert Ryan).

Black Rock works admirably as a thriller and was among the most interesting of early CinemaScope movies in its use of stylised groupings and elaborate dramatic compositions.[28] What is also of interest is that the film could never have been made at the time it was set in and was, I think, the first to touch upon the still highly controversial matter of the deplorable treatment Japanese Americans were subjected to during World War II. The producer was Dore Schary, who ten years before had sought to use the western genre for his wartime propaganda picture *Storm in the West*.

But what really concerns me here is the picture's attitude to the West. Despite an apparent absence of cattle, the Westerners are very insistent upon their status as cowboys. For example, the desk clerk at the unoccupied local hotel tells Tracy in a flat monotone that the hotel is 'reserved for cowboys, for their every wish and comfort' when they are in town. When Tracy gets a room he is ousted from it by the lethargically menacing Lee Marvin, who stretches out on the bed and tells him, 'These rooms are reserved for cowboys, for their every wish and comfort when they are in town, and I'm in town as any fool can see.' The snarling xenophobe Ryan tells Tracy, 'We're suspicious of strangers here – a hangover from the Old West,' to which Tracy replies, 'I thought the tradition of the Old West was hospitality.' And Ryan goes on to make a vicious little speech about the general public and their 'Wild West', the businessmen and their

28 The cameraman was the late William C. Mellor, a frequent collaborator of George Stevens; he also shot the most elaborately composed of all Anthony Mann westerns, *The Last Frontier*. The role of the cameraman is of paramount importance in the cowboy movie, indeed in the cinema generally, and I regret my incompetence to handle the subject adequately. The contributions to the western of Lucien Ballard (most of Peckinpah, several Boetticher films, *Will Penny, The Raid, The Proud Ones, True Grit*), Floyd Crosby (*High Noon, The Wonderful Country*), Charles B. Lang (*The Man From Laramie, The Magnificent Seven, One-Eyed Jacks*), James Wong Howe (*Hud* and *Hombre*), William Clothier (who has worked with Boetticher, Ford, Peckinpah, McLaglen, Wayne, Walsh and Burt Kennedy, as well as servicing exciting surprises from unknown talents like *Dragoon Wells Massacre* and *Firecreek*), and a dozen other cameramen, cannot be overrated – yet cannot be fully measured.

'undeveloped West', the writers and their 'romantic West' – 'To us this place is *our* West and I wish they'd leave us alone.'

The clear purpose of the film is to locate in the all-American figure of the cowboy some less attractive native traits: patriotism masking xenophobia, ignorance masquerading as intuitive common sense, mindless aggression concealed beneath virility, arrogance disguised as style. In addition they can't even fight fair, although a little skill at karate and a touch of intelligence by their one-armed opponent is more than enough to defeat them.

Hud Bannon (Paul Newman) would be very much at home in Black Rock, yet there is a genuine attempt in *Hud* to reveal this unattractive young Texan as a perversion of Western ideals, the decadent fag end of a tradition seen at its best in his father (Melvyn Douglas), a fine old rancher, who spurns the lure of oil and sticks to breeding longhorns 'to remind me of the way things was – everything we have comes from them.' The Western guitar music on the soundtrack belongs to the old man; the debased Country and Western music which issues from juke-boxes in seedy cafés and the radio in Hud's battered Cadillac reflects the ambience of Hud himself. The twentieth century they both reject overtakes them when their cattle are infected by foot-and-mouth disease. Hud's response is to try to evade the law by driving the stock elsewhere, his father's to face the consequences – which necessarily involves his death and the extinction of his world. Together they watch a bulldozer cut a pit for the cattle to be driven into, gunned down by government agents in hygienic masks and boots and then buried in lime. It is a sickening scene which speaks for itself without the old man's sententious gloss (not entirely uncharacteristic of Martin Ritt) that 'It doesn't take long to kill things like it does to grow.'

There are two other important figures in *Hud*. One is Alma, the ranch's housekeeper; in a performance of depth and maturity by Patricia Neal, this bruised and intelligent woman stands for the kind of complex absorption in modern life, that commitment to reality, which Hud and the old man have avoided. The other character, through whose eyes the action is mostly seen, is Hud's nephew Lon, who begins by hero-worshipping Hud and grows to see his desperate shortcomings. 'Little by little the country changes because of the men they admire,' his grandfather tells him. It is scarcely a coincidence, indeed it is part of the film's resonance, that Lon is played by the 20-year-old Brandon De Wilde, who ten years before appeared as little Joey, the child through whose eyes much of *Shane* is seen.

The Misfits and *Lonely Are the Brave* take a different, more romantic view of the cowboy, though they put him down in as unglamorous and rebarbative a world. Leaving aside the important aspect of *The Misfits* which concerns screenwriter Arthur Miller's attempt to explore the personality of his then wife Marilyn Monroe, the theme of the movie is the degradation and dissolution of the American Dream. And the chosen method is to concentrate on a party of rootless, aimless cowboys living around Reno, Nevada, divorce capital of America and graveyard of romance. The group is composed of the ironically named cowboy Gay (Clark Gable), a punch-drunk, mother-fixated rodeo rider (Montgomery Clift), a pathetic, garrulous aviator (Eli Wallach) who lives in a half-completed house, and a recent divorcée (Monroe) whose exterior *joie de vivre* conceals an emotional numbness. Together they set off into the mountains to hunt wild stallions with a truck and an aeroplane – a quest which is finally abandoned when the girl discovers to her horror that the object of this heroic exercise is to collect horse meat to be processed into tinned cat food. The film ends oddly, mystically, with Gay and the girl driving beneath the stars, having apparently discovered some peace in nothingness. At the time this scene, and the picture generally, seemed portentous and pretentious; over the years, however, *The Misfits* has gained an unusual and affecting depth as a work about the Monroe charisma (it was her last completed film) and the fading charm of Clark Gable, whose last appearance this was.

Jack Burns (Kirk Douglas) in *Lonely Are the Brave* is another misfit, a 'don't fence me in' cowboy almost identical to the barbed-wire-hating Dempsey Rae played by Douglas in *Man Without a Star* (1955). Only now he is in modern New Mexico, where jet vapour fills the sky, Boot Hill has been replaced by an automobile scrap yard, and motor highways have taken over from dirt trails. Subtlety is not exactly the most obvious quality of the film, and the makers do little to conceal their utter loathing of modern America and all its works. (The screenplay is by Dalton Trumbo, most talented of the 'Hollywood Ten', the first victims of the post-war Un-American Activities Committee witch-hunt.) On the other hand, apart from a sadistic prison guard, most of the other characters are approached sympathetically. The sheriff (Walter Matthau), who reluctantly heads the posse which pursues Burns when he foolishly breaks from jail, hopes that he will get away with his attempt to escape across the mountains. This lawman is disgusted with his lifeless, characterless police force as well as with the local army base, whose commanding officer sees the hunt as good practice for his helicopter pilots. The film is an early example of the use so often made since of the helicopter as a menacing symbol of totalitarianism and anonymous technology, and the sheriff anticipates the attitude of the reluctant leader of the posse (Robert Ryan) in *The Wild Bunch*, who says of the trash accompanying him, 'We're after men and I wish to God I was with them.'

Lonely Are the Brave could also be said to anticipate the climax of Peckinpah's *Cable Hogue*, for the film's structure is founded on the inexorable collision of Burns and his horse and a truck carrying a load of lavatory pans. We are introduced to this van when its indigestion-ridden driver stops in Joplin, Missouri, and announces he is heading for Duke City, New Mexico, and from then on the film constantly cuts back to this inelegant, impersonal juggernaut beneath whose wheels the doomed Burns will be sacrificed as he tries to ride across a rain-slick road to the Mexican border, All that remains after the dying cowboy has been driven off in an ambulance is his Stetson, lying in a puddle illuminated by the lights of passing cars.

In all the attention devoted to the hopeless rebellion of Burns, it is possible to overlook the rather unimpressive presence of his friend, a left-wing writer serving two years in jail for helping illegal Mexican immigrants. Offered as a practical rebel in contrast to the romantic intransigence of Burns, he has now decided to quit the wild life they both enjoyed and devote himself to working for social reform within the system. In the era of Kennedy and Martin Luther King, this seemed an obvious and desirable alternative; it still does, but it is a difficult thing to dramatise, and such a man has not been easy to accommodate in the western, nor has he appealed much to those creating the prevailing fashions in the radical, liberated Hollywood of the past ten years.

Unlike the other four modern westerns I have discussed, *Coogan's Bluff* is largely set in urban America after an opening sequence which locates the brutal, confident deputy sheriff Coogan (Clint Eastwood) in his natural habitat of rural Arizona. There we see him in a jeep tracking down a wife-murderer who has fled from a Navajo reservation and gone native. Cheerfully dispensing with the niceties of legal procedure which hamper his urban colleagues, he calls upon his pathetic victim, 'Put your hands up, Chief', and then knocks him down with the gun butt. Coogan's next assignment is to go to New York and bring back a fugitive prisoner, a drug-taking psychopathic hippie, and the events of this opening sequence are paralleled by the less happy, less successful progress around Manhattan, where he becomes embroiled in a world more complicated than his simple Western life and finds himself meeting a contempt similar to that he had shown his Indian prisoner. A black plain-clothes cop refers to him as 'Buffalo Bill with the fancy hat'; a witness he tries to railroad informs him, 'This isn't the OK Corral around here'; everybody calls him 'Texas', and a whore he rejects snarls, 'Texas faggot'.

His principal critic is the hard-pressed New York precinct cop Lt. McElroy (Lee J. Cobb), who looks at Coogan as if he's a primitive man from another time and place. 'What gives with you people out there – too much sun?' he asks, and when the injured Coogan tries to explain why he has to go after the prisoner whom he has foolishly allowed to escape, McElroy shrugs his shoulders with sardonic resignation and says, 'I know, a man's gotta do what a man's gotta do.'

The humour and criticism is not all directed at Coogan's gaucherie and the limitations of his crude, simple values. His genuine style is a challenge to the role-playing manner of so many New Yorkers he runs into; through his eyes we see the nastiness and run-down state of Manhattan. Some of this feeling is summed up in a close-up of his polished, pointed boot stepping out of a taxi into a pile of garbage in the street. And despite the patronising air with which he is greeted, his clothes and bearing have a powerful, in some cases almost fetishistic, appeal for many people he meets. Moreover, Coogan may have simple-minded and dangerous notions about life, but he isn't a naïve buffoon after the fashion of numerous cowboys in sophisticated urban comedies or *Midnight Cowboy*'s Joe Buck. The audience may be happy to see this arrogant Westerner disconcerted and humiliated, but we are also touched by his frustration and bewilderment.

Unfortunately *Coogan's Bluff* loses this critical balance about halfway through, and from being an intelligent, ironic movie it plunges into a crude thriller which intentionally or not appears to be a vindication of Coogan's aggression and crude 'law'n'order' tactics. Indeed quite a different mood takes over the later part of the film. Apart from a certain vague humanity (Coogan at the end gives his prisoner a cigarette, whereas he has refused one to his Indian prisoner at the beginning), the Arizonan appears to have learned nothing, and the New York cop seems only to have learned where Coogan comes from. 'Give my regards to Tex – I mean Arizona', is his parting shot in a rather sentimental closing scene. In fact, after the illegal procedures he has resorted to, Coogan would never have been able to leave New York with his prisoner, and that would have been a more interesting and logical ending. It was no doubt with this in mind that three years later Eastwood and his director Don Siegel made another police thriller, and in *Dirty Harry* the action turns precisely upon a dangerous criminal being set free as a result of the illegal means employed in making the arrest.

Between these two films Siegel had directed Eastwood in the stolid Mexican western *Two Mules for Sister Sara* and the subdued little Civil War Grand Guignol piece *The Beguiled*. On the side, Siegel had taken over and completed (without credit) the unsatisfactory but underrated Richard Widmark 'changing times' western *Death of a Gunfighter*, and advised Eastwood on his directorial debut, *Play Misty for Me*. While I regard *Dirty Harry* as a powerful fable and a dazzling display of film craft, I cannot say that I am entirely happy about the political and social implications of the film. Yet in making it, Siegel and Eastwood faced head on the problems posed by *Coogan's Bluff* – they could not possibly have resorted to the western for their solution without implying an observation of legal niceties wholly inappropriate to the genre and frontier life.

Like the makers of westerns, the genre's critics tend to locate their ideal in the past. George Fenin and William Everson, authors of the only major American book on the subject, *The Western from Silent to Cinerama*, would place the Golden Age around 1920, when their beloved William S. Hart was at his peak. For them the best westerns of the 1950s are Henry Hathaway's admirable *From Hell to Texas*, because of a script 'recalling at times the simplicity of William S. Hart', and *Shane*, 'which sent one's mind scurrying back to William Hart's *The Toll Gate*'. Both Robert Warshow and Harry Schein in their 1954 essays strongly implied that the genre was approaching its final sunset, and a dozen years later, in his 1966 radio talk *Decline of the Western*, Laurence Kitchin voiced a fairly general feeling that the great days were over, though just where the line should be drawn he left vague. All that weekly movie critics need is a succession of lousy cowboy films followed by an impressive 'anti-western' like *Hud* or *Monte Walsh* to turn their ready-made sermon on the subject into a reading of the last rites over the genre's sinking coffin. I mention this in no spirit of reproach, for the response is easily understandable.

This approach, however, flies in the face of the facts – by which I mean of course that it runs counter to my own opinion. As I have suggested earlier, the western seems to me far from moribund – indeed I should go so far as to regard it as one of the more vital centres of the cinema and the popular arts in our time. Admittedly, I think it is unlikely that we shall ever again see a director of John Ford's stature channel so much of his energy into the genre. From *Stagecoach* in 1939 to *Cheyenne Autumn* in 1964, he towered over the western, and for some time to come his presence will continue to be felt. In Ford's shadow, the 50s were dominated by Anthony Mann, Delmer Daves, Budd Boetticher and John Sturges, and the 60s by Sam Peckinpah. And to each decade Howard Hawks contributed a single movie, part of an evolving personal cycle with John Wayne always at the centre: *Red River* (1948), *Rio Bravo* (1959), *El Dorado* (1967) and finally *Rio Lobo* (1970). The plots and situations of the last three are almost identical – a pair of increasingly elderly lawmen accompanied by valetudinarian eccentrics and laconic, sympathetic youngsters upholding the law in the face of venal, faceless opponents. One has to view the films a second time and in the right order to appreciate that one isn't seeing a series of fading carbon copies where the comedy gets broader as the dramatic grip slackens, but rather a gradual digging deeper into familiar themes, where the looser surface conceals a profound pessimism, as if the ageing of Hawks and his heroes were being equated with the ageing, the loss of energy, of America itself.

There is now, I fancy, no need for any director to devote himself to the western. It is easier today to avoid getting typed, easier to raise money for personal movies which fit no particular genre. When a young unknown like Dick Richards makes *The Culpepper Cattle Company*, or an experienced producer like Stuart Millar elects to make his directorial debut with *When the Legends Die*, or Robert Altman comes up with *McCabe and Mrs Miller*, we know that they have deliberately chosen to make a western, that what they wished to say was peculiarly suited to that form and setting. And we do not necessarily expect them to return to the genre immediately, or at all. Of all major directors today, only Sam Peckinpah is totally identified with westerns, and on the two occasions when he has deserted the genre, the results have been disappointing (*The Getaway*, 1972) or disastrous (*Straw Dogs*, 1971); in each case the pictures failed to create a convincing world from the trappings of the chosen contemporary milieu (respectively, Texas and Cornwall), and both could

have been easily, happily, transposed to the West. Two other directors continue to specialise in westerns at a much lower, yet not
negligible, level – Andrew McLaglen, a protégé of John Ford whose
assistant he was on several occasions, and Burt Kennedy, screenwriter for Boetticher. They are hit-and-miss artists, notable more
for stamina than for consistent vision or imagination, though neither
is to be despised. Acolytes both, they loyally tend the flame at their
mentors' altars and seem unlikely to become high priests themselves.

Meanwhile the genre flourishes, some movies contributing to its
vitality, others merely attesting to its cultural centrality. As in the
past, almost as many films sink their vampire fangs into its body as
provide it with a transfusion of new blood. George Englund's
embarrassing hard-rock musical *Zachariah* (1970), for instance, is a
biblical allegory that announced itself as the first 'electric western'
and featured a number of pop groups in subsidiary roles. Another
biblical western is Robert Downey's immoderately ambitious
Greaser's Palace (1972), a random anachronistic satire in which a
zoot-suited Christ descends on nineteenth-century New Mexico
explaining his mission with the words: 'I'm on my way to Jerusalem
to be an actor-singer.' The Holy Ghost appears as a Lone Ranger
figure in white sheet and black Stetson, and God as a taciturn,
bearded old-timer. Christ moves among corrupt saloon owners,
permanently drugged Indians, homosexual Mexican dwarfs, restores
crippled pioneers, walks on the water, dances in a bar-room (the
Mary Magdalene figure complains that 'a man with holes in his hand
gets more applause than me'), before being crucified. *Greaser's Palace*
(the title, a pun on the grandiose 'Caesar's Palace', suggests Las Vegas
as the New Jerusalem) confirms the real difficulties of making a satirical western. The genre is riding a knife-edge all the time, and
Downey's parodies of *High Noon* and Peckinpah are crude to a
degree. Basically, it's the kind of thing that gives bad taste a bad
name.

As a director who has ascended from the underground movie into
the world of feature films, Downey provides a link between the
pretentious, biblical, showbiz conjunction of *Zachariah* and the flip,
lackadaisical, camp farrago *Lonesome Cowboys* (1968), in which the
stock company of the Andy Warhol factory go West to Arizona
under the direction of Paul Morrissey. This ludicrous movie is a
vague transposition of *Romeo and Juliet*. The film occasionally
suggests an exploitation of the latent homosexuality in cowboy
movies, but generally settles for predictable gay banter and

aggression. Inasmuch as the movie has a highlight, it resides in the scene where a former ballet dancer demonstrates – using a hitching rail as a dancer's exercise bar – how a cowboy should move and draw a gun.

Regrettably, Jean-Luc Godard's *Wind from the East* (1970) belongs right in there with *Zachariah, Greaser's Palace* and *Lonesome Cowboys.* According to James Roy MacBean in his introduction to the published screenplay of *Vent d'Est*, Godard 'systematically takes apart the traditional elements of bourgeois cinema – especially as exemplified by the western – revealing the sometimes hidden, sometimes blatant repressiveness which underlies it.'[29] The film is apparently set where the heroine's uncle 'managed the exploitation of aluminium for the Alcoa company near Dodge City' and features a sadistic cavalryman and a hapless Indian. It is nothing if not an elaborate political allegory or meditation inspired by the western. But it is a tiresome, hectoring film, alternating between the crude and the obscure, and painfully sad in coming from a director who has written so personally and sensitively about Ford, Mann and Peckinpah.

Discussing *Wind from the East*, one is reminded of a comment Godard made about Peckinpah in a 1962 interview. American directors, he said, 'have a gift for the kind of simplicity which brings depth – in a little western like *Ride the High Country*, for instance. If one tries to do something like that in France, one looks like an intellectual.' One cannot honestly say that by moving in the opposite direction Godard manages to be less of an intellectual than he has previously been, or shows any greater likelihood of contacting the large, popular audience which has always eluded him. A sojourn in America directing the kind of films he once admired but now professes to despise might well have benefited him and made it possible for him to operate within the central tradition of the cinema rather than on its uninviting, often justly ignored, edges.

Admittedly my politics are of a less extreme and ideological kind than Godard's, but having spent much of the first half of 1972 teaching at the University of Texas and travelling round the West, I don't find it impossible to combine my liking of westerns with my love for the 'Real West', my knowledge of frontier history, and an awareness of the contemporary world. I find little difficulty in reconciling Horace Gregory's attack on the commercial and political

29 Lorrimer, London, 1972.

exploitation of the 'cowboy cult' with Harry Schein's defence of the western movie. In his essay *Guns of the Roaring West*, Gregory wrote:

> More than anything else the cult expresses the desire to drama-tise a brightly surfaced and thin layer of American history, one that can be read at a glance with the mind untroubled by the need of serious understanding or research. It is a pictorial short-cut back to feeling very much at home in the United States.

Where Gregory's *Partisan Review* team-mate Robert Warshow calls the western 'an art form for connoisseurs' in that it allows the spectator to appreciate subtle changes and variations in familiar routines, rituals and patterns, Schein saw the genre as offering far more than aesthetic attractions:

> It gives us in fact the opportunity – unique in our culture and history – to experience how folklore is made, how it grows and takes shape. The roots of the mythology of Europe and the Near East are hidden in the past and can be only partially reconstructed today. But White America is no older than Gutenberg. It achieved economic and consequently cultural independence (an essential prerequisite for a mythology of its own) about the same time as the novel made its artistic breakthrough and started reaching a public. It is no coincidence that James Fenimore Cooper is America's first original contributor to literature. It is just as natural that the cinema embraced the Western from the start. In less than a lifetime of one generation it has developed from something seemingly insignificant to a tightly designed mythology following its own laws, to become the young America's own folklore.

The dialectical relationship between the opposing contentions of Gregory and Schein is neither purely aesthetic nor mythical; at the same time it cannot be regarded as a simple conflict between art and honestly recorded history. 'Humankind cannot bear very much reality,' observed T.S. Eliot (a poet born in St. Louis, the point at which the West begins); nor can the western. The genre can tolerate, indeed invites, transfusions of reality in the form of convincing psychological relationships and persuasively shoddy décor – every decade has its own standards in the matter of realism. Ford's *My Darling Clementine* looked pretty realistic by the prevailing norms of 1946, though it was at every point a total misrepresentation of the events leading up to the gunfight at the OK Corral, the year of which it even gets wrong. The subsequent versions of the same story move ever nearer to the known facts – John Sturges' *The Gunfight at the OK Corral* (1957), the same director's *Hour of the Gun* (1967), and Frank Perry's *Doc* (1971) – and each in turn presents a grubbier, more disenchanted view of life in Tombstone. But no version arrives at that quality of truth, albeit a bogus, mythic one, which Ford achieves.

The sordid real-life story of Wyatt Earp and Doc Holliday is largely of interest to us now for the light it throws on the way their legendary reputations have been shaped rather than for any intrinsic importance they had. The same is true of Billy Bonney and Jesse James, and in Arthur Penn's Billy the Kid film, *The Left Handed Gun* (1958), and Nicholas Ray's *The True Story of Jesse James* (1956), the central characters are examined in terms of, and personally confronted with, the myths which they became in their own lifetimes. In *The Man Who Shot Liberty Valance* (1961), which comes closer than any of his other westerns to a destruction of the myth, Ford presents two stories – the long-accepted one by which Senator Stoddard (James Stewart) brought law and order to Shinbone, and an account of the real events in which his dirty work was done for him by an old friend (John Wayne), on the occasion of whose funeral the past is observed in flashback. On being presented with the true story, the local newspaper editor tears up the reporter's notes, saying, 'This is the West, sir. When the legend becomes fact, print the legend!' The editor's comment may be cynical, but Ford's presentation of the story is far from being so.

However, a total take-over by a countervailing realism either threatens to destroy the western or replaces it with something new. Hamlin Garland's novels, for example, helped create a way of dealing with the pioneer experience which has little to do with the anterior traditions of the western movie (in heroic saga, dime novel, stage melodrama); and so did Willa Cather and the Scandinavian-American novelist O.E. Rölvaag. Following their example the Swedish directors Bo Widerberg and Jan Troell have made films with Western settings but deliberately outside the framework of the conventional horse opera. Widerberg's highly uneven biography of the immigrant Swedish union organiser *Joe Hill* (1971) owes nothing to the western, nor does *The Emigrants* (1971), the first of Troell's' lengthy two-part adaptation of Vilhelm Moberg's fictional tetralogy concerning a group of peasants who left Sweden in the mid-1840s and settled in Minnesota. *Joe Hill* is a piece of political myth-making, a celebration of lyrical socialism after the manner of Widerberg's earlier *Ådalen '31*; *The Emigrants* is a calculatedly downbeat attempt to re-create with maximum fidelity an important area of the nine-teenth-century proletarian experience. To be sure, their subject matter could easily have been rendered in terms of the traditional western, but the directors have chosen to create their own truths and not to present them in refracted fashion through Hollywood convention, or in conscious contrast to a series of existing expecta-tions, with a built-in resonance.

In this lies the partial failure of Troell and Widerberg. Their films stand alone. Whether American filmmakers will follow their example remains to be seen. Unquestionably, there is a vast area of American history that falls outside the purview of the western, but I doubt if it will prove all that rewarding. Robert Altman's *McCabe and Mrs Miller*, for instance, is a detailed, carefully thought out re-creation of pioneer life in a turn-of-the-century mining and timber settlement in Washington state. The central characters are the gambler McCabe (Warren Beatty) and his business partner, the skilled British cockney whore-cum-madam Mrs Miller (Julie Christie), and like the burgeoning frontier community which they exploit they are well within the framework of the western movie.

For a long time, though, we learn more about the economics of the town than anything else: if earlier horse operas have educated us in gunplay and ranch management, Altman's picture is at times almost a US Army Signals Corps instructional movie about setting up and running a brothel. We wonder indeed whether the film will actually become a western at all. We are eventually reassured by a beautifully staged cold-blooded murder of an innocent cowboy who falls off a rope-bridge into a frozen river, and this is followed by a remarkably sustained running gunfight in the snow. We are reminded of *High Noon* as the frightened McCabe and the three killers, who have been despatched by an anonymous mining company to put him out of business, stalk each other round town. Indeed, it is precisely because the film *is* a western that Altman can confer a heroic status upon a seedy pimp and an opium-smoking whore – two simple, community-minded entrepreneurs standing up against the inexorable pressures of the faceless corporate state.

Two remarkable recent films, Sydney Pollack's *Jeremiah Johnson* (1972) and Robert Benton's *Bad Company* (1972), are also sustained rather than diminished by gradually turning into westerns after

opening sequences which could have taken them along the same
trail as *The Emigrants* or *Joe Hill*. The central characters of both are
fugitives from war. When Jeremiah Johnson (Robert Redford)
arrives in Colorado territory on the last fringe of civilisation during
the 1840s, he is still dressed in army uniform. Some years later, after
painfully re-creating himself as a self-sufficient Mountain Man, he
encounters a party of cavalry and asks them about the war – is it
over? The soldiers are momentarily taken aback by the question: oh
yes, the Mexican–American War, it's long over, and clearly almost
forgotten. More explicitly, though not less centrally, the band of
teenagers led by the prissy middle-class farm boy Drew Dixon (Barry
Brown) and the sharp, working-class Pennsylvanian Jake Rumsey
(Jeff Bridges) in *Bad Company* join forces in St. Joseph, Missouri,
and head West, not as pioneers but as draft-dodgers from the Civil
War in 1863.

Traditionally in the movies and the more commercial aspects of
popular culture, history and the past in general provide occasions
for uplift rather than cynicism. The points of departure for *Jeremiah
Johnson* and *Bad Company* are only too obviously a prevalent feeling
about the Vietnam conflict, as are of course those for a number of
other films I have mentioned earlier. But as the researches of the
Chicago anthropologist Sol Tax have established, the Vietnam War
was not uniquely unpopular in American history. Viewing the situation in 1968, Dr Tax placed Vietnam as only the fourth least
popular war, coming behind the war of 1812, the Mexican War
(1846–8), which was denounced from numerous quarters, by
Lincoln, the Abolitionists and the Catholics, and the Civil War,
which led to anti-draft riots infinitely bloodier than anything seen
in twentieth-century America, and was termed 'a rich man's war
and a poor man's fight'.[30]

In an interesting article twenty years ago in *Sight and Sound*
(April–June 1953), written as the Korean War was drawing to a
close, Herbert L. Jacobson argued that a renaissance of the cowboy
picture took place during and immediately after World War II, and
that the genre had played a key part in sustaining American military
preparedness:

The seemingly miraculous transformation of the U.S. in two
world wars from a people with practically no army and a buried,

---

30 Quoted and discussed in *Rebellion on the Campus* by Seymour Martin Lipset
(Routledge & Kegan Paul, London, 1972), p. 12.

though glorious, military tradition, into a crushing military power, is due in no small part to the combative spirit kept alive in her youth by the cowboy tradition, itself constantly reflected in the American cinema...

In the light of much present-day thinking, such a comment sounds astonishingly naïve. Yet only on the surface do *Jeremiah Johnson* and *Bad Company* give the lie to it, and precisely because their makers are so knowing, so sophisticated. Johnson is rejecting a corrupt East Coast American civilisation and its politics, but after a winter of discontent up snow-creek in search of a counterculture without a copy of *The Last Whole Earth Catalog*, he becomes a legendary figure, a murderous Indian fighter. Admittedly, however, what triggers the change in his situation is the entry of the old world in the form of the US cavalry, who force him into conflict with the Indians by making him commit the unforgivable sacrilege of crossing their ancient burial grounds. Nevertheless, what he has taken with him to the West is a scarcely containable inner violence which the immensity, the awesomeness of the land itself and its native inhabitants inevitably draw out. This is the D.H. Lawrence theme which in similar fashion underpins Mulligan's *The Stalking Moon*.

Jeremiah Johnson is high mimetic in character, and the grandeur of the scenery (mostly shot in winter) matches the grandiose aspirations of the director and his writers. *Bad Company* is low mimetic – at every point traditional heroism is undercut, as might be expected in the directorial debut of Robert Benton, who scripted the picture with David Newman, his co-screenwriter on *Bonnie and Clyde*. Never have the West and its inhabitants appeared more uninviting – the weather is invariably bad, the food is sparse, the windswept, treeless grass plains stretch endlessly on, a pilgrim making his way back East offers his wife's sexual services at a dollar a time, homesteaders charge exorbitant prices for inedible meals, and a child gets the top of his head blown off for stealing a pie cooling on a window sill.

Bad Company is Tom Sawyer and Huck Finn out West, or perhaps even more a corrupt frontier version of *Oliver Twist* where the virtuous, hypocritical Drew plays Oliver to Jake Rumsey's Artful Dodger, and at the end the frame freezes on the two boys as they walk in with drawn pistols to rob their first Wells Fargo office. The screen also freezes on Jeremiah Johnson as he makes his final peace with the Indians. The fashionable device is the same in each film, but the meaning is different. True, both the Mountain Man and the pair of draft dodgers have become one with the land. But Johnson has been elevated to legendary status – he will ride off now up some frontier Olympus, freed by a violent transaction with the terrain and its remorseless guardians from his oppressive loneliness and selfhood. The boys in *Bad Company*, however, have been reduced – less perhaps at one with the land than with their society. They may be killed in the next minute; more likely they will meet their deaths in the succession of similar sordid robberies which will inevitably follow on from the present one. They have not transcended the violence of the world they sought to escape and which accompanied them to the West, but have gradually succumbed to it.

During the time I have been thinking about this book – roughly since 1963 when I began work on an uncompleted *Encounter* article looking at changes in the genre in the decade which has passed since Robert Warshow's famous essay in that journal – much has happened to the western movie.

At that point Peckinpah's *Guns in the Afternoon* had just introduced the sight of indoor plumbing into a cowboy picture, something which in Vidor's *Man Without a Star* (1955) had been a matter for incredulous sniggering among the cowhands and which was not shown to the audience. Peckinpah went one further in *The Ballad of Cable Hogue* (1970) and presented a stagecoach driver loudly urinating in the desert. Not long after this, Joseph L, Mankiewicz in his first western, *There Was a Crooked Man* (1970), staged a fight around the latrine in a frontier jail which concluded with the loser having his face ducked in a pool of urine. The floodgates, one might say, were then open: in *Monte Walsh* (1970) and *The Culpepper Cattle Company* (1972) the state of a cowboy's bowels becomes a matter of crucial dramatic importance. Other intimate aspects of frontier life such as incest, homosexuality and masturbation (discussed at length in *McCabe and Mrs Miller*) have become, or are becoming, commonplace. These are perhaps minor matters, though not easily dismissed as being the products of prurience, titillation or a taste for spurious realism. Yet they should not distract attention from the way in which the western has continued to dig away at the same old concerns, using a familiar range of situations and settings, and the way too that new westerns make us look again at and revalue those which have gone before. Perhaps the final word on the interplay between convention, myth and reality should be Marianne Moore's prescription for poetry, 'imaginary gardens with real toads in them'. One must naturally be aware of the danger of being deceived by real gardens populated by plastic toads.

If I have a major fear about the future it is that, in Britain at least, there won't be enough places left to see westerns in. As late as the mid-60s a Londoner could find virtually all the post-war pictures mentioned in this book, up to that time, showing over a period of a couple of months on weekdays and at Sunday screenings at little back-street cinemas and suburban movie houses in a sort of permanent repertory. Such is no longer the case, nor will it ever be again. As I write this, the picture palace at the end of my road has put up its shutters forever. A few weeks before it closed, I saw *When the Legends Die* there. Would that Stuart Millar's fine, elegiac film had been chosen, as Hawks' *Red River* was in *The Last Picture Show*, to end on – instead of letting the place die with the pathetic whimper of *Carry On Abroad*.

Back in 1962, in the high days of Kennedy's New Frontier, Fenin and Everson concluded their survey of over sixty years of westerns with the sanguine comment:

> It has been a distressingly long time now since such excellent westerns as *Shane* and before it *Wagonmaster*, *Stagecoach* and *The Toll Gate* appeared. But if a nation today can respond to the old values and spirit which made that nation great, then surely films will continue to be made by creative men depicting that history and the authenticity of the romance.

Even when I first read those words ten years ago, I had more faith in the western than I had in Western society, from the complexity and doubts of which the movies have drawn their strength. While I am a good deal more optimistic than many about the future of America, I do feel that the health and renewal of the genre over the past decade suggests that its development does not necessarily depend upon the prosperity and confidence of the United States. Equally, I should be more than a little surprised if the enlarged Common Market, for all the countervailing economic and cultural force which it is expected to become, will produce in the foreseeable future a cinematic form drawing on our shared European history which is likely to challenge the western.

Bibliography

The best, most easily available book on the West is the late John A. Hawgood's *The American West* (Eyre & Spottiswoode, London, 1967, published in the United States by Knopf as *America's Western Frontiers*). This is far and away the most comprehensive single work on the subject and contains a first-class bibliographical note which covers all the available literature up to that time. Of the hundreds of books Hawgood mentions, I feel it necessary to underline the importance to the serious student of the western of Henry Nash Smith's remarkable essay on 'The American West as Symbol and Myth', *Virgin Land* (Harvard University Press, Cambridge, MA; Oxford University Press, London, 1950). All British students of the West are in debt to Hawgood for his own scrupulous scholarship and for his editorship of Eyre & Spottiswoode's 'Frontier Library'.

As indicated in the text, I have found numerous books not strictly concerned with the West of great value – Howard Mumford Jones' *O Strange New World* (Chatto & Windus, London, 1965); John W. McCoubrey's *American Tradition in Painting* (George Braziller, New York, 1963); as well as several books by the late Richard Hofstadter, most particularly *Anti-Intellectualism in American Life* (Knopf, New York, 1963) and *The Progressive Historians* (Knopf, New York, 1968). Professor Hawgood's bibliography encompasses the principal texts on American Indians, but since then there has been a sizeable body of work which nobody interested in the subject should neglect: Alvin Josephy's *The Indian Heritage of America* (1968); *The American Indian Today*, edited by Stuart Little and Nancy O. Lurie (revised edition, 1968); *Our Brother's Keeper*, edited by Edgar S. Cahn (1969); Dee Brown's *Bury My Heart at Wounded Knee* (1971); and the three key polemical texts by Vine Deloria Jr. – *Custer Died For Your Sins* (1969), *We Talk, You Listen* (1970), and *Of the Utmost Good Faith* (1971).

The principal general book-length studies of the western are:

Agel, Henri (ed.), *Le Western* (Études Cinématographiques 12–13,

Lettres Modernes, Paris, 1969, revised and updated by Jean A. Gili, 1969).

Bellour, Raymond (ed.) *Le Western: Sources, Mythes, Auteurs, Acteurs, Filmographies* (Le Monde en 10/18, Union Générale d'Éditions, Paris, 1966, revised 1968).

Eyles, Allen, *The Western: An Illustrated Guide* (A. Zwemmer, London; A.S. Barnes, New York, 1967). This little handbook is an accurate and fairly comprehensive index, invaluable to the student of the genre.

Fenin, George N. and Everson, William K., *The Western: From Silents to Cinerama* (The Orion Press, New York, 1962).

Ford, Charles, *Histoire du Western* (Éditions Pierre Horay, Paris, 1964).

Parkinson, Michael and Jeavons, Clyde, *A Pictorial History of Westerns* (Hamlyn, London, 1972).

Rieupeyrout, Jean-Louis, *La Grande Aventure du Western* (Éditions du Cerf, Paris, 1971). This is the most ambitious book on the subject, a greatly extended and enlarged version of Rieupeyrout's 1953 book *Le Western*, which contained a preface by André Bazin subsequently reprinted in the third volume of Bazin's *Qu'est-ce que le Cinéma?* (1961).

There have appeared in recent years several studies of individual directors of which the best, and most germane, is Jim Kitses' *Horizons West* (Thames & Hudson, London, 1969), also a 'Cinema One' book, which deals admirably and lucidly, if somewhat solemnly, with the westerns of Anthony Mann, Budd Boetticher and Sam Peckinpah. In his 'Cinema One' monograph on *Howard Hawks* (Secker & Warburg, London, 1968), Robin Wood analyses with characteristic insight Hawks' *Red River, Rio Bravo* and *El Dorado*. Peter Bogdanovich's *John Ford* (Studio Vista, London, 1967), largely devoted to an unsearching interview, is full of information; John Baxter's *The Cinema of John Ford* (A. Zwemmer, London; A.S. Barnes, New York, 1972) complements it with shrewd criticism.

The periodical literature on the western, both in general and specialised journals, is immense and continually growing. The indexes of any of the world's leading film magazines will reveal numerous articles, interviews and reviews. I will content myself here with a list of five interesting pieces not aimed initially at movie fans:

Barr, Charles, 'Western', *Axle Quarterly*, No. 3 (London, 1963).

Gregory, Horace, 'Guns of the Roaring West', in *Avon Book of Modern Writing*, No. 2, ed. William Phillips and Philip Rahv (Avon Publications, New York, 1954).

Kitchin, Laurence, 'Decline of the Western', *The Listener* (London, 14 July, 1966).

Schein, Harry, 'Den Olympiske Cowboyen', *Bonniers Litterära Magasin* (Stockholm, January, 1954, translated as 'The Olympic Cowboy', *The American Scholar* (Summer, 1955).

Warshow, Robert, 'Movie Chronicle: The Westerner', *Partisan Review*, March–April, 1954, reprinted in *Encounter* (March, 1954) as 'The Gentleman with a Gun', and included in Warshow's *The Immediate Experience* (Doubleday, New York, 1962).

Afterword (1977)

Apart from correcting some minor errors of fact and adding new movies to the filmography, I have made no changes in a book completed in late 1972. This does not mean I still agree with everything I wrote then or even totally understand every line of it. Not surprisingly, my favourite pictures today differ considerably from the list in the 1973 Introduction. I now think Ford's best western is *The Searchers*, Hawks' is *Rio Bravo*, Penn's is *The Missouri Breaks* and Siegel's is *The Shootist*. Otherwise, I have no radical disagreements to record or reassessments to make.

The most obvious alteration the book might appear to invite would be some reconsideration of the Kennedy–Goldwater– Johnson–Buckley theory. When first committed to print (*The Times*, February 1971), the times were already getting a little complicated, and it was never my intention that this schema should be capable of endless readjustment to fit the prevailing political climate and new sets of characters. A conceit as relatively bold as that does not bear much tampering with if its author wishes to avoid both the charge of taking himself too seriously and the risk of modifying his thesis out of existence. Anyone who wants to can play the game of inventing a Carter or Brown western; we are at least spared the confusion of discussing a different type of Ford western. As for Richard M. Nixon, we have been given an excellent film about his coming and going. I refer not to Alan Pakula's estimable *All the President's Men*, but to Kirk Douglas' *Posse* (1975), which renders the political career of the former President in allegorical form through the political ambitions of Texas marshal Howard Nightingale, though in a manner its putative subject, for all his devotion to the genre, would not much care for.

Since the completion of *Westerns*, two notable things have happened to the genre. One is that the TV western, after producing an incalculable number of series from the late 1940s to the early 1970s, has come to an end. It is unlikely to return in its former abundance. The other is that the European western has run its course, after several years in the late 1960s when production in Italy alone exceeded fifty feature films annually. In the last three years, therefore, there have been fewer westerns than at any time since *The Great Train Robbery*. This has not prevented the 1970s from being one of the great periods of the genre. Indeed I would say that 1972 was as important for the western as 1950, and this explains the sanguine tone with which I concluded the book. It was the year that gave us *The Culpepper Cattle Company*, *The Cowboys*, *Jeremiah Johnson*, *Bad Company*, *McCabe and Mrs Miller*, the four modern westerns – *Junior Bonner*, *J.W. Coop*, *When the Legends Die* and that curious sport *Billy Jack*; as well as three minor masterpieces that did not reach Britain until the following year – Aldrich's *Ulzana's Raid*, which is perhaps the highpoint of the Vietnam pursuit cycle; Philip Kaufman's *The Great Northfield Minnesota Raid*, among the acutest studies of social banditry in the genre (see my review, *Sight and Sound*, Winter, 1973–4); and Clint Eastwood's *High Plains Drifter*. But whereas the half-dozen major westerns of 1950 were the tip of an immense iceberg, these films of 1972 virtually were the iceberg. In 1976 fewer than a dozen westerns reached British screens, but five of them must be reckoned among the finest pictures of the year – *Hearts of the West* (briefly seen in Britain under the flat, unappealing title *Hollywood Cowboy*), *The Missouri Breaks*, *Buffalo Bill and the Indians*, *The Outlaw Josey Wales* and *The Shootist*. The genre once resembled an immense cattle drive of scabby, indifferent animals led by a few fine steers; now it is like a luxuriant pasture occupied by a few prize animals, overfed perhaps but in radiant good health, who might drop dead tomorrow. A dearth of westerns, however, is not to be confused with the death of the western.

Although I have no major new insights, I do have a few further reflections which arise out of a most interesting and varied four years of moviemaking.

The Italian Western

From the mid-1960s the European western came in to make up the declining bulk in the world's cinemas of Hollywood westerns. It took from Hollywood, and also it gave back. Basically it took plots and situations, which were drained of too specific national meaning. What it returned to Hollywood was a taste for ultra-violence, a strong line in calculated sadism, a penchant for over-emphatic images, and overloaded sound tracks, a characteristically continental *nostalgie de la boue* that can pass for unflinching realism, and a slick line in simplified Marxism. These gifts could no doubt be phrased in a less pejorative fashion, and the Italian western did shake up the genre in a not unuseful way. It has been suggested that *The Wild Bunch* bears the mark of the Italian western; *Pat Garrett and Billy the Kid* certainly does. So the influence may have been filtered through Peckinpah.

What the Italian industry took principally from America, however, was Clint Eastwood, whom Sergio Leone borrowed from US television and returned home as the first major western movie star since the early 1950s. Through Eastwood's return to Hollywood one can trace the assimilation of the Italian western via stages of mere imitation, creative re-working and finally authoritative transcendence. In his first two Hollywood horse operas, Ted Post's *Hang 'Em High* and Don Siegel's *Two Mules for Sister Sara*, we have Italian westerns re-staged, the latter even having a score by Leone's collaborator, the prolific Ennio Morricone. The dullish *Joe Kidd* (1972) tempers the Mediterranean extravagance with some of John Sturges' characteristically chilly solemnity. With his confident first western as director, *High Plains Drifter*, Eastwood appeared in a highly charged morality tale which owes much to his mentor Sergio Leone in its pitiless allegory of an avenging angel returning to destroy a worthless community that had stood by while its sheriff was murdered. Three years later Eastwood directed *The Outlaw Josey Wales* which, while still clearly indebted to Leone, is a compassionate film, kindly without being unduly sentimental, and entirely rooted in the American experience. The Civil War, in the aftermath of which *Josey Wales* takes place, is clearly a substitute for Vietnam, and the shaping into a community of the disparate outcasts who join the fugitive Wales on his travels is a binding up of the wounds caused by the Indo-Chinese War and the social divisions of the 1960s. *Josey Wales* is a wryly optimistic picture (as is, in a different way, Penn's *The Missouri Breaks*), a film about the healing of a people and a land through suffering, endurance and mutual assistance.

The other major creation of the Italian western is Lee Van Cleef, who unlike Eastwood was to work with other European directors besides Leone (who brought him to Europe for *For a Few Dollars More*) and also unlike Eastwood did not prove profitable in his own land. In 1970 he returned home for his only Hollywood star role in *Barquero*, in which he played a New Mexico ferry operator holding off a psychotic Warren Oates and his gang. The skilled *pasticheur* Gordon Douglas managed to render it as one of the most Italianate of all American westerns, a pastiche of a pastiche as it were.

I now consider my earlier remarks about Italian westerns patronising and unduly dismissive, and feel that a major study remains to be written on the European western and its relationship to the American version. The chaotic *Italian Western: The Opera of Violence* by Laurence Staig and Tony Williams (Lorrimer Press, London, 1975) is not much of a start but better than nothing.

That discontent with Hollywood westerns – their values (whether conservative or liberal), their paucity of action and their declining numbers – played a major part in triggering off the Italian western is obvious, but the whole social and industrial history is worth examining. One thing I am fairly sure of is that no American director influenced the Italians more than Robert Aldrich. His *Vera Cruz* (1954) is a blueprint for the spaghetti western; and the baroque climactic gunfight in *The Last Sunset* (1961) between Kirk Douglas and Rock Hudson established the pattern for the standard rococo gun-down in Italian horse operas. Significantly enough, Aldrich's next assignment was *Sodom and Gomorrah*, filmed in Italy with Sergio Leone as his assistant. Shortly afterwards Leone made *A Fistful of Dollars*.

There is an intriguing reference to *The Last Sunset* in Bernardo Bertolucci's *The Spider's Stratagem*, made in 1970 but only recently (December 1976) seen for the first time in Britain. Bertolucci's film is in effect a Hollywood 40s *film noir* transposed to Italy and transmogrified by way of a short story by Jorge Luis Borges. The hero, while investigating the circumstances of his father's murder, visits an open air cinema where the picture being shown is *The Last Sunset*. The choice is clearly deliberate and while it obviously points to certain aspects of *The Spider's Stratagem* (the suggestion of incest, for instance), one suspects that it also refers to the special place Aldrich's film has in the affections of Bertolucci's friend Sergio Leone, with whom he worked on the script of *Once Upon a Time in the West* a year before the Borges adaptation.

Television
Twenty-five years of television westerns have left only faint memories. Rapidly the TV branch recapitulated the history of the movie western, coming from primitive two-reelers in the late 40s to the psychological and chamber western by the mid-50s, and then from the early 60s becoming pretty well stuck in a groove of well-meaning liberal westerns of the Kennedy variety. Their political and social outlook came in part from the kindly men who produced

them, and partly from the necessity to combine general inoffen-
siveness with social responsibility. There was also a formal
contribution. The family or group western arose in the late 50s when
there was a great cult of the family in America (this was the era of
McCall's, 'the Magazine of Togetherness', and the slogan 'the family
that prays together stays together'). This species inevitably (from its
convenient framework as much as its ideology) placed enormous
emphasis on stability, property, the ability of the little collective to
solve its own problems and those of others drawn into its circle. The
tragic sense of life, the idea that some problems are insoluble, was
thus excluded as much by the form as by the producers' own intentions. The forerunners of this series were *Gunsmoke* (which became
progressively blander and less violent, partly because of industrial
codes and pressures) and *Bonanza*, which established the pattern for
The Virginian, *The Big Valley* and *High Chaparral*. Like the Italian
western, the TV horse opera is still in search of its diligent historian.

In the 1950s Hollywood continually mocked television in its
movies, and whenever a TV set was seen it was pumping out some
undistinguished western – this is a cheap running joke in Nunnally
Johnson's *The Man in the Grey Flannel Suit* (1956), a picture with
little right to patronise anything. Later, in Richard Cawston's television documentary *Television and the World* (1961), what everyone
was watching from Chicago to Singapore was the same western,
never actually shown but represented by an archetypal soundtrack.
This commercial abuse of the medium was contrasted to ironic effect
with a class of illiterate Italian peasants learning to read through a
television educational course, and the first words of their text were
'Columbus discovered the New World.' The final bitter cut comes
in *The Shootist*. The past of the dying gunfighter, J.B. Books, is established by a montage of scenes from John Wayne movies starting
with *Red River* and working through *Rio Bravo* and *El Dorado*. The
film we are seeing, we readily infer, is as much about John Wayne
and the notion of heroism he represents in the cinema as it is about
this particular gunfighter, who like Wayne is also a sufferer from
cancer. The actors surrounding him bring to the picture a variety
of careers – for instance, James Stewart, the doctor, specifically refers
to the characters' (i.e., the actors') previous encounter in *The Man
Who Shot Liberty Valance* fifteen years before; Lauren Bacall, the
widow who solaces the dying Books, directs us to another aspect of
Hawks' work from Wayne's, and is of course the widow of her
Hawks films co-star Humphrey Bogart.

When it comes to the final gunfight in which Books/Wayne will
go out in a blaze of glory in the 'false spring' of a Western winter,
he is ranged against three challengers, all totally innocent except in
their aspirations. One is a young nonentity, who looks like the dark
side of Elisha Cook Jr.; the others are the ageing Richard Boone
and the still handsome Hugh O'Brian. Boone and O'Brian are character actors who never made it as fully-fledged stars in the cinema.
But for a while they were challengers to Wayne as television heroes
of the 1950s – O'Brian as the legendary marshal in the *Wyatt Earp*
series, Boone as the frontier knight-errant Paladin in *Have Gun Will
Travel*. TV's Wyatt Earp and Paladin are now long forgotten, though
millions watched them every week, more than were turning out to
see Wayne's movies. But Wayne survived, as cinema has survived.
He eschewed television. The screen was too small for him and apart
from a guest role in a 1960 episode of *Wagon Train* directed by John
Ford (he played General Sherman under his more-or-less real name,
Michael Morris) and a comic spot on *Laugh-In*, his appearances on
TV have largely been confined to self-consciously tolerant encounters with earnest liberal interviewers. Wayne of course guns down
O'Brian and Boone, before himself perishing at the hands of the
bartender, representative of a long-suffering trade at last given its
revenge here for all those shattered mirrors and wrecked saloons.

The Shootist, even if it doesn't prove to be Wayne's final western,
would be a fitting conclusion to his career, and is indeed his first
picture of distinction in the 1970s. In an essay on 'The Morality of
Poetry',[31] Yvor Winters distinguishes between a writer's 'morality'
and his 'theology', between the fundamental truths of experience
he incorporates into his poems and the body of received ideas he
imposes on them. Applying this same distinction to John Wayne's
career, one can see two lines of pictures. Films like *The Alamo*, *The
Cowboys*, his series with Andrew McLaglen (*McLintock!*, *Chisum*, *The
Undefeated*), express his theology, and they tend to be his most strident, least integrated works, where he is most in control as producer.
His finest films are his collaborations with Ford and Hawks, and
now *The Shootist* with Don Siegel, and these movies contain his
morality.

---

31 *In Defence of Reason* (University of Denver Press, Denver, 1947), p. 17 *et seq.*

Cops and Vigilantes

The quantitative decline of the western has been accompanied by the rise, or recrudescence, of two other types of film – the police movie and the vigilante film. Thematically and ethically they are closely related and spring from current frustrations of American urban life and the problem of law-and-order. As I have suggested elsewhere (see my article 'Cops' in *Sight and Sound*, Summer, 1974), the police cycle began in the late 1960s on both TV and in the cinema, and was given its greatest impetus through the success of *Dirty Harry* and *The French Connection*. Sam Peckinpah's *Straw Dogs*, made the same year (1971), helped the vigilante cycle on its way, though most of its films have been cheap down-market efforts, and the quite open way these films despise the ineffective upholders of the law has kept them off television, the medium in which the cop thrives.

Police and vigilante pictures are transpositions of the western into the modern world, and are taken by their most vociferous critics as bringing into question the western movie ethic and exposing its essential shallowness and even anti-social qualities. Looked at in another way, however, they confirm the value of the western in providing a suitably distanced and stylised framework for observing characters' behaviour, and recognising their involvement in symbolic transactions. Of numerous direct references to the western, those in three of these films are of particular interest. The first is one of the most likeable of the cop pictures, *Electra Glide in Blue*, where the director, James William Guercio, is determined to establish that his central character is a direct descendant of the heroes of the Old West. Consequently he begins his film in Monument Valley and ends it there with his diminutive motorcycle patrolman shot dead on the road, the camera drawing back to leave him among the familiar majestic buttes and mesas that define the West of John Ford. Moreover, the tiny cop identifies himself with Hollywood's shortest he-man star, Alan Ladd, and appropriately enough he is investigating the murder of Elisha Cook Jr., the perennial victim of American films and in this context specifically the man shot down by Jack Palance outside the saloon in *Shane*, the killing revenged by Alan Ladd in his most enduring film.

In the most profitable, most unctuously motivated vigilante film, Michael Winner's *Death Wish*, the protagonist is a liberal-pacifist architect (Charles Bronson) who goes out West on a professional assignment after his wife has been murdered and his daughter driven insane by muggers in New York. A quietly demonic Arizonan preaches him a sermon on self-help, takes him to a display of Western gun-fighting on a movie set and presents him with a pair of pearl-handled revolvers. Bronson goes back to Manhattan to become a one-man vigilante squad, battling against crime in the streets and subways and encouraging his fellow citizens to do like-wise. The place at which our gentle liberal undergoes his conversion is Old Tucson, the permanent western set built in 1940 for *Arizona*, and now used both for movie-making and as a tourist attraction. *Rio Bravo* was made there; so too during the past couple of years were Kirk Douglas' *Posse* and Andrew McLaglen's *The Last Hard Men*, and Old Tucson was the local community centre for the *High Chaparral* TV series. *Death Wish* draws on some very powerful associations that every viewer has with this particular Western town.

The third instance is the most distinguished movie the vigilante cycle has produced: Martin Scorsese's *Taxi Driver*, where we have the obsessional loner of the western located in the city and indulging in isolation his addiction to arms and gunplay. He is called Travis (the same name as the military commander of the Alamo); and when he eventually embarks on his orgy of retributive violence he shaves his hair in the Mohawk style as if making some symbolic transition into a cleansing, avenging Indian hero of a kind that would no doubt delight Leslie Fiedler.

Baseball

Three recent movies use the national game in its primitive nine-teenth-century form to interesting and contrasting effect. Aldrich's *Ulzana's Raid* (the second and best of three original western screen-plays written by the Scots novelist Alan Sharp, coming between *The Hired Hand* and *Billy Two Hats*) opens with a cavalry troop playing baseball at a dusty Western outpost. The camera contemplates them for some time, registering them as sportsmen from a painting by Thomas Eakins transposed from New England to the frontier. The effect of this organised game being played in the wilderness is absurd and melancholic; and it is quite clearly intended to make us think of American soldiers in Vietnam pursuing their curious pastimes in an alien land, thus creating the political ambience for the action that follows, where the Indians are equated with Asians, and American domestic colonisation with later imperial activities.

In *Posse* the fugitive outlaw Jack Strawhorn (Bruce Dern) arrives at a mountain hide-out to take charge of a new gang. He finds them playing baseball by a river – an unruly rabble of scruffy, innocent thugs, squabbling like children for the bat and ball, rolling over in the water while disputing the game. Soon they will be facing a small, trained, uniformed posse – and they will be dead.

In *The Great Northfield Minnesota Raid*, the James–Younger gang infiltrate the burgeoning middle-border town they intend to rob, and watch the confident citizens going about their business of creating the new settled America that will exclude them. Cole Younger (Cliff Robertson), the band's leader, comes across some sportsmen on the outskirts of town playing baseball. 'It's the new national pastime,' one of the enthusiastic spectators tells him. 'Our national pastime is shooting and always will be,' says Cole, and raising his shotgun blows the ball to pieces as if it were a clay pigeon.

Children

The 1970s began with two parallel movies released in early 1972, *The Cowboys* and *The Culpepper Cattle Company*, both related to the Vietnam experience. In the latter a young man is seen to be exposed to the corruption of adult life in the course of a cattle drive that is very evidently America on the move; he emerges annealed but undefiled. In *The Cowboys*, Wayne recruits a whole crew of children for a similarly symbolic journey. As he instructs them, first in a schoolroom and then on the range, he is teacher, father and (closely resembling his role in *The Green Berets*) commanding officer. When the parents see their children off, the tone of the scene suggests a departure to a war. The experience is thoroughly ennobling, and one is moved, while being aware, for all the sincerity of Wayne's performance, that one is being shamelessly exploited. Did the authors, Irving Ravetch and Harriet Frank Jr., feel the same? Perhaps. Certainly in *The Spikes Gang* two years later they wrote for director Richard Fleischer a screenplay that was *The Cowboys* stood on its head. They take three boys who leave their boring, narrow-minded homes in a frontier town after having helped a charming wounded outlaw (Lee Marvin). Meeting him again they take to a romantic life of crime (they've already accidentally killed a sheriff) which leads them down short inglorious paths to an early grave. This underrated little film ends with the eldest boy in a mutually fatal gunfight with the trio's one-time hero and mentor.

One thing that gives *The Spikes Gang* an added interest is the casting. The three boys are played by Gary Grimes – the exemplary teenager of *Summer of '42* and *The Culpepper Cattle Company*; Charlie

Martin Smith – the myopic born loser in *The Culpepper Cattle Company*, *American Graffiti* and *Pat Garrett and Billy the Kid*, in which he is the first of Billy's gang to die; and Ronnie Howard, also of *American Graffiti*. Howard was later to be given a crucial juvenile role in another western when he was cast as Lauren Bacall's son in *The Shootist*. There he became the beneficiary or depository of John Wayne's wisdom and experience; after killing the ageing gunfighter's invited assailant, he would renounce violence and live on in a sad twentieth-century world (the picture is set in the week following the death of Queen Victoria) denuded of clear-cut identifiable heroes.

New Faces of 1885

There has emerged during the 1970s a new group of western character actors, a new Hollywood posse as it were, riding behind the principals. They are an odd-looking bunch – quirky, dangerous, unkempt, wiry men, physically slight but coiled and ready to explode into laughter or violence at any moment. They dress in a weird array of battered headgear and greasy informal attire. Their prototypes are two character actors who became to their own surprise movie stars – Lee Marvin and Warren Oates. If the former was for a while during the overheated, Vietnam-haunted culture of the late 1960s the dove's favourite hawk, then Oates, the desperate hero-victim, was the Lee Marvin of de-escalation. Marvin emerged under the direction of Fritz Lang (*The Big Heat*, 1953) and Budd Boetticher (as the suave villain in the first Scott–Boetticher western *Seven Men from Now*); Warren Oates grew steadily, and the size of his roles too, through his long concurrent associations with Sam Peckinpah, Burt Kennedy and Monte Hellman.

The outstanding names in the new posse are Bo Hopkins, Geoffrey Lewis, Matt Clark (natural successor as life's fall-guy to Elisha Cook Jr.), Harry Dean Stanton, Luke Askew, John Quade and Wayne Sutherlin. Each of them figures in two or more of the following movies (Matt Clark is in six of them): *The Cowboys*, *The Culpepper Cattle Company*, *The Great Northfield Minnesota Raid*, *Pat Garrett and Billy the Kid*, *High Plains Drifter*, *Posse*, *Rancho Deluxe*, *Hearts of the West*, *The Missouri Breaks*, *The Outlaw Josey Wales*, *The Return of a Man Called Horse*. Whichever side of the law they're on, their appearance and demeanour is much the same, looking less honest than the bland, well-laundered lawmen and cowboys they succeed, and more individual than the plump, moustachioed villains they replace. Seeing *Rio Bravo* nowadays, one is struck by the almost comic collection of unshaven heavies from old B-feature days. No wonder audiences are so little disturbed by the extravagant way in which they are dispatched by sheriff John Wayne and his three jocular deputies. Their like could not be found today – their last symbolic representative was George Plimpton, doing one of his Walter Mitty acts as a central-casting villain in Hawks' final, anachronistic western *Rio Lobo*; and he is speedily given his quietus by John Wayne after uttering his single line, 'OK, Whitey.'

These actors help complete the movement through the 50s and 60s towards a more sharply etched, more individually realised background. Secondly, they represent a new kind of gritty, funky chic. Thirdly (and here they follow closely behind Marvin and Oates, as well as James Coburn and Jack Nicholson), they have finally obliterated the increasingly blurred physical distinction between the good guys and the bad guys. (Note, for instance, the way in which Bruce Dern gives much the same performance as the psychopathic hippie who menaces John Wayne and his assistants in *The Cowboys* and as the social bandit Jack Strawhorn in *Posse*, who only robs trains and lures Marshal Nightingale's discontented followers away from their discredited leader.) This doesn't mean that they have extinguished the distinction between right and wrong, good and evil, responsible and anti-social behaviour, ethical and unethical conduct. Far from it. What they have helped do away with is the easy identification of these moral polarities with the characters' demeanour and social roles.

One of the outstanding westerns of the 1970s, Peckinpah's *Pat Garrett and Billy the Kid*, is only fully to be comprehended through its actors. What concerns me here is not the roles assigned to Bob Dylan and Kris Kristofferson, or the one assumed by Peckinpah himself when he suddenly emerges from the darkness as the Fort Sumner coffin-maker urging Garrett to 'go in and get it done with', or the fact that the oft-referred-to demonic capitalist string-puller Chisum is never seen, and that we are expected to think of him as perhaps Richard Nixon, who back in 1970 used the John Wayne movie *Chisum* to preach a little lesson to the nation. What interests me is rather the fashion in which the picture deploys several generations of character actors. Reluctantly recruited by Garrett to help uphold the law, and in some cases doomed to die in the attempt, are Jack Elam, Slim Pickens, Richard Jaeckel and R.G. Armstrong, veterans between them of a hundred westerns. On the sidelines are old-timers Paul Fix and Chill Wills, newcomer Matt Clark, Katy Jurado (who deserted Gary Cooper at *High Noon* and now stands by her husband Slim Pickens, watching him die in silence in the film's most deeply affecting sequence) and Jason Robards. Riding with Billy the Kid are the bespectacled teenager Charlie Martin Smith, Luke Askew, Harry Dean Stanton, and a couple of other new faces, looking, as Eliot put it in *The Family Reunion*, 'so withered and so young'; and most of them survive.

Comedies

The most successful western of the 1970s has been Mel Brooks' comedy *Blazing Saddles* (1974). It has made more money than *The Missouri Breaks*, *The Shootist*, *Pat Garrett and Billy the Kid*, *Posse* and *Bite the Bullet* combined, and yet it cost less than half of any of these films to produce. Its success is difficult to explain, and the small handful of good jokes that can be snatched from the indiscriminately scattered buckshot of its comic fusillade are mostly fairly marginal to the genre. Which is not to say that the film isn't amiable or ingratiating, for it is both. The title itself is an amusing (and presumably intentionally anal) conceit, and the credit titles with their fiery lettering and wildly over-intense title song (sung in a Frankie Laine style by Laine himself, parodying his own performance of the songs of *Blowing Wild* and *3.10 to Yuma*) send up the cheap Technicolor westerns which Columbia and Universal churned out in the early 1950s. There are a number of acceptable jests here and there – particularly the tribute to the bearded Gabby Hayes-type old-timer whose unintelligible speech constitutes 'authentic Western gibberish'. But most of the jokes are thin and the surrealism second-hand. Even the much lauded scene in which the cowboys sit round the camp fire farting after their meal of tinned beans had been anticipated by Tonino Valerii's *My Name is Nobody* the previous year.

Nevertheless, *Blazing Saddles* captured the public imagination while virtually all other recent comedy westerns have fallen by the wayside. And this is odd, because the past four years have seen some of the most interesting comedies in the history of the genre – and audiences were invited to laugh at westerns not long after Broncho Billy Anderson exploded that minatory pistol in their collective face at the end of *The Great Train Robbery*.

The run-of-the-mill jokey westerns continue to be produced – Melvin Frank's *The Duchess and the Dirtwater Fox*, with George Segal and Goldie Hawn, Frank Gilroy's *From Noon Till Three*, with

Charles Bronson and Jill Ireland. But the really distinctive pictures
were made by directors and writers with a genuine feeling for the
genre, from which instinct the humour flowed – and invariably
rather painfully. Most celebrated of these failures is Robert Altman's
Buffalo Bill and the Indians (1976), a handsome bicentennial movie
asserting that all the world's a Western circus, the globe 'Cody-fied'
as one character in the film puts it. Yet underlying the technical
sophistication of Altman's film is an astonishing simplicity, not all
of which can be blamed upon Arthur Kopits' play *Indians,* first
performed by the Royal Shakespeare Company in London in 1968,
from which it derives. Paul Newman's William Cody is infinitely
more complex than the stage original, and the same can be said of
most of the white characters, but the Indians have become as dignified and wooden as effigies outside cigar stores, and the question of
white guilt, white bad faith and white cultural inferiority so manifest as scarcely to be worth arguing. Thus Altman's smooth dramatic
superstructure, enacted by a peerless team of performers, rests upon
a crude and flimsy socio-political infrastructure.

No one could actively dislike *Buffalo Bill*, and the same is true of
the other comedy westerns that gave so much more pleasure to the
limited audiences which paid to see them than to the generous
investors who paid to make them. James Frawley's *Kid Blue* (1973)
is a delightful movie about a failed outlaw (Dennis Hopper) in turn-
of-the-century Texas learning (by jumping on to the coal tender of
a moving train and falling off the other side) that he cannot earn his
living as a criminal, and attempting to settle down in the Texas
township of Dimebox. In this acutely realised frontier community
he finds no place to hide, and is driven into a corner from which
he can only escape by taking to the air – like Albert Finney at the
end of *Charlie Bubbles*. It is a sad little comedy, as too is Frank Perry's
Rancho Deluxe (1975), a western set in present-day Montana,
containing some devastatingly accurate scenes of life in the garish
modern West, and showing the way in which two anarchic outlaws
(Jeff Bridges and Sam Waterston) might function in the dehumanised corporate world of today. This engaging and confused picture
will endure as a commentary upon the screenplay by the same
writer, Thomas McGuane, for Arthur Penn's *The Missouri Breaks*,
where an almost identical plot and dramatis personae were treated
in rather different terms.

Two other comedies remain. One is Howard Zieff's *Hearts of the
West*, exhibited to disastrous box-office returns in Britain as

Hollywood Cowboy. This is a delicate tale (starring Jeff Bridges of *Rancho Deluxe* and many other distinguished flops) about an aspiring Western novelist who heads West in the early 1930s to soak up local colour and match the achievement of his hero Zane Grey. He finishes up acting in western movies on the Gower Gulch end of Hollywood's Poverty Row. In a few years *Hearts of the West* will surely find its place among the classic pictures about filmmaking (along with *A Star Is Born*, *Le Mépris*, *The Bad and the Beautiful*, *La Nuit Américaine*), and it will represent in the most kindly fashion the notion of the western as the representative American genre, encompassing the aspirations of an era. It would be a companion piece to the still unreleased *The Last Movie* (1971), in which Dennis Hopper savagely represented the making of a western in Latin America as just that.

Finally there is *My Name Is Nobody*, conceived by Sergio Leone and directed by his amanuensis Tonino Valerii. This exceedingly knowing picture shoots off in all directions, parodying Leone's own westerns and those he drew on and influenced. The film turns on the fate of ageing gunfighter Jack Beauregard (Henry Fonda), who is attempting to retire from a lifetime of frontier showdowns and catch a boat to Europe from New Orleans in 1899. What stops him is the western itself in the person of Terence Hill (screen name of Mario Girotti), the comic hero of the 'Trinity' films, the highly successful spaghetti western series which followed Eastwood's dour 'Man With No Name' trilogy.

In this picture, largely shot on American locations, Hill/Nobody protects Fonda from such varied heavies as R.G. Armstrong (a familiar overbearing figure in Hathaway and Peckinpah films) and Geoffrey Lewis (the wild, eye-rolling menace of the 1970s). He reveals to Fonda the name 'Sam Peckinpah' on a cross in an Arizona graveyard largely occupied by Western gunmen, and encourages him to take on 'the Wild Bunch', a hundred and fifty anonymous horsemen wearing yellow dusters and riding relentlessly in flattened telescopic focus to Ennio Morricone's parodic version of 'Ride of the Valkyrie', the ultimate horse opera theme. Fonda has his showdown with the bunch and enters history as a legendary figure, before taking part in a bogus shoot-out in New Orleans; following this he can slip off incognito to Europe, having passed on the burden of his role to his insouciant hippie successor. *My Name Is Nobody* is perhaps a rather indulgent picture, but its strength lies in the fact that its comic ideas almost without exception spring from a close study and understanding of the western movie and its underlying mythology. And like *The Shootist*, which it resembles, Leone's film is about the end of the movie genre.

Westworld

Michael Crichton's satirical thriller *Westworld* is one of the best science-fiction pictures of the 1970s. The setting is Delos, a super-Disneyland for adults in the Arizona desert where, for a thousand dollars a day, wealthy holiday-makers of the near future can realise their fantasies by entering a gun-toting Wild West (Westworld), decadent ancient Rome (Roman World) or chivalric Arthurian England (Medieval World). Only the visitors are human; the other figures are lifelike robots controlled by a team of technicians from an underground chamber. Everything in Delos is designed to provide excitement without danger or pain. The film's dislikeable Chicago lawyer hero (Richard Benjamin), who chooses Westworld, finds he can outshoot the resident android gunslinger (Yul Brynner), make love to electronic saloon whores, join in a bar-room brawl without getting scratched. As his companion reassures him: 'Why shouldn't you believe it? It's as real as anything else.' But things start going wrong, first in small ways (a mechanical rattlesnake really bites, a serving wench programmed for seduction slaps a lecherous $1,000-a-day monarch), then seriously. There is a murderous Spartacist uprising in Roman World, and the electronic gunslinger gets genuinely lethal, tracking the lawyer down from one world to the other, and finally into the subterranean control room. In the process he takes on some of the pathos of Frankenstein's monster, as we see the world through his stylised computer vision.

Westworld is a funny and chilling film that makes great play with our cinema-fed fantasies and with the way our planet has been turned into a vast tourist attraction. Crichton's imagery is richly resonant, and what gives the film its special poignancy is Westworld, where most of the action is set. A disappointing sequel, *Futureworld* (1976), has a brief scene in the ghost town which the abandoned Westworld has become, and a dream sequence in which the heroine has an erotic encounter with Brynner's android gunfighter, but they cannot save the film from being swamped by the flashy hardware of traditional science fiction.

The Missouri Breaks

Announced in 1967 on the dust jacket of the first Cinema One volume as *The Western*, this book was finally called *Westerns* for several reasons. First, there had already been a couple of books with that title (indeed it was the only title most previous students of the genre thought of using); secondly, *Westerns* sounded more casual, less definitive; thirdly, and most important, it suggested my feeling, or asserted my belief, that within the apparently monolithic genre were hosts of specific movies attempting to establish their individual identities. There is a contradiction here, or at least a fruitful tension, between works that exploit traditional material and conventional expectations and yet strive to be regarded as unique objects. But as I have sometimes explicitly stated, and I hope continually implied, this is the very strength of the western. The general shape of my monograph, however, ruled out close analyses of individual pictures, though throughout the book there are detailed descriptions of individual shots and sequences. In this respect therefore the title must seem a little misleading. Of course, considered critiques of single films abound in the periodical literature of the cinema. Still, I should like to conclude these additional reflections with some specific observations on one of the key movies of 1976, *The Missouri Breaks*.

Enormous things were expected of *The Missouri Breaks* in America, and when the picture was found to be flawed, which it is, and sometimes incoherent, which it also is, critics dismissed it as the cynical product of an agents' and producers' deal, of the kind that is said to be destroying Hollywood. There is perhaps some truth in this (though the fact that it is a cowboy movie may have exacerbated the criticism), and I heard it on all sides at a conference on western movies held at Sun Valley, Idaho, in June 1976, where I seemed to be the only person with a good word to say for the picture (and detractors included the novelist Thomas McGuane who wrote the screenplay; one of the character actors involved, who asked me if I could explain the film to him; and presumably Marlon Brando, who sent an anti-greetings telegram to the conference denouncing the gathering, western movies and the bicentennial celebrations). Yet considering the various talents involved, the movie deserves more sympathetic attention, and no one surely can fail to recognise at the very least an intermittent brilliance, or to be impressed by Michael Butler's fine photography, which creates a world somewhere between dreamy frontier romanticism and gritty realism – that ambivalence one finds in the paintings of Remington and Russell.

McGuane's original screenplay, as earlier suggested, is almost identical in plot to his modern western *Rancho Deluxe*. An autocratic businessman-rancher, tired of being robbed by a band of charming rustlers (who are in fact his neighbours), hires a stock detective. The investigator, a self-conscious performer, hunts his quarries with a variety of stratagems and eventually brings them to book largely for his own satisfaction, for along the way he has lost the confidence of his despised Eastern employer. In *Rancho Deluxe* the setting is contemporary Montana, the detective Slim Pickens, and the treatment casually comic with elegiac undertones. In *The Missouri Breaks* the setting is Montana in the 1880s, the detective, here called 'a regulator', is Marlon Brando (once kept under lock and key by a less congenial Slim Pickens in *One-Eyed Jacks*), and the mood casually tragic with comic overtones. In both films a liberated young lady plays a mediating role – in *Rancho Deluxe* she is the stock detective's alleged daughter, who helps destroy the gang with her sexual wiles; in *Missouri Breaks* she is the rancher's daughter (the delightful newcomer Kathleen Lloyd), deserting her father and finding love with the leading outlaw. In both films Harry Dean Stanton rides with those engaged in ripping off the ranchers. The two films are graced by McGuane's creative ear for idiosyncratic Western speech. No sentence is ever predictable unless that is the very point, as when at the wake for the slain ranch foreman (to avenge whose death the regulator is hired) a guest sententiously observes: 'He personified the American West in the days of its rowdy youth.'

Looked at in another way, as an Arthur Penn picture, the plot of *The Missouri Breaks* takes on a different significance. Whatever Penn may have felt about the importance of this particular film, its basic structure is much the same as that of all his movies – *Bonnie and Clyde*, *Alice's Restaurant* and *Night Moves* as obviously as his two previous westerns, *The Left Handed Gun* and *Little Big Man*. This is to say that two cultures confront each other – a settled, social world growing increasingly authoritarian, and a free-wheeling anarchic community becoming increasingly corrupt. Between these two irreconcilable milieux a pair of contrasted (and mutually antagonistic) figures come and go, in often unhappy alliance with those they serve or affect to show allegiance to. In a simple, straightforward fashion they are Pat Garrett and Billy the Kid in *The Left Handed Gun*; in a less immediately obvious way they are Annie Sullivan and Helen Keller in *The Miracle Worker*.

Jack Nicholson brings to the role of Tom Logan, leader of the horse thieves, his own peculiarly compromised brand of Hollywood anarchism, seen at its most commercially strident in *One Flew Over the Cuckoo's Nest*, its most quizzically uncomprehending in *Chinatown*, its most institutionally frustrated in *The Last Detail*. But one must remember that ten years before Nicholson was involved as writer, producer and actor in the making of a pair of low-budget westerns, two of the most remarkable ever realised in the genre, and drawing consciously on Camus and Beckett – Monte Hellman's *The Shooting* and *Ride in the Whirlwind*. Both films underpinned their absurdist plots with the kind of elusive (because never explained) historical and social detail in which *The Missouri Breaks* abounds.

The introduction of Brando into the scheme is the joker, or perhaps the One-Eyed Jack. Twenty years ago Brando could hardly bring himself to tell Truman Capote that his first independent production was to be a cowboy picture. Now Brando returns, after a second western playing another masochistic border outsider hero in *The Appaloosa* (aka *Southwest to Sonora*), to the genre he despises, fortified by his passionate commitment to the American Indian cause. Unfortunately there are no Indians in the film for him to orient himself by, and there is apparently nothing positive (morally, that is) for him to seize on in the character of the regulator, Robert E. Lee Clayton. So he transforms Clayton into a self-loathing eccentric who hates his employer Braxton even more than the horse thieves he is hired to exterminate.

In turning against himself in such a histrionic fashion, Brando has stumbled across – consciously or not – one of those key figures which recur in American literature and illuminate the national character. This is the confidence man, the charismatic chameleon of Twain and Melville who turns up in Barth, Pynchon and Nabokov, as well as in such movies as *Little Big Man* and Hellman's *Two-Lane Blacktop*. As Tony Tanner observes in his *City of Words* (1971):

> In many recent American novels we will find the hero in quest of identity confronting a Protean figure whose quick metamorphoses seem to make him enviably well adapted to reality; but the hero seldom takes him for a model, no matter how much he may learn from him, for that way lies chaos, the nightmare jelly, the ultimate dissolution of self.

Thus Brando is never the same from one scene to another. He arrives in Indian dress hidden behind his horse, and proceeds to disrupt a wake by dragging the corpse out of its ice-filled coffin. Subsequently he dons a series of wild, though by no means arbitrary, disguises – the stiff white hat and lace shirt of an effete Southern gentleman, the coolie head-dress of a Chinese railroad labourer, the conservative garb of an itinerant preacher, the fantastic drag get-up of an old pioneer lady in a poke bonnet. And in these outfits he relentlessly hunts down the gang of happy horse thieves in poetically or sadistically varied fashion. One victim is cast loose from a rope to drown in a fast-flowing river. Another is killed in a privy at long range with a Creedmore Sharp hunting rifle, and a third is murdered with the same weapon while making love to a farmer's wife against the wall of her shack. (It is clearly no accident that the impotent assassin should choose to eliminate his distant, unaware victims while they are defecating and fornicating.) A fourth target is burnt up in a hut and then skewered against a tree with a cruciform hunting knife. This particular killing is carefully calculated to invoke the napalm bombing and bizarre weaponry employed in Vietnam, for *The Missouri Breaks* is as much a response to the aftermath of the Indo-China war as Eastwood's *The Outlaw Josey Wales*. Brando played a not wholly dissimilar role in Penn's *The Chase* (1966), where he appeared as a Texas sheriff employed to do the bidding of the rich ranchers and oil-men whose notion of law-and-order rules the local community. But there the Brando character at first attempted to hold the ring, and then, after taking a characteristically cathartic beating, climbed down off the cross to help the bunch of proto-anarchists (a prophetically emblematic group led by Jane Fonda and Robert Redford) defy the mob. In *The Missouri Breaks* he allies himself with the autocratic rancher Braxton and perishes at the hands of Jack Nicholson.

Braxton (amply embodied by John McLiam, who played the intransigent land baron in *The Culpepper Cattle Company*) is first seen in the opening sequence as he leads a condemned horse thief to his execution through the verdant grasslands of Montana, pausing to inform his prisoner proudly that in his first year in the state he transformed scrub into pasture and in the second he introduced '8,000 Texas half-breed cattle and 3,500 volumes of English literature in my library'. To his daughter he is obsessed with percentages, with the abstractions of commerce and a faceless, godlike justice. After the undramatic hanging he returns home, removes his boots and asks the daughter for his favourite novel, *Tristram Shandy*, the book which undermines literature, just as Braxton's behaviour calls established society into question.

The names Robert E. Lee Clayton for the regulator and Tom Logan (a raffish Irish version of Lincoln, one infers) for the Nicholson character suggest the Civil War being carried on out West in distorted, parodic fashion; tragic history being repeated as farce. Brando represents the death of Southern chivalry, identifying with the authoritarian macho-culture of Braxton and embracing sterility and extinction. Logan on the other hand, 'the last, best hope on earth' as Lincoln once said of America, turns to the daughter, a figure of fecundity and wry hope with whom he has one of the tenderest love affairs in any recent western. He quits, though does not betray, the sodality of his criminal comrades. Choosing the company of women and the cultivation of the land, Logan survives. There is a suggestion here of two ways open to America, though they are not unduly emphasised, and at the end we are left with Logan and the rancher's daughter parting and only tentatively contemplating the possibility of a reunion. But before then, far more decisively, we have had the climactic encounter between Nicholson and Brando. This is no orthodox, traditional gunfight. Brando has been preparing hideous traps for his victims and picking them off at a distance, then sending their horses home with his trademark, a spent bullet, attached to the bridles. Now he lies sleeping in a forest clearing, accompanied by his horses, the only creatures with which he can establish any kind of relationship; in his way he figures as the last of the big western hippophiles. In large close-up he wakes in the dark to be asked what woke him up; he coughs and is told by Nicholson's off-screen voice that his throat has been cut. From the remote killings of Brando's buffalo-hunting gun – the male, organised, detached murder by the Establishment's agent – we have moved to the intimate, personal, silent, feminine death-stroke of the knife.

The Missouri Breaks is a funny, touching movie which uses the western as a true forum for the confrontation of contemporary issues and talents. And the film is as resonant as the multiple puns of its title – which refers to a geological formation in Montana, to the symbolic fracturing of the fluvial axis of America, to the cruel burden placed by the West upon its hopeful pioneers (a brilliant speech given by McGuane to a hard-pressed farmer illuminates this),[32] to a

---

32 'They call this country Hell's Gate and that's what it has been for the earliest

crucial division in American experience, and, in the immediate context of Penn's film, to the ironic luck and licence of the central characters.

---

people in here. When my dad came in here it was nothin' but a bunch of savage Indians and Jesuits. Ole Thomas Jefferson said he was a warrior so his son could be a farmer so *his* son could be a poet. And I raise cattle so my son can be a merchant so *his* son can move to Newport, Rhode Island, and buy a sailboat and never see one of these bastard-ass sonofabitchin' mountains again.'

More Books

Professor C. Northcote Parkinson might well argue that the production of academic treatises on any given subject is in inverse ratio to the subject's continuing social importance. A sign of an area's declining importance, therefore, would be the interest taken in it by universities. Unquestionably as the number of westerns has steadily decreased so the number of books and articles about them has grown. My own is part of this flood. Nearly all the books, however, arise from a newly awakened American academic interest in indigenous genres. It was inevitable of course that the recently created departments of film studies had to discover Hollywood cinema and make it respectable, for they could scarcely attract sufficient students with the diligence and ability to equip themselves with the knowledge of foreign languages and cultures that would be necessary for a proper study of the cinemas of other countries.

A useful guide to the available literature on the subject in English is *Western Films: An Annotated Critical Bibliography* by John G. Nachbar (Garland Publishing, New York and London, 1975). Nachbar has also edited *Focus on the Western* (Prentice-Hall, Englewood Cliffs, NJ, 1974), which contains a number of valuable essays by various authors, including John G. Cawelti (two excellent pieces) and John Tuska. Tuska's piece now forms part of a lengthy, meandering but enjoyable stroll through western movie history: *The Filming of the West* (Doubleday, New York, 1976), in which he includes material from interviews with numerous western moviemakers ranging from Hoot Gibson to John Wayne. One of Cawelti's essays is drawn from his elegant monograph *The Six-Gun Mystique*, which is both a good book on the western and a shrewd critique of methodology in the study of popular culture. Published by the Bowling Green University Popular Press in Ohio, it is undated, though Nachbar's *Annotated Bibliography* gives the date as 1971, and Nachbar should know because he heads the Center for the Study of Popular Culture at Bowling Green State University.

An ambitious, not to say arrogant, and by no means entirely convincing academic treatise is *Sixguns and Society* by Will Wright

(University of California Press, Berkeley, CA, 1975), which employs the techniques of Claude Lévi-Strauss to make 'A Structural Study of the Western' and advance an all-encompassing theory about the relationship of Hollywood westerns to American society over the last forty years. (See my review, *Sight and Sound*, Spring, 1976.) There have in addition been a clutch of undistinguished large format picture books on the western, and the new edition of Allen Eyles' guide *The Western*, to which I looked forward in *Westerns*, has now appeared (The Tantivy Press, London; Barnes & Noble, New York, 1975). Also available at last in English are two classic essays by André Bazin, 'The Western or the American Cinema par excellence' and 'The Evolution of the Western' in *What is Cinema?* Volume II, selected and edited by Hugh Gray (University of California Press, Berkeley, CA, 1972).

PART TWO

Westerns Revisited
(2004)

Introduction

There have been five American presidents in the twenty-seven years since the revised edition of this book, four of them from west of the Mississippi (Gerald Ford was born in Nebraska, but grew up in Michigan) and thus identified by cartoonists around the world as Stetson-wearing, gun-toting cowboys. The fifth, Jimmy Carter from Georgia, was not so characterised and caricatured. He cultivated peanuts on a farm, not steers on a ranch, and during his ineffectual presidency was not involved in bellicose language or sabre-rattling. He did, however, when John Wayne died in 1979, speak of the star's heroic achievements on the screen as if they had been truly enacted, thus conflating the cinema and real life in a manner that was to be habitual with his successor Ronald Reagan. 'John Wayne,' Carter said, 'was bigger than life. In an age of few heroes, he was the genuine article. But he was more than a hero – he was a symbol of the most basic qualities that made America great. The ruggedness, the tough independence, the sense of personal conviction and courage – on and off the screen – reflected the best of our national character.' His predecessor, Gerald Ford, paid a similar tribute: 'John Wayne was a unique, magnificent person, who met every challenge in his own life and responded to the nation's problems with courage, wisdom and conviction.'

Reagan was mocked in his lifetime and by numerous liberal columnists at his death as a B-feature actor and western star, a combination considered to render him ineligible for high office. In fact, although he presented the TV series *Death Valley Days* shortly before giving up acting for full-time politics, he only appeared in a half-dozen westerns. Interestingly the long-time, recently retired projectionist at the White House's private cinema has revealed that more movies were shown there during the Carter regime than any other these past forty years. He also recorded that the most requested picture over this period was Fred Zinnemann's liberal *High Noon*, written by one of the most celebrated victims of the House Un-American Activities Committee. Quite evidently a succession of embattled presidents has identified with Gary Cooper.

John Wayne has been dead for a quarter of a century, and *The*

Shootist proved a suitable film to go out on – an elegy for both his career and the genre. It was the last western of James Stewart as well, though he was to live for a further twenty years, and Henry Fonda, Randolph Scott, Joel McCrea and Gregory Peck are also dead. So is Steve McQueen, whose penultimate movie (his final picture is better forgotten) was the elegiac western *Tom Horn* (1980) in which he played a gunfighter in a changing West who chooses to super-intend his own execution rather than submit to a hangman chosen by a community he despises. Indeed, all but one of *The Magnificent Seven* (1960) are now dead, the only survivor being Robert Vaughn, who in 1980 parodied his earlier role in a low-budget science-fiction version of *The Magnificent Seven* called *Battle Beyond the Stars*. Although Kevin Costner was thought of early in his career as the natural successor to Gary Cooper and has appeared in four west-erns, two of which he directed, he is not considered a western star. In fact the only living actor who is so regarded, Clint Eastwood, established this reputation in the 1960s, and has only appeared in two westerns – *Pale Rider* (1985) and *Unforgiven* (1992) – since *The Outlaw Josey Wales* (1976).

But the spirit that informs the genre, along with its legendary characters, myths, historical associations, values and contradictions, is far from dead, though often turning up in unexpected forms and in previously unvisited places. During the first sixty years of the Academy Awards, a single western, *Cimarron* (1931), won an Oscar. In the 1990s two movies, *Dances With Wolves* and *Unforgiven*, won both the Best Film and Best Director awards. Until 1980 just one western, *Bad Day at Black Rock* (1955), which was not generally regarded as a western, was shown in competition at the Cannes Film Festival (and brought Spencer Tracy the Best Actor award). Since then four have competed for the Palme d'Or: Walter Hill's *The Long Riders*, Michael Cimino's *Heaven's Gate*, Eastwood's *Pale Rider* and Jim Jarmusch's *Dead Man*, all of them going away unrewarded. And the context is the paradox that people the world over have adopted some modified form of cowboy clothes as their informal dress, and continue to use the image of the cowboy to mock and even vilify America's political leaders and those who ally themselves with their policies.

This notion of middle-class citizens around the world obsessed with the West is cleverly used in Jim Goddard's British thriller, *Parker* (1986). The film opens with a party of cowboys riding in the mountains at dusk and then making camp for the night. They seem to be viewed through the trees at a little distance. Is it an Indian ambush? Are they about to be bushwhacked? No, they're being watched by a British businessman who has been abducted in Munich and then released in the Bavarian Alps, and the ruggedly authentic-looking Westerners are in fact well-heeled Germans spending the weekend playing at being cowboys. Since the early twentieth century the German fascination with the West has been greater than that of any other European country and in July 2004, a little north of Berlin, an enormous western theme park opened called Silverlake City. Named for a fictional frontier town in the western novels of the cult German writer Karl May, it was built on a 70,000 square foot site at a cost of £12m.

1 Waiting for the End

Opening three years after America's military withdrawal from Vietnam and a year after the North's final victory over the South, Eastwood's *The Outlaw Josey Wales* was the last western to allegorise Vietnam. It was given its world premiere at a conference held in Sun Valley in the week of the bicentennial celebrations of 1976, referred to in the Afterword. Its theme was 'Western Movies: Myths and Images', and it was sponsored jointly by the National Endowment for the Arts and the Levi–Strauss Corporation, the so-called 'Cowboys' Tailors' of San Francisco. It was an astonishing gathering of actors, filmmakers, historians, sociologists, writers and critics, ranging from Blanche Sweet, a Biograph star and a leading lady in D.W. Griffith films before World War I, and Buster Crabbe, the Olympic gold-medallist and B-feature star of westerns and sci-fi pictures, to Warren Oates, Peter Fonda and of course Clint Eastwood. A strong contingent of Indians, as they were then called, included Chief Dan George, the Pulitzer-prize winning novelist Scott Momaday, and the radical lawyer and specialist in Indian rights, Vine Deloria Jr. Everyone tried to be optimistic and upbeat, but there was a clear sense that we were more concerned with the past than the future. A feminist from the University of California, Berkeley, opined that there would be no real breakthrough for women in the genre 'until the essentially male linear narrative patterns are smashed', though the cultural historian Richard Slotkin (author of *Regeneration Through Violence: The Mythology of the American Frontier*, and *Gunfighter Nation: The Myth of the Frontier in Twentieth-Century America*) believed that 'when capitalism comes out of its present crisis, the western will return'. I recall it as an elegiac occasion, though more nostalgic than funereal. Consciously or unconsciously this seemed to be the view of the convenors, as I was invited to chair the final panel held on the morning of 4 July on the vague topic, 'Seventy-five Years of Westerns, a Perspective' on which the speakers were the 68-year-old critic and historian Arthur Knight, the 69-year-old Indian actor Iron Eyes Cody, the 82-year-old King Vidor, the 85-year-old Colonel Tim McCoy, who entered films as an advisor on *The*

Covered Wagon (1923), and the 88-year-old Henry King, who had flown his own plane from Los Angeles to Idaho. Immediately the debate had concluded, we all drove over to Hailey, birthplace of that great modernist Ezra Pound, to see cowboys and cowgirls perform at a flagwaving Fourth of July rodeo. All five panellists are now dead, as indeed are most participants.

Some months later Jimmy Carter was elected President, and there were, as most people at the conference had predicted, the smallest trickle of American westerns during his occupation of the White House. No more than one or two a year, and most of them with modern settings, until 1980, when there were a half-dozen. There was, however, as anticipated, a cycle of movies about Vietnam. While the war was in progress there was a single mainstream picture dealing explicitly with the conflict, *The Green Berets* (1968). Co-directed by its star, John Wayne, it alluded to the western in naming the isolated Special Services headquarters in the Indo-China boondocks 'Fort Apache'. (The title *Fort Apache, the Bronx* was given in 1980 to a thriller about an isolated police station in a district of New York where law and order had broken down.) The movie was picketed everywhere, and banned or driven off the screen in several countries. Now the war was over there was no need to treat it obliquely, and in rapid succession came two relatively cheap movies, Sidney J. Furie's *The Boys in Company C* and Ted Post's *Go Tell the Spartans* (both the work of directors who'd made westerns), and then three major pictures by filmmakers who'd never been associated with horse operas – Michael Cimino's *The Deer Hunter*, Hal Ashby's *Coming Home*, and Francis Ford Coppola's *Apocalypse Now!*. All of these movies proved successful at the box-office and picked up awards. They seemed to clear the air as they engaged with the Vietnam experience, directly and critically, demonstrating the absurdity of the conflict and the traumatic consequences for its participants.

As I've said earlier, *The Outlaw Josey Wales* was a movie about healing wounds and binding a nation together. The Vietnam movies differed greatly in this respect, and Michael Cimino, whose *The Deer Hunter* picked up Oscars for Best Film and Best Direction, went straight on to direct a deeply pessimistic western, which turned out to be the most controversial and widely vilified cowboy movie of all time. A critical and commercial disaster, *Heaven's Gate* was held responsible at the time for destroying its production company, United Artists, and finally burying the western for good. As we know, neither of these outcomes exactly came about. In fact, at the time *Heaven's Gate* went into production, United Artists was in a state of disarray and indecisively led after the departure of its chief executives to form their own studio, and UA's parent company, the TransAmerican Corporation, was keen to divest itself of its troublesome filmmaking arm.

The film overran its budget of $7m and eventually cost $35m, a vast sum in those days. It was shown for a few days in late 1980 in Cimino's own cut of 219 minutes, then, after the unfavourable press reaction, withdrawn and released some months later cut to 149 minutes. This version was only briefly shown in US cinemas, and was the one exhibited in Europe where it opened in competition at the 1981 Cannes Festival. Subsequently a restored version was made, roughly the same length as the original, though oddly enough lacking a few shots that were in the truncated film, but as this print was available only in 70mm it could not be widely shown.

Like a good many westerns, *Heaven's Gate* is based quite closely on an actual event, the so-called Johnson County War of 1892, the inspiration for a number of films, the most famous of which was *Shane*. The Cattle Growers' Association of Wyoming, run by rich ranchers and representing absentee landlords and major investors on the East Coast, had for some years been troubled by rustlers stealing their cattle on the open range. They were mainly sheep farmers and sodbusters cultivating small patches of land. When a few 'regulators' (gunfighters hired to intimidate or kill cattle thieves) failed to control the rustling, the Association, with the connivance of state or federal authorities, recruited a vigilante force of around fifty, including mercenaries from as far away as Texas. They drew up a death list of over a hundred people in Johnson County, the centre of the greatest number of offenders, and moved in to kill them. They were, however, met by a posse of around 200 people, and the invaders became the quarry and were only saved by a troop of cavalry sent by the governor. A mere handful of people were killed, and despite arrests and indictments, no one was convicted.

Cimino has taken these events and, using the names of several actual participants, has shaped a radical story directed against the Wasp ascendancy and their plutocratic collaborators who have usurped the law and subverted the democratic system. The settlers in Johnson County are almost entirely recent immigrants from Eastern Europe, few of them with any knowledge of the English language, and they've been driven to rustling to feed themselves and their families during the course of several terrible winters. In a pair of parallel scenes there are two roll calls. In the first the smartly dressed Cattle Growers in their elegant club in Caspar, Wyoming, assent to the illegal homicidal action by answering to their names, all of them Anglo-Saxon. In the second scene, the names – all Eastern European – are read out from the death list in a bare temporary hall to a gathering of the roughly dressed immigrants and intended victims of the Association. When they eventually gather to face the enemy, the battle is ferocious with major losses on both sides. The central action of the movie takes place over a mere three days.

At the centre of this conflict Cimino has located a triangular affair in which two men, the sheriff Jim Averill (Kris Kristofferson) and Nate Champion (Christopher Walken), a regulator for the Cattle Growers, compete for the love of Ella Watson, a young French-born brothel owner (Isabelle Huppert). She accepts payment in cash or stolen cattle, and is despised by both the Association and the puritanical immigrants. Averill and Champion are both specifically identified as class traitors, the former a wealthy Harvard graduate who has gone West and taken the side of the immigrants, the latter the son of immigrants (probably from Hungary) who has taken lucrative, lethal employment with the upper classes. Why Averill has chosen the course he has is not spelled out, but one infers that it might be connected with the sentiment expressed by Theodore Roosevelt in the 1880s when he wrote to Henry Cabot in Boston from the ranch he managed in Dakota Territory: 'The statesman of the past has been merged, I fear for good, into the cowboy of the present.'

The chief representative of the cattle barons is Frank Canton (Sam Waterston), a real-life figure whose father was a cabinet minister under President Harrison, but transformed here from the itinerant lawman of dubious reputation that he was into a xenophobic upper-class snob. When he leads his little army into Johnson County, his dress (black fur hat, fur-trimmed coat and black boots) makes him look like one of the vicious Cossacks from whose persecutions the immigrants have fled. He is thwarted but not defeated, and one of his potential victims despairingly remarks that Canton's side will win 'even if it takes a hundred years'.

The film has a prologue and a coda set in the East. In the prologue, Averill and his best friend Billy Irvine (John Hurt) graduate from Harvard in 1870. Ignoring the call to devote themselves to the high ideal of 'the education of a nation', Irvine, as class orator, makes a supercilious, complacent speech about finding it unnecessary to make changes to 'what seems well arranged'. In the event Irvine becomes an effete, ineffectual drunk and is shot dead with a hip flask in his hand, while Averill turns into a romantic, ineffectual idealist. In the film's coda Averill is to be found in 1903 on his palatial yacht off Newport, Rhode Island, married to a languid beauty of his own class who looks as if she might have posed for John Singer Sargent.

Heaven's Gate is visually stunning, beautifully photographed by Vilmos Zsigmond and superbly designed by Tambi Larsen. The interiors are dark, sepia-toned, illuminated by shafts of blinding light from the chilly mountain world outside. The creation of the frontier town of Caspar, its few brick buildings rising from the muddy, bustling streets, the air polluted by billowing chimneys and the trains passing through its centre, is magnificently achieved and of unusual conviction. The film has all the ingredients one asks of a superior western, but its succession of sustained set-pieces like the opening dance to a Strauss waltz in the open-air at Harvard, make one think of Luchino Visconti. The handling of the Eastern European peasants and the staging of the battle between the immigrants and the raiders bring to mind the Soviet cinema of Donskoi and Eisenstein. The film has certain longueurs, some of the editing seems a trifle abrupt, and in any version I've seen, the actors' naturalistic diction makes the dialogue at times difficult to follow. It is, however, a movie of epic grandeur, one of the most powerful and thoughtful westerns ever made. Why then did the movie fail, not merely badly, but catastrophically?

There was a variety of factors, and without implying the existence of a conscious conspiracy, I would suggest there was a general will in America in 1980, some expression of the collective unconscious, that *Heaven's Gate* should fail, just as there was a general consensus the following year that *Raiders of the Lost Ark* should succeed. The first was unwittingly swimming against the national tide, the latter knowingly being borne along by it. A couple of years earlier, Jane Fonda conducted a campaign against Cimino's *The Deer Hunter* on the grounds that it was a racist Cold War movie, and she was given support in this by the Eastern bloc who forced it to be withdrawn from competition at the 1979 Berlin Film Festival. Fonda was a somewhat interested party as she was simultaneously promoting her own Vietnam film, *Coming Home*, which took an explicitly hostile attitude to the war and its participants. Far subtler than *Coming Home*, and without any preaching, *The Deer Hunter* took a similarly radical approach to its working-class characters of Eastern European origin as it did to the immigrants from an earlier generation who also become victims of the system in the stylistically similar *Heaven's Gate*. We never, of course, see the people who have been exploiting them, and indeed the movie only dwells on the characters' working class steel town community when the three heroes demonstrate their patriotism by leaving the inferno where they work for the hell of war in Vietnam. The game of Russian roulette they play with their Viet Cong captors and later at a club in Saigon shortly before the city falls, is a metaphor for the madness of war into which they have been led and not, as many left wing writers were to claim, an indictment of the enemies' sadism.

The film critics, whose praise had created the atmosphere that had made *The Deer Hunter* a box-office success and the recipient of three of the major Oscars for which it was nominated, were (consciously or not) looking for an opportunity to apologise to Jane Fonda, an astonishingly influential figure at the time, a social heroine vindicated for her courageous opposition to the war. They found their target in Cimino's next film and they really went to town. The nature of their animus was clearly expressed in the review by one of the most influential of their number, Vincent Canby of *The New York Times*: 'It fails so completely that you might suspect Mr Cimino sold his soul to the devil for the success of *The Deer Hunter* and the devil has just come around to collect.'

A second reason for the hostility was the feeling shared by the Hollywood studio bosses, the film critics and the public at large about the hubris of the generation of young directors who had been assuming control of Hollywood in the 1970s. Their films were extravagant, self-indulgent, pretentious, constantly running over budget. They lacked fiscal prudence and a proper managerial sense. Moreover their behaviour on and off the set was said to be fuelled by cocaine. The general view was that the lunatics had taken over the asylum (a term first used in 1919 when Chaplin, Griffith, Fairbanks and Pickford combined to launch United Artists, the producers of *Heaven's Gate*) and some drastic action had to be taken to bring the reckless rebels to heel. The overreaching Cimino was to be the sacrificial victim.

The radical critics, who a few years earlier might have embraced a movie of such an obviously left wing, quasi-Marxist character, found themselves standing shoulder to shoulder with conservative forces that objected to the movie for the very reason that it was politically subversive. These reactionaries were partly reflecting the changing mood of a nation that was turning its back on the spirit of the 1960s and looking for stability after the crisis of Watergate. Finding itself reeling under the humiliation of the Iranian occupation of the American embassy in Teheran that Carter seemed incapable of resolving by force or diplomacy, the country rejected him after a single term and elected Ronald Reagan. Indicative of the national mood was the popularity of *The Great Santini*, the hero of which was a Marine Corps major unable to settle down after his time as an ace fighter pilot in the Korean War and deeply disappointed by his studious, non-aggressive son. The movie failed in 1979, but re-released after Robert Duvall was nominated for an Oscar, it became one of the major surprise hits of 1980.

The reputation of *Heaven's Gate* was altogether different in Europe, starting from a few minutes after the first screening at Cannes in May 1981. At the press conference immediately following the film (at which Cimino, Kristofferson and a United Artists representative were present) the chairman, Henri Béhar, who is principally a writer on film industrial affairs rather than a critic, immediately embarked upon what he called 'Heaven's Gate – l'affaire'. There was an immediate intervention by France's most respected film critic, Michel Ciment of the monthly *Positif*, who insisted that what we should be discussing was 'Heaven's Gate – le film', which he immediately pronounced a masterpiece. His intervention was enthusiastically applauded, but Béhar was determined to pursue the controversial news story. Before there was an opportunity to talk about the picture, the representatives of the popular press were allowed to lay into Cimino with such questions as how did he feel about driving a film company to the wall, and was it true that cases of champagne were shipped to the film's remote locations in Montana to celebrate the exposure of the first 200,000 feet of film. Thus it was always to be – the controversy first, followed by a discussion of the film as a footnote to a scandal. No wonder that Cimino's career was crippled and that his only subsequent excursion into the West has been *The Sunchaser* (1996) in which a deeply discontented oncologist reluctantly accompanies a dying half-Indian patient on a mystical journey from Los Angeles to a sacred Native American site in the mountains of Colorado.

It might well be noted that a British director, Hugh Hudson, who had also enjoyed early success and won an Oscar for *Chariots of Fire*

(1981), was to suffer a disaster comparable to *Heaven's Gate* with a similarly expensive historical epic, *Revolution* (1985), about three people caught up in the War of Independence. It too ran over budget, lost virtually every penny put into it and more or less ended its director's promising career.

2 Television

The television western as it proliferated in the 1950s, 60s and 70s exists no more, though from time to time there are one-off films, mostly mediocre works like the various lacklustre re-makes of, or sequels to, such classics as *High Noon*, *Shane* and *True Grit*. The big screen's desperate search for material with a built-in nostalgic appeal has led to numerous big-budget film versions of old TV series like *Mission: Impossible*, *Star Trek* and *Charlie's Angels*. Inevitably this has extended to the western with expensive treatments of two shows from the 1950s and 60s – *Maverick* (1994), with Mel Gibson replacing James Garner as the eponymous itinerant gambler, and *Wild Wild West* (1999), in which Will Smith and Kevin Kline take over from Robert Conrad and Ross Martin as the secret federal agents on special frontier assignments. The extravagant inventions of Kline's character and the pair's mad antagonist (Kenneth Branagh) fly in the face of the low-tech aspect of the western that makes the genre so attractive. Both films are heavy-handed comedies (the first, and better, scripted by William Goldman who won an Oscar for writing *Butch Cassidy and the Sundance Kid*) and proved surprisingly popular at the box-office.

There have, however, been several mini-series. I have not seen the twenty-hour version of James H. Michener's blockbuster novel *Centennial* (1978) though it has been well spoken of. But I have seen and admired two remarkable TV mini-series – Simon Wincer's *Lonesome Dove* (1988) and John Milius's *Rough Riders* (1997) – that are as good as the best westerns of the previous three decades, and in contrast to most of them they are upbeat, celebratory, un-ironic in their attitude to heroism. The first is a masterpiece, the second extremely fine.

Adapted from Larry McMurtry's Pulitzer Prize-winning novel, *Lonesome Dove* is in three parts – 'The Leaving', 'The Plains', 'The Trail' – and follows a 3,000-mile cattle drive in the early 1890s from the most southerly part of the United States along the Rio Grande in Texas to the farthest northerly point in the Montana territory near the Canadian border. The film is epic in conception and execution, the eight-hour duration allows for a leisurely pace that reflects the months involved and the distance travelled in taking 2,500 steers across America. Titles superimposed on the screen mark the stages of the journey, and the film combines the modern and the traditional. In a modern mode there is a lack of formal exposition that leaves us to fill in details of past and present relationships from the characters' actions, conversations and behaviour, as well as elliptical jumps that force us to infer a deal of what has been happening along the trail. In traditional terms the narrative, in which several strands cross and re-cross over a vast area, resembles that of an expansive Victorian novel (or, somewhat later, Boris Pasternak's *Dr Zhivago*) where coincidence becomes a tapestry of fate.

The central characters are two former captains in the Texas Rangers, Woodrow Call (Tommy Lee Jones) and Augustus McCrae (Robert Duvall), now middle-aged, who, having rid Southern Texas of predatory Comanches and Kiowas as well as of outlaws, have settled for an unexciting life selling cattle and hiring out horses. Appropriately enough they live in a one-whore town called Lonesome Dove, the name reflecting desperate isolation and peace. The one whore is Lorrie (Diane Ladd), an illiterate sweet-natured girl beloved, in the absence of any competition, by every man in the neighbourhood. Her full name is 'Lorena', eponymous heroine of the love song sung on both sides of the Civil War, and the theme attached indelibly to the contested character played by Natalie Wood in Ford's *The Searchers*.

A long absent younger associate of Woodrow and Gus, Jake Spoon (Robert Ulrich), who's more interested in gambling than raising cattle, returns to Lonesome Dove after nine years away to tell them of the opportunities up north in Montana for cattlemen to exploit virgin land. Of course it's a long way off, there are rivers and badlands to be crossed, renegade Indians and marauding outlaws to be confronted. Woodrow is a humourless, stern figure, a disciplinarian and born leader, dedicated to the protestant work ethic. Gus is a humorous, kindly, philosophical ironist, a cultivator of leisure, 'a rake and a rambler', as a former lover says. They are loners of different sorts. The first is the kind of man who made life in the West possible. The second is the free spirit who made it bearable. They are complementary, symbiotic figures, as close as an old married couple, but there are no homoerotic undertones. They recall the ageing marshals in Peckinpah's *Ride the High Country*, though their relationship is more subtly developed, but structurally they resemble John Wayne and Montgomery Clift in *Red River*.

Woodrow sees the drive north (taking cattle and horses rustled in Mexico) as both a challenging adventure and the opportunity to establish himself as a cattle baron in Montana. Gus, whom we so often see relaxing in saloons or up to his neck in water, goes along out of friendship and as an opportunity to have a reunion with the love of his life, Clara (Anjelica Huston). She now lives a settled life as a rancher's wife in Nebraska, and he hasn't seen her for eighteen years. Joining them on the journey are Jake Spoon and the whore Lorrie, who has attached herself to him, various cowhands including a pair of young Irish brothers, and the black cowboy Josh Deeds (Danny Glover). Josh wears what appears to be a Confederate soldier's cap, and as he has worked for Woodrow for thirty years, we assume he was initially his slave. In two separate strands, which gradually join up with the main line of the action, a husband and wife go in different directions. The husband, a young sheriff from Arkansas (Chris Cooper), goes south in reluctant pursuit of Jake the gambler on a trumped-up murder charge. Meanwhile his pregnant wife (Glenne Headley) goes north in the hope of re-joining her former lover. They are both frustrated as a result of the men they seek being hanged, one summarily, the other judicially.

The journey north is punctuated by a succession of deaths and burials, of brutal encounters with thieves and hostile Indians, of storms and drought. A young cowboy, afraid of water, dies when he's attacked in a swollen river by a nest of poisonous snakes. Lorrie is abducted and raped by an evil half-breed, Blue Duck (Frederick Forrest), a malevolent figure of consciously irredeemable evil who combines the worst of European and Native American cultures. There are also idyllic interludes, most especially several sojourns at Clara's ranch, and there's a running sub-plot concerning whether Woodrow will acknowledge that the teenage ranch hand Newt (Ricky Schroder) is his son by a prostitute who died a dozen years before.

Although *Lonesome Dove* recapitulates the plots and incidents of most westerns you've ever seen, it doesn't have the self-consciously synoptic character of *How the West Was Won*, and it ends without any sort of triumphalism with the successful conclusion of the drive and the first winter in Montana. Before completing the journey, Gus dies – choosing death rather than losing a second leg from blood poisoning caused by Cheyenne arrows. To fulfil a deathbed promise, Woodrow decides to make a return journey, riding alone, taking his friend's body to be buried in Texas. This is a heroic personal undertaking, and dramatically it relates to Gus's semi-comic lament that the two of them have been forgotten because they're still alive, so haven't become legends and thus the stuff of song. But as Gus's body is transported from one end of the country to the other, Woodrow becomes an instant legend on the frontier, greeted everywhere as a hero. And when finally he reaches Lonesome Dove, a young reporter is there from a San Antonio newspaper to interview him, a scene designed to evoke John Ford's *The Man Who Shot Liberty Valance*.

The power of *Lonesome Dove* derives from several sources. First there's Bill Whitliff's eloquent script. Second, the acting is outstanding, with Robert Duvall and Tommy Lee Jones anticipating the roles they were to play fifteen years later in respectively Kevin Costner's *Open Range* and Ron Howard's *The Missing*. In an interview in *The Times* (8 August 2004), Duvall picked his role as Gus McCrae as his favourite from the eighty-four movies he'd made up to that time. Third, there is the sympathetic direction of Simon Wincer, the Australian filmmaker who had shown his skill in handling action sequences in an awesome landscape in *The Lighthorsemen* (1987) set in Palestine in World War I, and was to go on to make the Australian western *Quigley Down Under* (1991) and the para-western *Harley Davidson and the Marlboro Kid* (1991). Finally there is the outstanding cinematography by Douglas Milsome and the second unit cameraman, Dean Semler. No film has been so assiduous and successful in capturing on celluloid the dusty, pastel-toned paintings of Frederic Remington. TV films rarely look this good. Semler was to win an Oscar two years later for *Dances With Wolves* and Milsome was to give the West a magical aura in Cimino's *The Sunchaser*.

Rough Riders is a long, intelligent film about the hand-picked volunteer cavalry regiment that Teddy Roosevelt recruited from the Western states and territories, to take part in the liberation of Cuba in the brief Spanish–American War. The movie builds up to the bespectacled Colonel Roosevelt (Tom Berenger) leading his Rough Riders with his drawn sabre in the battle of San Juan Hill on 1 July 1898, and concludes with his return to the States as a hero, ready to become Governor of New York, and eventually President of the United States. It's an exciting movie, made with loving care, idolising Roosevelt as the politician and intellectual as man of action, the decisive leader capable of both winning a war and a Nobel Peace Prize. The picture provides a historical link between the concept of

Manifest Destiny and the winning of the West (the title of a three-volume history of the frontier that Roosevelt wrote in the early 1890s) and America's emergence as a great imperial power. Back in 1975, Milius had written and directed *The Wind and the Lion*, a film about a later incident in Roosevelt's career, when as President in 1904 he sent a detachment of US Marines to rescue an American woman and her children taken hostage by a rebellious Arab band in Morocco. Arising from the Vietnam experience, it's an elegiac movie about America's need to use her power to intervene on the world scene. At the same time there's a recognition that Roosevelt (Brian Keith), the romantic warrior, has more in common with his rebellious Arab quarry (Sean Connery) than either has with most of those around them. This is a relationship between apparent enemies that is to be found in other Milius pictures and in Walter Hill's *Geronimo* which Milius co-scripted.

3 Comedies

Over the years it has been virtually obligatory for screen comics to go West at some point in their careers, from Chaplin in *The Gold Rush* to the British 'Carry On' repertory company with *Carry On Cowboy*. Most of these movies, whether locating their heroes as incongruous figures on the frontier or attempting to parody the conventions of the genre, have been feeble. The best jokes are those that occur in a serious context (Robert Duvall is brilliantly funny as a jester among gunfighters in *Lonesome Dove*) and the best western comedies are light-hearted dramas like *Support Your Local Sheriff*, rather than outright farces. But the immense success of Mel Brooks' *Blazing Saddles*, which he claims to have undertaken out of dire necessity after two ambitious failures, has encouraged others to follow his hit-and-miss approach with its mixture of low comedy and surrealism.

Influenced by both *Blazing Saddles* (particularly the scene in which the heroes ride out of the Hollywood studio into the real world) and *Hearts of the West*, Hugh Wilson's *Rustler's Rhapsody* (1985) has the clever premise of taking Tex O'Herlihan (Tom Berenger), the singing cowboy hero of black-and-white B-movies of the 1930s and 40s and suddenly shifting him forward three decades. In mid-reel he finds himself appearing in Technicolor in a version of the 1880s in which his simple honourable values (he only shoots at his opponents' hands) and his fancy clothes make him a weird anachronism. There are some smart ideas here about the hero's sexuality, the problems that arise when two 'good guys' confront each other ('the most good guy will win') and how he reacts when he finds himself in a situation where the style and politics have become those of Leone and Peckinpah. But the film never reconciles its protagonist's ability to foresee plot developments (deriving from the endlessly repetitive films in which he has figured) with his naiveté about changing times. Despite its frequently embarrassing longueurs, this is an oddly endearing picture. Largely shot in Spain by José Luis Alcaine (Pedro Almodóvar's regular cameraman), it rapidly disappeared from the box-office radar, and its director retreated into the more conventional urban comedy of the long-running *Police Academy* series. Hugh Wilson did, however, return to the western as co-writer with John Milius on *Rough Riders*.

A year after *Rustler's Rhapsody* came John Landis's less interesting, but not dissimilar, knockabout comedy *Three Amigos!* starring Chevy Chase, Steve Martin and Martin Short as a trio of singing cowboy stars, albeit from Hollywood's silent days. Mistaking their screen performances for genuine heroism, they're invited by Mexican peasant fans to do a *Magnificent Seven* act and protect them from a gang of marauding bandits. It's a confident mess, short on purpose and long on borrowed jokes, and also indebted to *Blazing Saddles*.

Andrew Bergman, author of the original scenario, had apparently thought of *Blazing Saddles* as essentially a comedy of a black American who accidentally becomes a sheriff in the West. But the movie was offered to Mel Brooks, who was in financial straits at the time and took it on for the money. By casting himself as a state governor and Gene Wilder, an actor associated with playing neurotic Jewish nebbishes, as the alcoholic gunfighter known as the Waco Kid, Mel Brooks turned the film into a Jewish western. This wasn't apparently, as one supposed, a strategy but the result of expediency, because Brooks initially offered the role of the Waco Kid to Dan Dailey and John Wayne (who is said by Brooks to have loved the script but rejected it for image reasons). It was only when Gig Young, cast because he was a genuine alcoholic, had to fall out on the day shooting began for being drunk and incompetent, that Wilder got a role he craved.

Wilder's presence is part of the movie's strength, arising from the popular perception that the American Jew (Wilder's father was a Russian immigrant) is the antithesis of the traditional Wasp hero of the western, the former defensive, gregarious, loquacious, urban, the latter aggressive, solitary, taciturn, rural. The Borscht-belt comedian Phil Leeds had a song called 'Irving the Jewish Cowboy' in his repertoire, and there was published in the mid-1960s a slim volume entitled *How to Shoot a Jewish Western* which featured stills from westerns accompanied by speech balloons containing inappropriate Jewish sentiments (e.g. Jeff Chandler as Cochise in *Broken Arrow* asks prospective son-in-law James Stewart: 'What are your business prospects, Mr Bloomingdale?'; Barbara Stanwyck, dressed all in black, her hands clutching her gun belt, stands defiantly before some cowering lawmen in a still from Samuel Fuller's *Forty Guns*, demanding: 'OK, so who said my gefilte fish was lousy?'; a dying outlaw, clutching his gut, says: 'You can't trust the chopped liver in Tombstone'). Of course we know that 'Broncho' Billy Anderson, the world's first western star, was born Max Aronson, and a number of his successors were also Jewish (most famously Kirk Douglas and Paul Newman), and that numerous Jews have directed, written and produced westerns. But stereotypes die hard.

It therefore seemed obvious that there was rich comic material to be mined from the story of a gentile (Harrison Ford) reluctantly escorting a hopelessly unworldly young Polish rabbi (Gene Wilder) across the nineteenth-century West. The plot of Robert Aldrich's *The Frisco Kid* (1979) resembles S.N. Behrman's World War II comedy *Jackobovsky and the Colonel*, and Wilder plays Avram, the accident-prone innocent sent from his Polish seminary to care for a new congregation in San Francisco. After being robbed by con men, he is forced to put himself in the hands of Harrison, a grumpy outlaw. Along the way he meets Amish people, teaches friendly Indians new dances, has his faith tested in an alien context and has a gun put in his hand by the outlaw to see if he'll use it. What might have been an amusing fiddler on the hoof sadly turns out to be a perfunctory, heavy-handed piece of work, sentimental and full of misfiring jokes.

Rather more successful along similar trails, but in modern America, is Ron Underwood's *City Slickers* (1991), scripted by two of Hollywood's most dependable formulaic comedy writers, Babaloo Mandell and Lowell Ganz. Billy Crystal, Bruno Kirby, and Daniel Stern play middle-class New Yorkers, all experiencing mid-life crises and struggling with unrewarding, well-paid jobs and stale marriages. We first see them aping Papa Hemingway at the running of the bulls in Pamplona and following similar macho weekend pursuits. At the age of 39 they decide to go West and join a pair of black dentists, a couple of overweight Jewish ice-cream tycoons and an attractive young woman (Helen Slater) on a two-week cattle drive from New Mexico into Colorado. Whinging and wise-cracking, they hit the trail under the tutelage of an almost parodic super-cowboy named Curly, marvellously played by Jack Palance, who can strike matches on his cheek. When Curly suddenly dies, they're forced to go on alone, facing the ultimate tests and gaining character and the movie becomes a cross between *Red River* and *The Cowboys*. What is most striking is the moral seriousness that runs through this romantic picture. Sometimes it surfaces as sentimentality. More often it resides in the way the movie grasps the central preoccupations of the western, among them the contest between the desire for independence and the demands of community, and the discovery of what it is to be a responsible, inner-directed man. There was a poor sequel two years later.

The most affectionate western spoof of the past couple of decades is the third instalment of Robert Zemeckis' *Back to the Future* trilogy (1990), in which Michael J. Fox as Marty McFly, the film's teenage hero, goes back to the nineteenth century to rescue the stranded Doc Brown, his time-travelling inventor friend and surrogate father (Christopher Lloyd), who's trapped in the 1885 version of their hometown, Hill Valley. Using Doc's time-travelling DeLorean car, Marty heads at rapidly accelerating speed towards a drive-in cinema resonantly located in Monument Valley which is showing the low-budget 1955 horror flick *Tarantula*, featuring at the bottom of the cast list the unknown Clint Eastwood. At the point of collision with the drive-in's screen the DeLorean passes through the time barrier and lands in the Old West just as an Indian war party is being pursued by the US cavalry. In this frontier community Marty encounters the first generation of the McFly family lately arrived from Ireland, and gives his name as Clint Eastwood. What he has stumbled into is less the real West than the world of the classic western.

Back to the Future III alludes to and evokes numerous famous westerns, and sitting in the local saloon are several celebrated cowboy movie actors including Harry Carey Jr., whose career and that of his distinguished father cover the history of the genre. As Marty and Doc Brown prepare for their return to 1985, they draw on their knowledge of the western. Doc, who finds a common bond with the town's new school marm (Mary Steenburgen) in their mutual love of Jules Verne, overcomes his bashfulness and starts to court this exotic outsider by carefully imitating the way Henry Fonda's Wyatt Earp escorts Cathy Downs onto the dance-floor in *My Darling Clementine*. Marty survives a gunfight by remembering Eastwood's cunning strategies in *A Fistful of Dollars*.

But for Marty, the 1985 teenager, John Ford westerns are as distant a part of the past as the historical West itself. The genre's values seem to him both comic and romantically appealing, and that gives an edge to the proceedings, and takes us to the *Back to the Future* trilogy's central joke about rapid social change and historical discontinuity. There is in the movie a central contradiction that's both comic and revealing. The supporting characters behave according to a traditional European view of society, which believes that your ancestors and your progeny are likely to be much like you. The bullies in 1985, for instance, are the great-great-grandchildren of pioneer scoundrels, and in the twenty-first century their children will still be bad apples. Yet though young Marty's jeans determined his name when in the Trilogy's first episode he returned to 1955 (he was dubbed Calvin Klein), his fate is not determined by his genes. He has that American belief in the ability to challenge fate and re-shape his life by an act of will.

Much of the film, as I've said, is set in Monument Valley. Conscious of its iconic significance, Zemeckis was to have his Candide-like twentieth-century American everyman played by Tom Hanks in *Forrest Gump* run through Monument Valley on his journey through the experience of our time.

4 The Italian Western

Since the earlier editions of this book, the Italian movie industry and the nation's popular cinema have gone through a series of crises into near terminal decline, and the idea of a Hollywood-on-the-Tiber has become a matter of history. The serious study of the Italian western I said was needed in 1976 eventually appeared in 1981 as *Spaghetti Westerns: Cowboys and Europeans from Karl May to Sergio Leone*, written by Christopher Frayling, who as a student in the 1960s may well have coined the term that gave his book its title. As a result of his book (much revised in 1998) and the availability of Italian westerns on video and DVD, a small canon has been established that consists principally of Sergio Leone's *Dollar* trilogy and his *Once Upon a Time in the West*, and a couple of films by Sergio Corbucci, most notably his influential *Django* (1966), long banned in Britain for its violence, and *The Big Silence* (1968).

Once Upon a Time in the West, which did not reach Britain in its complete form until 1984, is a towering movie, one of the greatest ever made. It might now be seen as the centrepiece in a trilogy of political movies about the fight over land and water in the American West, flanked by John Sturges's *Bad Day at Black Rock* (1954) and Roman Polanski's *Chinatown* (1974). Itself full of references to numerous American westerns and now easily identifiable to audiences around the world, it has been much copied and parodied. Leone's opening scene, where three gunfighters lie in wait for the hero to arrive, is recapitulated in the subculture of Californian bikers at the beginning of Walter Hill's *Another 48 Hrs*.

What is generally regarded as the final spaghetti western, Monte Hellman's *China 9, Liberty 37* (1978), consciously evokes *Once Upon a Time in the West* and various other westerns. Shot in Spain with studio work in Rome, the film stars Fabio Testi as Clayton Drum, a legendary gunslinger spared from the gallows by the intervention of a railroad boss who wants him to kill Martin (Warren Oates) whose land they need. But Clayton takes a liking to Martin and leaves after having a fling with his young wife Catherine (Jenny Agutter). When she thinks she has accidentally killed her brutal husband, Catherine attaches herself to Clayton and they find themselves caught between Martin's band of brothers and the railroad's hired guns.

This is a curt, elliptical film full of visual and verbal violence, and charged with a lyrical eroticism close to soft-core pornography. It's a slightly chaotic affair, not unlike Hellman's two earlier westerns in this respect, and punctuated by bizarre moments. The film has a dusty, forlorn look. It's the only western shot by Italy's most celebrated cameraman, Giuseppe Rotunno, and he made it between working on Lina Wertmuller's *A Night Full of Rain* and Bob Fosse's *All That Jazz*. The weirdly resonant title (the picture is also known as *Amore, Piombo e Furore, Clayton and Catherine*, and *Clayton Drum*) refers to a road sign pointing to the two small Texas towns where much of the action takes place.

The Fabio Testi character shares the odd name of a cowboy in Hellman's *The Shooting*. Martin talks of having been a hired gun for the railroad and killing a whole family for his ruthless employers, an exact account of the murders carried out by Henry Fonda in *Once Upon a Time in the West*. Martin's drunken, rapacious band of brothers is intended to recall the dangerous Hammond brood to which Warren Oates belonged in Sam Peckinpah's *Ride the High Country*. Peckinpah himself makes a brief appearance as Wilbur Olsen, a dime novel writer who wants to 'buy the legend' by signing up Clayton for the rights to his name and adventures to sell to readers in the East, to give them 'the lies they need, we all need'. Hellman had been associated with Peckinpah five years earlier when he'd been on the point of following up his greatest film, *Two-Lane Blacktop*, with a movie scripted by the same avant-garde writer, Rudolph Wurlitzer, *Pat Garrett and Billy the Kid*. But *Two-Lane Blacktop* flopped and *Pat Garrett* was assigned to Peckinpah. He too, neither for the first nor the last time, had trouble with the producers, who re-edited his picture and removed twenty minutes from it. It is possible therefore to see in *China 9, Liberty 37* a fable about moviemaking in which the gunfighters are the directors and the cynical, manipulative railway magnates are the producers.

Of recent movies, the film most influenced by spaghetti westerns is Sam Raimi's *The Quick and the Dead* (of which more later). A runner-up is Martin Campbell's *The Mask of Zorro* (1998), a sequel of sorts to Rouben Mamoulian's *The Mark of Zorro* (1940), the classic swashbuckler about the masked aristocratic avenger who fights on behalf of the oppressed common folk against their Spanish exploiters in early nineteenth-century California. In Campbell's film a long-

imprisoned Zorro (Anthony Hopkins) escapes to seek revenge on
the evil governor who killed his wife and abducted his daughter
(Catherine Zeta Jones). He trains a young bandit (Antonio
Banderas) in swordsmanship and self-control to join him in the
enterprise. It is less the plot that brings to mind the spaghetti western
than the tone and appearance. The outlaw played by Banderas is
initially involved in scams resembling those of *The Good, the Bad
and the Ugly*, and in addition to a James Horner score that echoes
Ennio Morricone, there's that familiar spaghetti setting of a hellish
goldmine worked by Indian slaves, and the anachronistic notion of
Mexican priests inspired by liberation theology.

The finest, most touching reference to the Italian western during
the 1990s was the dedication in the final credits of Clint Eastwood's
Unforgiven 'To Sergio and Don' – they're of course his mentors
Sergio Leone and Don Siegel.

5 Westward the Women

In his contribution on 'women in western history' to *The New Encyclopedia of the American West*,[33] the historian Joseph E. Taylor writes: 'As late as the 1970s the general understanding of women in the American West could have been summed up in three stereotypes: "Molly, Miss Kitty, and Ma".' He refers to Molly, the schoolmarm in Owen Wister's novel *The Virginian*, Miss Kitty the whore turned saloon keeper played by Amanda Blake in the TV series *Gunsmoke*, and the dedicated, long-suffering mother in *The Little House on the Prairie*, the enduringly popular children's novel by frontier writer Laura Ingalls Wilder, which became a long-running TV series in the 1970s and 80s. 'These stereotypes shaped not only hundreds of Western tales, novels and movies but what passed for history as well,' he continues. But recent historical scholarship has challenged the centrality of men in frontier history, and 'replaced the old stereotypes with a much more sophisticated understanding of the place of women in the American West'. Indeed, the earliest of the revisionist texts cited by Professor Taylor is a documentary work of 1977 edited by Christiane Fisher appropriately called *Let Them Speak for Themselves: Women in the American West 1849–1900*.

Not surprisingly the variety of academic studies has scarcely been reflected in the western over these past thirty years. With inevitable nods in the direction of feminism the vast majority of movies ring variations on the familiar roles assigned to women, digging deeper, and presenting them in such a manner as to suggest a greater sense of personal freedom or at least an awareness of victimhood. At a very simplistic level, we have in *China 9, Liberty 37* the heroine ironically lamenting to her lover when he asks what she'll be doing now she is (or at least thinks she is) a widow: 'What choice do I have – whoring or teaching school?'

Low-budget movies viewing the West from a determinedly feminist perspective have tended to take on a stoical or tragic cast.

---

33 Ed. Howard Lamar, Yale University Press, New Haven and London, 1998, p. 1230.

Richard Pearce's *Heartland* (1979), based on the journals of a frontier wife, is a bleak, authentic story of a woman (Conchita Farrell)
coming with her daughter to early twentieth-century Wyoming to
work as housekeeper for a dour widowed farmer (Rip Torn) whom
she later weds to share a loveless, hardscrabble life. As Christopher
Peachment acutely observed in his *Time Out* review, 'it's the kind
of western that Ken Loach might make'. Equally depressing, and
honest, is Jon Sanders' *Painted Angels* (1997), an authentic, wholly
unromantic account of life in a frontier brothel of the 1880s. The
title is one of those awful Victorian euphemisms for whores. Brenda
Fricker is the stern, kindly Irish madam, herself a victim of an
exploitative social system who must act ruthlessly to please her clien-
tele and satisfy her employers. The only hopeful way out is through
marriage to an admiring client, most probably middle-aged. The
more likely way out when she is no longer attracting sufficient clients
is to be cast into the back streets to sell her body for booze, opium
and a few cents before dying of disease, malnutrition and exposure.
Ada (played by Anne Mottram, the director's wife and co-author
of the script) loses her position as the house's chief attraction, and
is replaced by her daughter, scarcely into her teens. This is the cul-
mination of movies about life in frontier bordellos that, following
the final abandonment of the Hollywood Production Code in 1968,
lead through *The Wild Bunch*, *McCabe and Mrs Miller*, *The Great
Northfield Minnesota Raid* and *The Long Riders*, to *Unforgiven*.

No less pessimistic but rather livelier is *The Ballad of Little Jo*,
written and directed by Maggie Greenwald. It is inspired by a true
story of a New England woman (Suzy Amis), who heads out West
in the late 1860s after being seduced and abandoned by her lover
and rejected by her middle-class family. Josephine disguises herself
as a man, Little Jo, to make a living as a small-scale rancher in a
brutal, xenophobic, masculine world that proves as hostile to her as
to her gentle Chinese lover.

These three films are only borderline westerns, nearer to the
novels of Hamlin Garland, O.E. Rölvaag and Willa Cather than to
those of Zane Grey and Louis L'Amour. Their feminist impulses
deny the essential violence of the genre, whereas the heroines of the
mainstream western merely challenge it, allowing the gunfights and
bloodletting to continue to their exhilarating and dramatically satis-
fying conclusions. In the mainstream films the best roles are those
played by Cate Blanchett in Ron Howard's *The Missing* and by
Annette Bening in Kevin Costner's *Open Range*, both released in

2003, of which more later. Their performances are different from those where women assume traditionally male roles, found chiefly in pictures celebrating such legendary cross-dressing frontier figures as Calamity Jane and Belle Starr. One of the more remarkable instances is a film I neglected in the earlier editions of the book, Louis Malle's *Viva Maria!* (1965), which has a place in both the development of the European western and the role of women in the genre. A comic melodrama with surreal touches, the film casts the French cinema's greatest female stars of the day, Jeanne Moreau and Brigitte Bardot, as two beautiful girls called Maria, the former a professional singer working with a travelling circus in Central America, the latter the daughter of an Irish Republican terrorist who is killed attempting to blow up a bridge in a British colony in Latin America. The pair join forces as a singing striptease duo, become involved with guerrilla forces in a fictitious dictatorship and are transformed into revolutionary heroines. While writing the script, Malle and his co-writer Jean-Claude Carrière had in mind a distaff version of Robert Aldrich's *Vera Cruz*, which as I mentioned earlier was a major influence on Sergio Leone.

Viva Maria! was extremely popular everywhere except in the United States, and although intended by Malle as a light-hearted romp after the tragic *Le Feu follet*, it anticipated what were shortly to be major political considerations of the radical young – female empowerment, and the choice between violent revolution and political persuasion. Its plot was more or less borrowed by Leone for his fourth and final western as director, *Giù la testa!*, and its use of the machine gun influenced subsequent westerns, European and American. Gatling guns and similar automatic weapons in the West go back to Cecil B. De Mille's *North West Mounted Police* (1940), where Gary Cooper seizes a machine gun about to fall into Indian hands. But the manner in which Bardot and Moreau turn such a gun on their enemies – Moreau rather nervously feeding the belt of bullets, Bardot expertly firing – gave it a dramatic vitality that later directors found irresistible, Leone, Corbucci and Peckinpah among them.

The machine gun is also a major weapon in the most determined of 1990s mainstream Hollywood westerns to embrace feminism – Jonathan Kaplan's *Bad Girls* (1994). Cody (Madeleine Stowe), Anita (Mary Stuart Masterson), Lilly (Drew Barrymore) and Eileen (Andie MacDowell) are spirited whores maintaining their self-respect while working upstairs at a saloon in a Colorado mining town. They're the objects of demonstrations by local puritans, and when Cody is on the point of being lynched for killing a hypocritical local bigwig in self-defence, the other three rescue her and they ride off, followed by Pinkerton agents hired by the victim's vengeful widow. Their journey takes them to Texas where they're wrongly accused of bank robbery and become involved with Kid Jarrett and his band of psychopathic outlaws with whom Cody once rode. The movie is full of references to other westerns (most particularly the acquisition of a Gatling gun from a military train near the Rio Grande which they first trade to a criminal band, then use in the finale). But the names of Cody and Jarrett direct us elsewhere, though to what purpose is unclear. They're obviously intended to evoke Raoul Walsh's 1949 gangster picture *White Heat* where James Cagney's psychopathic hoodlum is called Cody Jarrett.

Bad Girls is a flat-footed, indifferently plotted movie with a fashionable feminist thrust in the way it presents the women characters as both a quartet of mutually caring, sexually liberated sisters and a bunch of women victimised and demeaned at every turn. All four have back-stories of the troubles that drove them into prostitution like the whores narrating their sad stories in John Cleland's *Fanny Hill*. Cody was an orphan working as a skivvy before being abducted by outlaws and then turning to prostitution. Lilly worked with her father's travelling acrobats until being left by his sudden death to pay off heavy debts. Eileen's rancher father had a heart attack after the banks foreclosed on his mortgage. Anita's husband died of cholera on the Oregon Trail. Two of them are raped and badly beaten, all are accused of crimes they didn't commit, and they're subject to constant humiliation by respectable citizens and outlaws alike.

Only two young men – a naïve rancher and a gunfighter out to revenge his parents' death at the hands of the Jarrett gang – show them respect. As the widow says when a smug lawyer tells her that only her husband could lay claim to their land in Oregon: 'Yes, I understand that. I was worthless until I got married. So now, I guess, I'm worthless as a widow. Funny I had some value as a whore. Did I shock you? You expect me to cry over your big desk? So if your laws don't include us, then they don't apply to me either.' She exits, throwing the fee the lawyer demands on the floor before him. It's a forceful scene and the movie inevitably creates a moral framework that permits them to retaliate, though this being a traditional western, gauged to entertain, they act according to the cowboy code.

Cody takes her revenge on her ravisher in a fair fight, even providing a round for his empty gun. This isn't presented in a parodic or ironic or post-modern fashion. In fact one of the most attractive aspects of the picture is its lack of cynicism. Another is the sheer style of these four good-looking, elegantly dressed young women as they ride together like the gunfighters in *The Magnificent Seven* and then walk into the final bloody showdown like William Holden, Ernest Borgnine, Warren Oates and Ben Johnson in *The Wild Bunch*. Fortunately they survive, with one staying behind with the young rancher and the other three riding off into the most glorious frontier sunset you ever saw.

Bad Girls was almost entirely the work of men behind the camera – male writers, cinematographer, composer, and a director, Jonathan Kaplan, who began his career making exploitation pictures. The same is true of *The Quick and the Dead* (1995) made the following year, where the director is Sam Raimi, who made his name with low-budget horror flicks. The moving force behind the picture was unquestionably Sharon Stone, who co-produced (on the strength of her commanding appearance in *Basic Instinct*) and stars as a strident, sexually empowered participant in a lethal competition staged in a stylised frontier township by psychotic gunfighter Gene Hackman. It's the ultimate post-modern homage to Leone, photographed by the Italian cinematographer Dante Spinotti, and drawing in a cast of old western hands and such neophytes as Leonardo DiCaprio and Russell Crowe.

6 Legends Re-examined

In the 1930s, before the cinema discovered the flawed hero or the anti-hero, the legendary figures of the West were invariable seen in a heroic light either doing their duty in bringing civilisation to the frontier as trailblazers, wagon masters, lawmen, cavalry officers, or as misunderstood outlaws. But as I pointed out earlier, the movies have taken an increasingly critical view of the famous names, and each generation has come up with new interpretations suitable to the mood of the times but often offensive to those adhering to received opinion.

The Alamo

A much restored version of the fortress and former Spanish mission, where Davy Crockett, Colonel William Travis and Jim Bowie died along with nearly 200 others in March 1836 facing the Mexican army, stands as a 'shrine to Texas liberty' and a major tourist attraction in San Antonio. A version of it is to be found on a ranch near the Mexican border at Brackettville, Texas, where the set built for John Wayne's 1960 epic still stands for the benefit of tourists and moviemakers. (*Bad Girls* was shot there, and so was John Ford's *Two Rode Together*.) The mythology surrounding the Alamo was well under way before the Civil War. The Texans' rallying cry 'Remember the Alamo' entered the language (with later crises making such versions of it as 'Remember the Maine' and 'Remember Pearl Harbor'), and President Teddy Roosevelt staged a reunion of his Rough Riders in front of the Alamo in 1905.

The earliest film of the siege was shot in Texas in 1915 and partly locally financed. Among those that followed were two films of 1955, Frank Lloyd's mini-epic *The Last Command* featuring a lacklustre cast headed by Sterling Hayden as Jim Bowie and Arthur Hunnicutt as Davy Crockett, and *Davy Crockett, King of the Wild Frontier*, starring Fess Parker and cobbled together from a three-part Disney television series for kids. It is, of course, John Wayne's 1960 film that, though not a great commercial success, stamped its simplistic, patriotic, rightwing view on the public mind. In the years since then the distinctive façade of the mission-fortress has established itself as an icon.

In Jerry Paris's *Viva Max*, a lumpen comedy of 1969, Peter Ustinov played a jokey present-day Mexican general who leads his troops into Texas to reoccupy the Alamo. Eagle Pennell's *Last Night at the Alamo* (1984) is a rather good low-budget picture scripted by Kim Henkel, co-author of *The Texas Chainsaw Massacre*. Shot in grainy black-and-white this truthful film takes place in the Alamo, a sleazy bar in suburban Houston, frequented by deadbeats, no-hopers and assorted rednecks. The bar is to be razed to the ground the following day to make way for a high-rise apartment block. It recalls the changing times of the Lone Star State similarly signalled in *The Last Picture Show*. 'Make Way for Tomorrow' says the demolition company's sign, stuck up against the Alamo's façade, which is a clapboard version of the iconic silhouette of the Alamo Mission, the cradle of the Texas Republic defended by Bowie and Crockett.

The Alamo crowd are as desperate as the barflies living on pipe dreams in Eugene O'Neill's *The Iceman Cometh*, and their equivalent of the charismatic Hickey is a posturing oilfield roustabout nicknamed Cowboy and significantly surnamed Regan, whose never-removed Stetson conceals a balding head. Cowboy (well played by local Texas actor Sonny Davis) has fantasies of becoming a Hollywood star ('they need men like me out there') and he believes that a political contact in the state capital can save the Alamo. When he eventually gets through to Austin, his side of the telephone conversation goes: 'No, Sam Houston never slept here... not *exactly* historical... at least eighty years ago... No, I don't think anyone famous ever came through.' A drunken Cowboy eventually gets his gun, but it's no match for the wrecker's ball.

A similarly satirical and ironic reference is made in Louis Malle's masterly *Alamo Bay* (1985), a film in the old Warner Brothers social-conscience style based on a true story. Set in the eponymous fictitious port on the southern coast of Texas, it turns on a confrontation between xenophobic local fishermen and Vietnamese refugees whom they believe to be threatening their already failing livelihood. Ed Harris plays Pearce, their redneck leader (nicknamed Shang Pearce after the famed Texas cattle drover Shanghai Pearce) who imagines himself under siege from foreigners and leads a Ku Klux Klan assault on the intruders. The film appeared in the middle of the Reagan era and on the tenth anniversary of the fall of Saigon and was subjected to a critical drubbing that suggested that a

Frenchman had no right making a film in America along these lines.[34]

In the TV film *Lonesome Dove*, the two old-timers, played by Robert Duvall and Tommy Lee Jones are riding past the crumbling ruins of the Alamo in the San Antonio of the early 1880s. They ask themselves why their own heroic careers as Texas Rangers are not remembered and Duvall comes up with the theory that it's because they weren't killed in the line of duty.

In this light it strikes one that a new, possibly iconoclastic look at the Alamo and the sacred cows gathered within its walls might be long overdue, and it was expected that this movie might be John Lee Hancock's *The Alamo* (2004). Made in the wake of the cataclysmic events of 9/11, this film tries to be even-handed and manages for most of the way to avoid the strident patriotism of the Wayne movie in its treatment of the heroic, martyr-creating defeat at the Alamo, and eschews any exaggerated triumphalism in its treatment of Sam Houston's crushing victory over Santa Anna's Mexican army at the battle of San Jacinto which brought about Texas independence the following year. The latter event was not covered except by way of a concluding statement in Wayne's picture. The price Hancock and his co-authors, Leslie Bohem and Stephen Gaghan, pay for trying to be revisionist without offending traditional Texan sensibilities is to end up with a picture uncertain in tone and somewhat muffled in its statements about history.

Whether for commercial reasons or deliberate effect, efficient actors of no great heroic presence were cast in the leads. The roles played back in 1960 by Wayne, Richard Widmark, Laurence Harvey and Richard Boone, all imposing stars, were taken in the 2004 film by low-key, physically unimpressive figures – Billy Bob Thornton (Crockett), Jason Patric (Jim Bowie), Patrick Wilson (garrison commander Lt. Colonel William Travis), and Dennis Quaid (Sam Houston, first President of Texas). They are not men self-evidently keeping a rendezvous with destiny. Crockett, having lost his seat in the Senate, has come to Texas to get one of the patches of land freely offered in Washington to any chancer prepared to throw in his lot with this rebellious corner of Mexico. He isn't expecting to fight and only stays because he's a prisoner of his own myth; he wears a coonskin cap because this is how the actor impersonating him on stage back East dresses. Dying of consumption,

34 Philip French (ed.), *Malle on Malle* (Faber & Faber, London 1993), pp. 146–54.

Bowie is permanently drunk, and has come to San Antonio to reclaim the garrison's artillery for Sam Houston. The politically ambitious Travis has just got a divorce from a constraining wife, obtained custody of his son, and comes to the Alamo to advance his political ambitions. Unexpectedly, he finds himself in charge when his superior officer leaves to attend to urgent business elsewhere, and he has difficulty asserting his authority.

But they rise to the occasion, and the fall of the Alamo and the battle of San Jacinto are handled in a solemn fashion with funereal music by Carter Burden that denies the audience anything approaching visceral enjoyment. Few bones are made about the commercial, expansionist aims of the Texan leaders. While bickering goes on among the leaders of the competing factions at the Alamo, an observer on the fringe, speaking in Spanish, describes the future martyrs and their followers as 'lowlifes' and opines: 'Santa Anna only wants to rule Mexico; these people want to rule the whole world.' But Santa Anna is presented, not unjustly, as a brilliant, arrogant military leader, a preening monster with contempt for the lives of his men whom he employs as suicide bombers. After his initial triumph at the Alamo he enters into a running war with General Sam Houston, now commander of the rebel army of Texas, who abandons the bottle and his irresolution to conduct a campaign in which he is reminiscent of the Duke of Wellington luring the Napoleonic Santa Anna into inevitable defeat.

The film's thrust is that this is a war that should not have been fought, but once embarked on against a deadly enemy it must be pursued, however reluctantly. This is the way the picture reflects the temper of the time in a guarded revisionism, a decent half-hearted liberal affair that satisfies neither hawks nor doves. In this reading the drunken, ineffectual Sam Houston is Bush, the Alamo is his Twin Towers, a tragedy created by his inactivity, after which he pulls himself together to seek just vengeance. The Battle of San Jacinto is the invasion of Afghanistan and Iraq; Santa Anna is a combination of Bin Laden and Saddam Hussein. In the movie Sam Houston proclaims the battle cry that has echoed down the years, 'Remember the Alamo!' (actually spoken by a certain Colonel Sidney George Sherman) which was evoked again after the Twin Towers assault. This movie, in which we see Colonel Travis make his now legendary appeal for reinforcements for the Alamo, gives a fresh resonance to the understated message sent by the commander of the Apollo 13 mission to NASA in 1970, 'Houston, we've got a problem.' Perhaps this movie should have starred Tom Hanks as Colonel Travis.

Wild Bill Hickok

The union soldier, cavalry scout, lawman, gambler, ace gunslinger and dime-novel hero James Butler ('Wild Bill') Hickok (1837–76) was apparently the childhood hero of Dwight D. Eisenhower, and he was as identifiable by his long hair as by the twin pistols he kept quite high on his waist with the handles facing his opponents. In *The Plainsman* (1936), Cecil B. De Mille's epic treatment of the winning of the West, Hickok is portrayed by a quiet, unflamboyant, dignified Gary Cooper who plays down the customary wildness. Jean Arthur as his long-time friend and sometime lover Calamity Jane is a cheerful, kindly outdoor girl. Twenty years later, during Eisenhower's first term as President, Hickok and Calamity Jane were domesticated in the Warner Brothers musical *Calamity Jane* (1953) modelled on *Annie Get Your Gun*. A clean-shaven, short-haired Howard Keel (who had played Frank Butler in *Annie Get Your Gun*) was Hickok and a buckskin- (and occasionally gingham-) clad Doris Day was a pert, strident girl-next-door version of Calamity Jane.

In *Little Big Man* (1970), Arthur Penn's satire on the West, on American bellicosity at the height of the Vietnam War, and on the counterculture, Hickok is one of the legendary figures that the centenarian fabulist Jack Crabbe (Dustin Hoffman) claims to have met during his youth roaming the frontier. Although he appears only briefly, when Crabbe is a witness to his murder in a Deadwood saloon, Wild Bill is given an impressive presence by the great character actor Jeff Corey, who the previous year had been the unscrupulous killer of the heroine's father in *True Grit*.

Since the first edition of my *Westerns*, Wild Bill has been impersonated twice in films that treat him as a doomed, world-weary hero stuck with his legend and confronting his imminent and early death. Both make a big point of his failing eyesight (as does William S. Hart in the 1923 film *Wild Bill Hickok*). Directed by J. Lee Thompson, *The White Buffalo* (1977) is an ambitious movie inspired by Herman Melville's *Moby-Dick*, though presumably embarked on as a major production by Dino De Laurentiis to cash in on the success of *Jaws*. Instead of a great white whale there is here an albino buffalo of immense size and ferocity that stalks the plains and is clearly a symbol for the spirit of the land or the troubled, vengeful soul of America. Wild Bill Hickok (Charles Bronson at his most saturnine), who's going blind in late stages of syphilis, dreams of this fearsome animal and returns to the West for one last hunt after the humiliating experience of performing twice nightly in Buffalo Bill's touring Wild West Show. The picture opens impressively with Hickok (prematurely aged and wearing smoked glasses) waking on a westbound train from his nightmare of the charging, red-eyed, white-skinned beast, and firing off his six-shooters into the bunk above him, which is fortunately unoccupied. He alights from the train beside a mountain of bleached buffalo bones, all that's left of the mighty herds that were slaughtered to feed railway workers.

Another legendary Western figure, the great Sioux chieftain Crazy Horse, is after the buffalo which destroyed his village, and to redeem himself he must wrap his dead child's body in its hide. He's played by Will Sampson, who was Chief Brogden in *One Flew Over the Cuckoo's Nest*, as well as the translator in *Buffalo Bill and the Indians* and a Texas brave in *The Outlaw Josey Wales*.

It is a good set-up and there's a strong cast of familiar character actors, John Carradine as a cadaverous undertaker and Slim Pickens as a creatively foulmouthed stagecoach driver among them. There is also a touching performance from Kim Novak as an old flame, Pistol Jennie, who cheerfully comments, when hearing of Wild Bill's terminally ill state, 'Probably gave it you myself.' But the film is poorly scripted and J. Lee Thompson, in one of his more interesting late pictures, can't reconcile the various conflicts between the naturalistic and the highly stylised, the amusingly scabrous and the portentously sombre, the social and the metaphysical. Its pessimism about the end of the West is ultimately enervating rather than bracing. The grittily authentic sets and décor by Tambi Larsen (who had designed *The Outlaw Josey Wales* and was to receive the one Oscar nomination bestowed on *Heaven's Gate*) are impressive. But the picture is finally sunk by the white buffalo itself which ends up as neither magical nor realistic, and as unconvincing as the whale in John Huston's *Moby Dick*.

Less ambitious but infinitely more satisfactory is *Wild Bill* (1995), adapted by its director Walter Hill from a play and a novel by two distinguished American writers, respectively Thomas Babe's *Fathers and Sons* and Pete Dexter's *Deadwood*. The first thing we see in the film is Hickok's coffin being taken out of a hearse at Deadwood's Mt. Moriah cemetery. The story is then narrated in flashback by his drunken English friend, Charley Prince (John Hurt in a role similar to the one he played in *Heaven's Gate*), using a formal, deliberately

sonorous Victorian style. The movie is in effect a series of short
scenes, most of them violent encounters thrust upon, or invited by,
the explosive Wild Bill (Jeff Bridges), and leading up to his assassination in a Deadwood saloon by a disturbed young man called Jack
McCall, whose mother Wild Bill deserted fifteen years before. The
trigger-happy Bill is inclined towards self-justification, frequently
asserting that 'you should know better than to touch another man's
hat', and that this is as good a reason as any for getting killed. Nobody
talks of anything else but their recollections of and relationships with
Wild Bill, including Calamity Jane (Ellen Barkin), the rough, tough
love of his life, a drifter, sharpshooter and legendary figure herself,
with whom he has a reunion in Deadwood. For reasons that aren't
made explicit – impotence, guilt, an inability to allow anyone close
to him again – he rejects her advances.

By the time he has come to Deadwood after years of rambling,
he's a frontier legend, immediately recognisable for his flamboyant
appearance and a target for the indignant, the inferior and the
searchers after instant celebrity. A comic interlude with him
performing with Buffalo Bill's Wild West Circus in the East shows
us that he cannot simulate, he can only enact what he has become,
and he lacks that American ability to transform himself by an act of
will. 'He has discovered that being Wild Bill was a profession in itself,'
the narrator says. There is a good deal of emphasis on religion in
Hill's movie including a hot gospel service conducted by a manic
preacher played by the former evangelist, Marjoe Gortner. When
they arrive in Deadwood, Charley remarks that the wide-open
scenes remind him of the Bible. 'Which part?', Bill enquires. 'The
part before God gets angry,' Charley replies. But Bill cannot bring
himself to seek the redemption that western heroes often strive for.

A physician tells Bill that glaucoma, probably resulting from 'too
much closeness to infected females', is causing the failing eyesight
that is likely to end in blindness. And like the Wild Bill of *White
Buffalo* he has monochrome dreams of his past which occur most
powerfully when smoking opium in Deadwood's Chinatown. The
casting of Bridges, an actor usually associated with cheerful,
everyday extroverts, as a doomed, inward-looking man, trapped by
his legend, was a shrewd move, suggesting a smouldering violence
and a sense of tragic destiny residing in the soul of the average
American male.

It is perhaps not too fanciful to see this film as reflecting the mood
of a post-Cold War America where the enemy is no longer defined,

and the righteous hero has no obvious place to exert himself. Or associating Wild Bill with Bill Clinton. This is a dark, complex picture – fierce, elegant, self-conscious, not a little mysterious. Popular neither with critics nor the public, it was a commercial disaster of almost *Heaven's Gate* proportions, and was made by the same company with two of the same stars.

Deadwood (2004), the most notable TV western series after *Lonesome Dove*, took its cue from the cinema by engaging Walter Hill, the director of *Wild Bill*, and his cinematographer, Lloyd Ahern, to make the first episode. In *Wild Bill*, Keith Carradine took the minor role of Buffalo Bill. Here he plays Hickok, but in this Deadwood, though he's a charismatic character, he's not the dominant figure and indeed is murdered in the fourth episode and ceremoniously buried in the fifth. As played by Carradine he is a quiet, majestic figure, conscious of his legend and dangerous, yet anything but wild in his demeanour. He is also enigmatic, possibly uncertain of what he is to do with what he knows to be at best his last few years. His companion, Charles Utter, despairs of steering him away from the gambling tables, where his fortunes fluctuate, and towards the possibility of striking it rich as a prospector. He has also, we learn, recently married a woman working in a travelling circus, and is off-hand but not rude in his dealings with Calamity Jane (Robin Weigert), his devoted admirer, who is far from glamorous here. Indeed she resembles the scruffy, sun-burnt Annie Oakley as played by Betty Hutton, stumbling out of the backwoods in the opening scenes of *Annie Get Your Gun*, and before she receives a makeover to become the peaches-and-cream blonde star of Buffalo Bill's Wild West Circus.

Created by David Milch and the work of nine writers and seven directors, *Deadwood* begins in 1876, the year of the national centennial celebrations and two weeks after the the disaster of Custer's Last Stand less than 200 miles away. Deadwood, centre of a major gold strike in the Black Hills of Dakota, is an illegal town on an Indian reservation, outside the jurisdiction of either state or territorial authorities, and though rapidly growing in population is invariably called a camp. 'No law at all in Deadwood,' says a man who's hanged as a horse thief before he can get there. The opening episode is dark and dense, the ultimate 'dirty western' in appearance and disturbing in several ways. First, there are a number of different characters and story lines with very little formal exposition. Second, the language, replete with obscenities, is more rebarbative than anything previously heard on television or in a theatrical western. Third, there appears to be no moral centre of any kind. In fact what we seem to be seeing is not an innocent Eden about to be corrupted, but rather that medieval world without order of which Thomas Hobbes writes in *Leviathan*: 'No arts, no letters, no society; and which is worst of all, continual fear and danger of violent death; and the life of man, solitary, nasty, brutish and short.' This Deadwood, where men are free to do as they will, is in fact an image of unrestricted laissez faire capitalism where the strong and unscrupulous thrive and the weakest go to the wall, or if killed are fed to the swine belonging to a Chinese pig farmer. Or it could be a metaphor for the film business: one of the directors who figures in this book remarked to me some years ago that Hollywood is the last surviving example of unbridled capitalism.

The town is largely run by the saloon owner and whoremaster, the explosive, ruthless, foul-mouthed, Machiavellian Al Swearengen (Ian McShane) and his murderous myrmidons. From his headquarters at The Gem he also controls the outlaws known euphemistically as road agents, who prey on wayfarers, and he cheats prospectors and manipulates bogus claims. He conspires with the corrupt hotel owner, E.B. Farnum, and is challenged for control of the town by the suave Cy Tulliver (Powers Boothe), who arrives to open a smarter gambling den-cum-brothel, the Belle Union, to compete with The Gem. There is a variety of incidents and story-lines, but the chief one running through the first series concentrates on a small girl, the sole survivor of a Norwegian immigrant family bushwhacked by Swearengen's outlaw associates on their way back to Minnesota, disgusted by Deadwood. The massacre, carelessly disguised as an attack by Sioux, is investigated by Wild Bill Hickok and Seth Bullock (Timothy Olyphant), both former marshals, and they find the child. She's cared for by the tough, hard-drinking Calamity Jane and the town's general practitioner, Dr Cochran (Brad Dourif), an honest man cowed by Swearengen. Later Alma Garret (Molly Parker), New York socialite widow of a fortune seeker dude killed by Swearengen, and the abused prostitute, Trixie, join in caring for the girl and protecting her from Swearengen. In this way *Deadwood* is less cynical than the earlier western it inevitably brings to mind, Robert Altman's *McCabe and Mrs Miller*, in which Keith Carradine also appears.

Gradually an odd alliance grows up between these people, helping them cope with various threats as well as with the murder of Wild Bill, thus demonstrating the resilience of a natural human decency under pressure. The town survives an outbreak of smallpox, and ahead of it lies a great fire, a flood and finally extinction as the gold is exhausted and the miners move on, leaving Deadwood to become a legend and a museum like Tombstone down south in Arizona. With a complexity and moral density found in few other westerns, *Deadwood* creates a cautionary metaphor for the America of George W. Bush.

The James–Younger Gang

Jesse James is America's Robin Hood, named as such in his lifetime, and until the 1970s his activities and those of his outlaw band have been treated in the cinema pretty much with the indulgence and affection accorded to the Merry Men of Sherwood Forest. Two films at the beginning and end of the 1970s, directed by two of the brightest moviemakers to emerge in that decade, played with the myth and reality of the James gang to considerable effect – Phil Kaufman's *The Great Northfield Minnesota Raid* (1971) and Walter Hill's *The Long Riders* (1980). Both are fables full of authentic period detail and realistic violence in the Peckinpah manner. They pick up the gang fairly late in their careers, in the centennial year of 1876, when they headed 400 miles north from their base in Clay County, Missouri. This clannish community of poor farmers, mostly former confederate supporters, admired James for taking action against banks and railway companies run by eastern outsiders who threatened their land and way of life. The gang's destination was the bank in Northfield, Minnesota, an area regarded by them as foreign Union territory. The raid, of course, is a disaster and brings about the end of the gang.

In Kaufman's film, reflecting the anarchic mood of the Vietnam era, there is a clash in the gang between the nominal leader, Jesse James (Robert Duvall) and his Bible thumping brother, Frank (John Pearce), and the second-in-command Cole Younger (Cliff Robertson) and his two brothers. James is a zealot, a violent psychopath still fighting the Civil War and regarding their train robberies and bank hold-ups as legitimate guerrilla raids. He steals the idea of robbing the Northfield Bank from Cole, but in the ranting style of a hot-gospel evangelist he claims to have received the plan in a vision. Duvall's performance at this point anticipates the roles that would bring him an Oscar (*Tender Mercies*) and an Oscar nomination (*The Apostle*).

Cole Younger is a cool, self-mythologising ironist, who knows himself to be the gang's brains, and wants to accept the amnesty offered by the state and abandon the life of crime. But when their sworn enemy, the Pinkerton Detective Agency, bribes the speaker of the state legislature to thwart the amnesty, he goes along with their operation. He even tricks the unscrupulous bank manager into conspiring to fill his safe with gold lured from local merchants who don't trust the banking system. The film is a Brechtian satire on capitalism and on American hypocrisy in which the vindictiveness, violence and self-justification of the outlaws is perfectly matched by those of the Pinkertons and the venal, vengeful civic leaders of Northfield. At the end Jesse escapes from the scene disguised in the clothes of an elderly widow he's first helped then murdered, while a badly injured Cole, being carried away in a prison wagon, raises himself up in his cage to acknowledge the cheers of the poor folk in the streets.

The movie is both comic and cruel. *The Long Riders* is equally detached and unsentimental, but altogether more serious and romantic. More than incidentally Kaufman went on to make a light-hearted film about New York street gangs in the 1960s, *The Wanderers* (1979), while Hill preceded *The Long Riders* with a mock epic about gang warfare, *The Warriors*, that transposed Xenophon's *Anabasis* (about Greeks making their way home through hostile Persian territory) to a stylised twentieth-century New York. It could easily have been a western.

The Long Riders announces its central theme from the beginning by casting four sets of real brothers as Jesse and Frank James (James and Stacey Keach), Cole, Jim and Bob Younger (David, Keith and Robert Carradine), Clell and Ed Miller (Randy and Dennis Quaid), who constitute the gang's central core, and the treacherous Bob and Charlie Ford (Christopher and Nicholas Guest) who kill Jesse. This is no gimmick because it's a movie about families, family obligations and the rootedness of a threatened clan. As with Francis Coppola's *The Godfather*, it deals with crime as a way of life, accepted by the women who stay at home and the surrounding community. The greatest offence of the Pinkertons, hired by the railroad company to destroy a gang that has been marauding the middle-border ever since the Civil War, is to have killed Jesse's retarded teenage brother and maimed his mother in an attack on the family home. When they're not robbing trains and banks, the gang are involved in domestic and community activities.

The dour Jesse is a settled family man whose place is at home. He's contrasted with the flamboyant Cole Younger, a long-haired, bearded hedonist and drifter, whose natural habitat is the brothel. The nearest Cole gets to a settled life is the meetings over the years with the prostitute and bandit Belle Starr (Pamela Reed) who bore his child. For this gang the Northfield robbery is to be that traditional movie event – the last big job before retirement. Doom hangs over their lives, and while the movie opens with a slow motion shot of the gang riding in silhouette on the horizon to Ry Cooder's jaunty, folksy fiddle music, a dark tone is emphasised by the numerous scenes set in the rain and in forests, and the long grey cattlemen's dusters and black hats the gang wear as a sort of uniform.

The film relates to the post-Vietnam spirit and the degeneration of the counterculture in the late 1970s. Referring to the Civil War, a badly injured Cole says: 'I spent four years in the army and eleven years trying to get out of it.' Its final image and comment on family life is of Jesse being shot from behind by his latest recruits, the Ford brothers, as he adjusts the sampler 'God bless our home' on his living room wall. They shout out 'I shot Jesse James' as they fire their pistols. At this point the man becomes myth, and the celebrated 'Ballad of Jesse James' plays over the credits. Kaufman's *The Great Northfield Minnesota Raid* denies Jesse this dignified, possibly tragic exit. Instead we see this very sampler in the home of the widow that Jesse is shortly to kill, and as he rides away in drag he's talking hopefully of putting together a new gang and recruiting those promising Ford brothers. *The Long Riders* was shot partly in Georgia, home state of President Carter, and partly in California, home state of his successor.

Ang Lee's *Ride With the Devil* (1999) can be seen as an informal preface to the movies about the James–Younger gang, dealing as it does with the Southern guerrilla bands fighting against Northern irregulars during the Civil War. Set west of the Mississippi it's much closer to a western than to a Civil War movie like *Gone With the Wind* or *Glory*. The Southerners in this bloody sideshow were called Bushwackers, the Northerners Jayhawkers. They were a mixed bunch of schoolboys, farmers, idealists, chancers and psychopaths, and riding with them were men who were to become legendary post-war outlaws, among them the James brothers and the Youngers.

All of the action is seen from the point of view of Jake Roedel

(Tobey Maguire), the decent son of a German immigrant. His father is a Union sympathiser, but out of friendship for Jack Bull Chiles (Skeet Ulrich) Jake joins a band of Bushwhackers, whose first task is to avenge the death of Jack's father, a well-off farmer, killed in cold blood by Jayhawkers. 'Some friendliness may be lost to your kin,' a Union prisoner tells Jake, and shortly thereafter his father is brutally murdered to pay for the sins of his son.

The first ninety minutes of *Ride With the Devil* feature a succession of brilliantly staged ambushes and battles, culminating in the appalling massacre on 21 August 1863 when the charismatic madman William Clarke Quantrill led a small army of 500 southern guerrillas in an attack on the abolitionist community of Lawrence, Kansas. The raid resulted in the deaths of more than 150 innocent male civilians and the town being put to the torch. This sequence invites comparison with the opening of Peckinpah's *The Wild Bunch*, but Ang Lee never resorts to lyrical slow motion. As a dazed Jake wanders through the nightmarish horrors being inflicted around him in Lawrence, he becomes aware of the absurdity of the Civil War and is disgusted by the brutalising effect it has had on him and his comrades in arms. Accompanying him is his new friend, the freed slave Daniel Holt (Jeffrey Wright). Out of allegiance to an aristocratic friend, he has also allied himself to the Southern cause. Only when death ends these commitments can Jake and Holt be liberated.

The 19-year-old Jake has killed fifteen men but never made love to a woman, and the final forty-five minutes of the picture are about his spiritual healing, partly through the kindly agency of Sue Lee (played by the singer Jewel), a sensible twice-widowed woman scarcely more than a year his senior. But the earlier part of the picture is not all fighting. Between the skirmishes there is time out of war around the campfires, in primitive winter quarters, and on visits to sympathetic farmers giving assistance to the Bushwhackers. In these scenes the young southerners reveal themselves as trying to live up to an ideal. They conceive of themselves as chivalrous men of honour, their stylised speech (much of its drawn from Daniel Woodrell's novel, *Woe to Live On*, on which the film is based) stemming from their reading of the King James Bible, Shakespeare and Walter Scott. They are, however, committed to a lost cause, as a landowner explains to them in a forceful address.

As in his *Sense and Sensibility* and *The Ice Storm*, Ang Lee shows himself sensitive to the language and culture of a particular time and place, an uncommon thing in movies made by foreign directors working in Hollywood today. The film convinces both in its feeling for the milieu and in its intense physicality – the pain of gunshot wounds, for instance, and the discomfort of days spent out of doors in inclement weather. Like all Lee's pictures it's about families, real and surrogate, under stress, breaking up and making up, taking in new members. But in this case one of the families involved is the United States itself. So in addition to being a story of friendship, there's a strong political aspect.

The earlier westerns it brings to mind are Robert Benton's *Bad Company* and Eastwood's *The Outlaw Josey Wales*, both made in the 1970s in response to the Vietnam War. Lee's film is something of a commentary on the internecine conflicts of the 1990s, especially those attendant on the end of the Cold War in the former Soviet Union and the former Yugoslavia. America itself, *Ride with the Devil* tells us, went through a similarly painful civil war with its concomitant atrocities and divided loyalties, and though there were moments of glory it was no glorious experience. But people did survive and many of them lived more sensible, sensitive lives as a result. Some of course did not – the James brothers and the Youngers, for instance.

Billy the Kid
The Lincoln County War, a long-running, highly violent, extremely complicated dispute in northeastern New Mexico between 1878 and 1881, was conducted initially between the great cattle baron John Chisum and the businessman Lawrence G. Murphy who had a virtual monopoly of commerce in Lincoln County. It came to involve rival factions of small ranchers and the so-called Santa Fe Ring of corrupt politicians and government officials in the state capital. But it is best known as the backdrop to the short career of the cowhand turned outlaw William Bonney known as Billy the Kid, who was gunned down by his friend turned lawman, Pat Garrett, in 1881 at the age of 22. Billy is second only to Jesse James as a cold-blooded killer transformed by dime novels and popular myth into a folkloric hero who had been driven into a life of crime by social circumstances. Most early screen versions of Billy romanticised him and featured actors too old and too good-looking for the part (even the youthful looking 33-year-old Paul Newman was too old in *The Left Handed Gun*). Probably the only truly realistic treatment of his character is Stan Dragoti's *Dirty Little*

Billy (1972) which dealt with his early, pre-Lincoln County days, with the unprepossessing Michael J. Pollard (the dim-witted C.W. Moss in *Bonnie and Clyde*) portraying him as a seedy, half-sharp psychopath.

On either side of *Dirty Little Billy* came Andrew V. McLaglen's *Chisum* (1970) and Sam Peckinpah's *Pat Garrett and Billy the Kid* (1973). *Chisum* was carefully designed for John Wayne by his producer son Patrick, and the screenwriter Andrew J. Fenady, to express Wayne's political views. Wayne's Chisum, the most powerful man in his part of New Mexico, is a paternalistic capitalist with a true stake in the land standing up for the little people against a predatory business tycoon and distant, conniving bureaucrats. In this context Billy the Kid – a sweet-natured, good-looking, sharp-shooting lad employed by Chisum's ally, John Tunstall – is a minor figure, as is his subsequent nemesis Pat Garrett.

Chisum is a positive, celebratory movie, and I think more highly of it now than I did in 1970, possibly because it was so liked then by Richard Nixon. *Pat Garrett and Billy the Kid* is quite the oppo-site, though only since what seems to be Peckinpah's original cut was discovered in the late 1980s have we been able to judge it prop-erly. (It's 20 minutes longer than the 106-minute version released in 1973).) This elegiac movie takes place after Billy (Kris Kristofferson) has become an outlaw, cut off from both factions involved in the Lincoln County War, and it's about death, corrup-tion and the end of the West. In the restored version it unfolds from the murder of the ageing Garrett (James Coburn) in 1906 in myste-rious circumstances, but suggesting this is something that had been waiting to happen. And we infer that what we see are the dying thoughts and memories of Garrett himself. Everyone involved is preparing to face death, and though Billy and Pat are in one sense victims of the exploitative system that put them on different sides of the law, they are also tragic heroes enacting an unavoidable fate that draws them together.

Kristofferson and Coburn have a weight and nobility that is not to be found in any other treatment of this story, certainly not in the two more recent versions of the Lincoln County War and its after-math, Christopher Cain's *Young Guns* (1988) and Geoff Murphy's *Young Guns II: Blaze of Glory* (1990). In Cain's film Billy Bonney is played by Emilio Estevez as an edgy charmer, fascinated by his growing legend and demonstrating that when the bullets start to fly a near-psychopath might be more useful company than a reasonable citizen. This Billy is just one of the six young 'regulators' employed by the English rancher John Tunstall (Terence Stamp at his most socially and sexually ambiguous) to protect his cattle from the massed forces of the corrupt robber baron Murphy (Jack Palance). Murphy has the territorial governor in his pocket and is backed by the Santa Fe Ring of fellow businessmen in his campaign to monopolise the range. A kindly, almost Dickensian figure, Tunstall is taking these wayward boys in hand, educating them in good citizenship and the responsible use of power. When he's murdered, the young gunslingers first seek to bring his killers to justice, then (egged on by Billy's ferocity and the unyielding opposition) turn to revenge and outright war.

In addition to the well-staged set-pieces, the dusty, wintry, subfusc look (achieved by Dean Semler, among the best western photographers), and the fine ensemble acting, *Young Guns* is probably the most accurate account there has been of the Lincoln County War. It has a narrative coherence lacking in Peckinpah's movie, and situates the characters within the currents of the times. In allegorical terms the film touches, unconsciously perhaps, on American attitudes of the time in which it was made. This was the moment when the presidential baton was passed from Ronald Reagan to George Bush, and Thatcher was the morally dominant figure in the Atlantic alliance, and this seems to be reflected in the relationship between John Tunstall, the patriarchal/matriarchal figure, and his admiring American apprentices.

The sequel, *Young Guns II: Blaze of Glory*, was directed by the New Zealander Geoff Murphy, who had taken the western down under with the Maori War movie *Utu*. His film (scripted by Joe Fusco who wrote *Young Guns* for Christopher Cain and photographed again by Dean Semler) covers much the same ground as Peckinpah's *Pat Garrett and Billy the Kid*. The gracefully staged action sequences are set to music by Alan Silvestri and Jon Bon Jovi, a score much influenced by that of Bob Dylan for Peckinpah's film. Where *Pat Garrett and Billy the Kid* was framed in extended flashback by the death of Pat Garrett in 1908, Murphy's movie begins with a bespectacled old-timer emerging from the New Mexico desert in 1950, claiming to be Billy Bonney. He engages a young lawyer to press for the state pardon Governor Lew Wallace had promised him and reneged on in 1879, and then tells his story about friendship, legend, betrayal and staying alive. Peckinpah makes a definitive statement. *Young Guns II* poses a series of questions. Is the seemingly authentic depiction of frontier life true? Is it the tall tale of a liar, the fantasy of a man who has convinced himself he is Billy?

Tombstone and the Earps

Advertising itself as 'the town too tough to die', Tombstone, Arizona is now a commercialised time capsule that has been saved from being a ghost-town by a single event – the gunfight that took place near the OK Corral on 26 October 1881, lasting a matter of seconds and in which three people were killed and two wounded. The encounter captured the public imagination and was to confer legendary status almost comparable with that of Don Quixote and Sancho Panza on the itinerant lawman Wyatt Earp and his friend, the tubercular gambler, gunfighter and former dentist, Doc Holliday.

The Wyatt Earp myth was given its definitive form in John Ford's *My Darling Clementine* (1945), which I've already mentioned several times. This film, portraying Earp as a wholly good man and his opponents at the OK Corral, the Clanton gang, as irredeemably bad, reflected the hopes of a nation seeking to settle down in peace after World War II, a conflict that was considered as just as it had been long and sacrificial. (To appreciate how good Ford's film is, compare it with Louis King's lacklustre *Powder River*, a 1953 re-working of the same script with names and locations changed so that few people at the time even recognised it as a re-make.) By the 1960s, in *The Hour of the Gun* (1967) and Frank Perry's *Doc* (1971), the events were seen in a realistic, cynical light appropriate to those times. Eventually in the 1990s there was to be a serious revaluation of the Earps and Tombstone.

But the two 90s films were immediately preceded by a nostalgic comedy-thriller that cleverly played with the fact that in his twilight years Wyatt Earp visited Hollywood and may have met the silent cowboy star Tom Mix, who had been born the year before the Gunfight at the OK Corral. In Blake Edwards' *Sunset* (1988), the ex-marshal, now 82 and confidently relaxed, is played by James Garner, who had portrayed him as stern and vengeful in *The Hour of the Gun*, while Mix is impersonated by a genial Bruce Willis. The year is 1929 and the film's villain is a sadistic studio boss called Alfie Alperin (Malcolm McDowell), a cross between Harry Cohn and Charlie Chaplin. The monstrous Alfie compels the flamboyant Mix, one of his contract performers, to make his talking-picture debut as Wyatt Earp, overriding the star's protest that 'I didn't become *numero uno* by being someone else.' As a publicity stunt Alfie engages the former marshal as technical adviser. It transpires that the producer's abused wife (Patricia Hodge) is an old flame of Earp's from Denver, and she persuades him to look into a blackmail threat to her son. But no sooner has the ex-lawman started on his investigation than the boy is accused of murdering the madam of Hollywood's most prestigious brothel, a fancy place where all the whores are parodic lookalikes of movie stars. (Such an establishment existed, and a similar one employs Kim Basinger in a later film knowingly drawing on Hollywood scandals, Curtis Hanson's *LA Confidential* [1997]).

So Earp and his new sidekick Mix go down the mean streets of LA together to help clear the lad, and they're impeded every inch of the way by the industry's front-office men, the local cops and the criminal underworld. Though this is a light-hearted picture, the setting isn't the innocent Hollywood of *Hearts of the West* or *Singin' in the Rain*. Beneath the celluloid glamour and the Art Deco glitter, there is appalling corruption and exploitation of the sort Edwards maliciously observed in *S.O.B.*, his rancid portrait of Hollywood in the 1980s. But the movie manages to be affirmative in a way *S.O.B.* didn't, and this comes from the way Garner plays the 82-year-old Earp as a witty, laconic man of probity and massive dignity, yet with a roguish charm. In the famous distinction made by David Riesman in *The Lonely Crowd*, he belongs to the dying breed of 'inner-directed' men, who answer to personal moral imperatives and principles, as opposed to the 'other-directed' types as represented by the glamorous show-off Tom Mix, who look outside for their values and constantly seek the approbation of contemporaries. At the end Earp travels by train into the sunset and impending death while Mix rides alongside, waving his white ten-gallon Stetson and performing tricks on his horse, Tony.

The 90s films about the Earp family were ambitious works, epic in scope and deeply serious in intent – George Pan Cosmatos's 129-minute *Tombstone* (1993) and Lawrence Kasdan's 189-minute *Wyatt Earp* (1994). *Tombstone* is the least fictionalised account to date of the events leading up to and following the OK Corral shoot-out. No characters are invented though the film conflates the love of Wyatt's life, Josephine Marcus, whom he didn't meet until after he left Tombstone, with an actress known only as 'Clara', who was the subject of contention between Earp and the county sheriff of Tombstone. For the first time a movie identifies the conflict between various competing factions within Tombstone on the one hand, and a group of loose cannons known as 'the Cowboys' on the other. Estimated to number between 30 and 500, this odd confederation of anarchic predators lived by rustling cattle and horses and robbing stagecoaches and miners. They were led by Old Man Clanton and a psychopath with the misleadingly gentle name of Curly Bill Brocius (played with a terrible ferocity by Powers Boothe). The debonair Earps in their fancy city clothes are here presented as opportunistic townees, gamblers and entrepreneurs, as opposed to the wild and raffishly dressed Cowboys who live outside town. The film resembles *The Missouri Breaks* in the way it contrasts two kinds of American violence – that which allies itself with so-called progressive, respectable society and that which opposes it.

At best the Earps are defending the bad against the worse. Finally when the gloves are off and the time of reckoning comes, all civilised constraints are put aside for a climactic bloodletting of a primitive, tribal kind. This isn't the Tombstone of John Ford, it's the cruel world of Leone, Peckinpah and Eastwood.

With an enormous cast of named characters and a labyrinthine plot, Cosmatos' film suggests – intentionally or by accident, through its disjointedness and confusion – the political and moral complexity of the background to the OK Corral. Kurt Russell as Earp is less saintly than Fonda, though less corrupt than Harris Yulin in *Doc*. Clearly by 1993 a man can have many flaws yet remain a romantic hero. The film was made shortly after Eastwood's *Unforgiven* and after the election of Bill Clinton, seen at the time as charismatic but flawed, and later to retain his heroic status after the revelations of behaviour that in earlier times would have destroyed his reputation. Val Kilmer's Doc is a reckless, dangerous character, as always a foil to the calculating Earp, and much is made (as in *Hour of the Gun*) of Earp's presence at his deathbed in a Colorado sanatorium in 1887. There are hints that their relationship is the legend's true love story. A tale initially told in black and white, then in various shades of grey, can now have its touches of pink.

None of *Tombstone*'s principal actors had been in a western before, but the producers dotted the background with some notable old-timers. Robert Mitchum handles the narration, Charlton Heston plays an elderly rancher, and most significantly the 73-year-old Harry Carey Jr., a former member of John Ford's repertory company, appears as the elderly sheriff whose death at the hands of Curly Bill Brocius brings Wyatt Earp into the fray. His father, Harry

Carey, was born the year silver was discovered at Tombstone, and he appeared in Ford's first film, knew Wyatt Earp in Hollywood, and played a character based on Earp in the 1932 movie *Law and Order*.

Like *Tombstone*, Lawrence Kasdan's *Wyatt Earp* is a handsomely designed, realistic film that sets out to locate Earp in the context of his times. The film begins in sombre fashion as Earp (played by Kevin Costner as simultaneously ordinary and charismatic) sits in a Tombstone saloon before going out to face the Clanton gang at the OK Corral. As he rises to join his brothers and Doc Holliday (Dennis Quaid), Kasdan cuts back to 1863 and the 15-year-old Wyatt on his father's farm in Iowa, dreaming of glory and envying his brothers fighting with the Union army. His efforts to join them are frustrated by his father (Gene Hackman), a stern Protestant patriarch whose wanderlust is part of an incurable belief in the beauty of life west of the Mississippi. In addition to this belief in the infinite promise of the West, Dad instils in Wyatt three precepts, all of which might be seen as expressing the political and social beliefs, still very much in the air, of Ronald Reagan and his British mentor, Margaret Thatcher. First, that family is everything, the rest of society are strangers. Second, that the law is all that holds a society together. Third, that when confronting vicious men you must strike first.

After drifting around the post-Civil War frontier, Wyatt settles into a quiet married life back in Midwestern Missouri, aiming to be a lawyer. But when his pregnant wife dies of typhoid, he turns to drink and horse-thieving in Arkansas Territory, and is saved from the gallows by his father. He heads west again in search of redemption, reconstructed as a 'deliberate man', his heart hardened. In an odd way this development has parallels with the career of George W. Bush.

The first hour of *Wyatt Earp* is the most considerable and original part of a lengthy film that is nearly halfway through by the time Earp strikes up his odd friendship with the amoral Doc Holliday. Quaid plays Doc, the aristocratic Southerner, as a man of mordant wit and with a death wish. He gives depth and style to the role. Kasdan begins to rush things when Earp gets to Tombstone, and Cosmatos's movie is clearer on the town's politics, fairer to the Earps' enemies, and better on the extraordinary character of the place itself. But the accumulation of telling social and psychological detail in Kasdan's picture is remarkable, and both films are unflinching in the way they show the Earp wives (most of them former prostitutes) being treated as chattels. And both are unromantic in their handling of violence. The young hero in *Wyatt Earp* vomits after seeing a messy gunfight in a dusty cow town. Yet both Cosmatos and Kasdan avoid the cynicism usually found in revisionist westerns.

Ultimately a question mark hangs over Kasdan's Earp, and in a touching coda set at the turn of the century, the ageing ex-marshal approaches Alaska by sea, still searching for his El Dorado, and a young man approaches him and his third wife to raise memories of Tombstone. In this scene homage is once more paid to *The Man Who Shot Liberty Valance* and the questions Ford raised in that film about fact and legend.

7 The Modern West

The two films set in the West of the relatively recent past that are closest to being actual westerns in the conduct of the characters and the gunplay are both about soldiers returning from World War II hoping to find life unchanged: Alan J. Pakula's *Comes a Horseman* (1978) and Stephen Frears' *The Hi-Lo Country* (1998).

Comes a Horseman is well underway before we discover that this is not the Old but the New West. The opening military funeral that two horsemen pass by is for the son of a local cattle baron (Jason Robards). The boy's body has been brought back from a World War II battlefield to this remote corner of Montana. (This is odd, because in reality soldiers were customarily buried where they fell, but maybe this is gestural or metaphoric.) The time is 1945, the Russians are approaching Berlin. A modest homesteader, Ella (Jane Fonda), and a recently discharged veteran (James Caan) wounded in action, to whom she has sold a small parcel of land, are standing out against the ruthless cattle king's attempt to take them over. Provided they can round up enough stock each year to sell at seven cents a pound, they can survive.

This is a commercial range war, because Robards has over-reached himself to maintain the extensive spread created by his grandfather after the Civil War. He is now the vassal of an oil company that seeks to exploit the valley's mineral resources in anti-cipation of the post-war power boom.

The film has the essential elements of a western – cattle-drives, a savage barroom brawl, an open-air hoedown, a climactic show-down, a philosophical old-timer (Richard Farnsworth). It also has a lean, tanned Jane Fonda, her hair dangling in a braid behind her Stetson. At 41 she's much the age her father was when he worked with John Ford on *Young Mr Lincoln*, *Grapes of Wrath* and *My Darling Clementine*, and she's powerfully evocative of him in her appearance, posture, and vocal timbre. She has never been more handsome, more appealing.

Fonda's burgeoning love affair with Caan is at the centre of the film. She's a range-reared tomboy, aggressive, stern, tough. He is a veteran of the Italian campaign, gentle, compromising, laconically humorous. 'Lady, you've got balls the size of grapefruit,' he says grudgingly. Their relationship grows to the rhythm of work – she laughs for the first time while they're branding cattle; they first embrace as he mends the farm's wind-pump; they go to bed after rounding up their shared herd following a night-time stampede; they confirm their independence while bargaining with a crafty stock dealer; finally they kill together.

The film is set in a verdant valley in the Rockies beneath a vast, often dangerously lowering sky. The interiors are almost stygian in their darkness. Always, just beyond the frame, danger lurks. We're reminded that Pakula's previous movies are forceful studies of paranoid city life – *Klute*, *The Parallax View*, *All the President's Men* – which were also photographed by the gifted Gordon Willis, the patient, painterly cameraman on this film, and on numerous pictures by Francis Coppola and Woody Allen.

But before he turned director, Pakula produced *The Stalking Moon* (referred to earlier), a fine western directed by his longtime collaborator Robert Mulligan. In this 1969 picture a murderous unseen Apache tracks Gregory Peck and Eva Marie Saint across Arizona. In crucial ways *Comes a Horseman* echoes the earlier film as years go by and different people enter into moral contests for the possession of the land.

The Hi-Lo Country was a cherished project of Sam Peckinpah that he never got to make, and the script (adapted from former cowboy Max Evans' 1961 novel by Walon Green, who wrote *The Wild Bunch*) eventually ended up in the competent hands of Stephen Frears. The film is about two close friends from New Mexico, both cowboys, the roistering extrovert Big Boy (Woody Harrelson) and the quiet, introspective Peter (Billy Crudup), who volunteer for military service immediately after Pearl Harbor. Big Boy serves in the Pacific with the Marines, Peter joins the army and goes ashore at Omaha Beach, and they don't meet again until they return home in 1945 to a much-changed West. The area is now dominated by ranch owner Jim Ed Love (the suave, gravel-voiced Sam Elliott), a hard-faced man who's done well out of the war, having used the profits from the high cost of beef to buy out local outfits. He drives a white Cadillac, regards himself as a businessman and employs Big Boy's weak brother.

Big Boy and Pete refuse to sell their small spreads to Big Ed and become his hired hands. Instead they join forces, for independence and smaller rewards, with a traditional rancher (James Gammon) so they can drive cattle to railheads rather than put them on trucks. The movie looks unflinchingly at the restrictive life of the cowboy, largely confined to brawling, boozing, gambling and chasing women. But it also sees what is attractive – the graceful practice of traditional skills, the camaraderie of the range, and the landscape in which it is conducted. 'This is what I was born to do,' says Pete. The movie has a dark brooding quality similar to that of *Comes a Horseman*, and there's a lot of pain in it. Pete, starting with the opening credits, is doomed to a lifetime of being bruised and scarred through falls, fights and encounters with barbed wire, while Big Boy is haunted by the belief that like his father and grandfather before him he's doomed to die a violent death.

The film has an elegiac quality, underlined by the presence as a fortune teller of the 72-year-old Katy Jurado, who stoically watched her men die in a succession of westerns from *High Noon* to *Pat Garrett and Billy the Kid*. The film is dedicated to Frears' mentor Lindsay Anderson, author of an affectionate monograph on John Ford, and to his late friend, the independent filmmaker Maurice Hatton, whose best known movie, *Long Shot* (in which Frears makes a brief appearance) is about an attempt to produce a picture in Scotland called 'Gulf and Western', an action movie about oil-rig workers in the style of Howard Hawks.

Possibly more ambitious but less successful than these two are a couple of films set in the modern West, one rather earlier, the other slightly later in the century, both based on books by notable Western novelists – Edward Zwick's *Legends of the Fall* (1994), adapted by Susan Shilliday and Bill Wittliff (co-screenwriter on *Lonesome Dove*) from Jim Harrison's novel, and Billy Bob Thornton's *All the Pretty Horses*, adapted by Tom Tally from the novel of Cormac McCarthy.

Legends of the Fall is a sprawling, self-consciously lyrical family saga that recalls those romantic silent movies such as *The Four Horseman of the Apocalypse* and *The Big Parade* about young men volunteering to serve in World War I, known until 1941 as the Great War. It also illuminates the background to the atrocities by backwoods defenders of American values committed in Oklahoma City shortly before the film opened. It suggested that the perpetrators, far from representing some unfathomable aberration, are an extreme embodiment of something deep in the American grain. Around 1890 the patriarchal Colonel Ludlow (Anthony Hopkins) resigns from the US Cavalry in disgust over the Federal

Government's betrayal of the Indians, and settles in Montana to escape a loathsome civilisation. When his prim wife returns to the East, he is left to raise their three sons as free spirits, in close touch with the land and Indian lore.

But in 1914, on the outbreak of the Great War, and against their father's wishes, they enlist in the Canadian army. A young Boston woman (Julia Ormond) becomes successively the fiancée of the youngest son, who's killed on the Western Front, the lover of the wild middle son, Tristan (Brad Pitt), who leaves her in 1918 to roam the Pacific, and the wife of the reliable eldest, Alfred (Aidan Quinn). The Colonel puts a curse on Alfred for betraying the family's independence by becoming a Congressman in Washington, and when the idolised Tristan returns in the early 1920s his father encourages him to restore the family fortunes by defying Prohibition to become a big-time bootlegger.

At the end, Alfred and his father are reunited by jointly killing a policeman, a sheriff and a local politician who come to the ranch to arrest Tristan for murder. The charismatic Tristan lives on for a further forty years, settling in the woods as a heroic renegade, an inspiration no doubt to the Montana militia. The values and behaviour of the Ludlow clan go unchallenged in this humourless, unironic, seemingly unintentionally revealing work. Wrestling with grizzly bears is what manhood is about, the film states, not wrestling with moral dilemmas and historical contradictions.

All the Pretty Horses is set like *The Hi-Lo Country* in the aftermath of World War II and involves two young men dedicated to the traditional cowboy life, knowing it is soon to end. The movie also has Penélope Cruz, in a similar role to the one she plays in Frears' film, as a fetching heroine constrained by the conventions of Hispanic family life. After John Grady Cole (Matt Damon) discovers he isn't to inherit the family's ranch in West Texas, he heads south to Mexico with his friend, Lacey Rawlins (Henry Thomas), in search of adventure, and on the way they reluctantly admit to their company the stubborn teenage runaway Lucas Black (Jimmy Blivens). During a storm Lucas loses his horse and in attempting to retrieve it from a band of Mexicans he disappears into the night. For Mexicans, going north and crossing the Rio Grande is a journey towards economic liberation. Traditionally, in literature and drama at least, to go south across the Rio Grande is for American citizens to be liberated from puritanical Anglo-Saxon repression, but also to enter a dark and dangerous world – old, Catholic, superstititious.

Cole and Rawlins are warmly received by a wealthy landowner, Rocha (Rubén Blades), who commutes by private plane from Mexico City to a vast ranch that has been in his family since the eighteenth century. Impressed by Cole's way with horses, Rocha gives them jobs. But Cole becomes entangled with Rocha's daughter Alejandra (Penélope Cruz), and this leads to their employer getting them arrested for horse theft and murder, crimes actually committed by their erstwhile companion Lucas while trying to recover his horse. In fact the boys had been intending to steal the sixteen mustangs that, in a beautiful sequence, they break in during four hectic days, winning the admiration of their Mexican colleagues.

After being made to confront the killing of Black by a vindictive, corrupt police captain, Cole and Rawlins are thrown into a horrendous penitentiary to undergo a purgatorial experience that ends with the near-death of Rawlins in a fight and Cole killing a thug in self-defence. After their release, further trials confront them, including Alejandra's renunciation of Cole, before the two young men are reunited back in Texas on a near-derelict homestead that symbolises both the reality of their failure and the triumph of their spirit. The movie sticks quite closely to the novel, and takes in a deal of the terse dialogue embedded in McCarthy's often purple prose. It is also superbly photographed with lyrical images of horses galloping free, of riders dwarfed by the mountains around them or shown in their smallness in the landscape that stretches out before them. But the performances lack depth and definition, and the action is frequently abrupt, oddly paced, and sometimes mystifying, probably because over an hour was removed from director Billy Bob Thornton's original three-hour cut.

Surprisingly, Robert Redford never returned to the historical western after *Butch Cassidy and the Sundance Kid* and *Tell Them Willie Boy is Here*, but he did appear in Sidney Pollack's *The Electric Horseman* (1979) and directed and starred in *The Horse Whisperer* (1998), based on a best-selling novel by the British author Nicholas Evans. The better of the two by some way is *The Electric Horseman*, which borrows themes and incidents from several downbeat modern westerns of the 1960s – tales of doomed present-day cowboys like *The Misfits* and *Lonely Are the Brave* – and treats them in the optimistic manner of Frank Capra's populist comedies of the 1930s. Redford plays Sonny Steele, a drunken ex-rodeo star engaged to promote the Ampco Corporation's Ranch Breakfast cereal on the big trail around supermarkets and shopping malls. The latterday East Coast journalist waiting to be softened by his brand of folksy sincerity (the Jean Arthur character of the New Deal era) is played by Jane Fonda. She's a New York TV reporter visiting Las Vegas to cover an Ampco sales convention where Sonny is scheduled to ride another tame animal from the conglomerate's 'Stable of Corporate Symbols', a thoroughbred racehorse called Rising Star, at Caesar's Palace.

Finding that the beast is as full of tranquillisers and steroids as he himself is of booze, the disgusted Sonny rides the stoned creature out of the casino, and down the neon-lit Vegas strip. Then he unplugs the apparatus that makes the pair of them look like a mobile Christmas tree, and heads through the dark into the Nevada desert, bent on giving Rising Star his freedom among the wild mustangs of Utah. Sonny's employers go berserk, and the boss (played by John Saxon in the kind of rimless glasses associated in the movies with the Gestapo) orders a vast manhunt. But the ingenious journalist tracks him down and joins forces with the fugitive to exploit his rebellion on the air and to assist his mission. This canny film plays off nicely its conventional contrasts – the gutsy individuals against the faceless conglomerate, the pristine grandeur of the Western landscape against the vulgar excrescence of Vegas, the horse against the automobile, the honest outlaw against the corrupt lawmaker. There's enough irony and reticence to keep excessive sentimentality at bay, while the movie asserts that sometimes you *can* beat City Hall, and that, contrary to the title of an earlier Pollack picture, sometimes they *don't* shoot horses.

The Horse Whisperer is an altogether more solemn affair with a monumentally self-regarding performance from Redford who's frequently shot with the sun catching his hair from behind to give him the appearance of a saint or a Greek god. The story is in effect much like *The Electric Horseman* in the way it pits the city (artificial, corrupt) against the country (natural, honest) through the characters of Annie (Kristin Scott Thomas), an Englishwoman editing a smart New York monthly, and Tom Booker (Redford), a Montana cowboy who 'helps horses with people problems'. This is conjoined with the therapeutic mysticism of the West that's found in Michael Cimino's *The Sunchasers* and a couple of Oliver Stone pictures (*The Doors*, *Natural Born Killers*) where the heroes commune with Indian shamans.

Leaving her husband in Manhattan, Annie brings her 13-year-old daughter Grace (Scarlett Johansson), crippled after a horrendous riding accident, and the traumatised horse, Pilgrim, to the West to meet this legendary healer. We never actually hear him whisper to the horse, though at one crucial moment he does say to Pilgrim: 'There's something you've got to do tomorrow.' Predictably, he gets the horse on his feet, Grace back into the saddle and Annie to see the limitations of her big city ways. Tom and Annie fall in love, but never get any further than a moonlight kiss and some close dancing at a hoedown. Tom, it transpires, is too much in love with his ex-wife, a Chicago cellist. 'When she played, something went right through me,' he recalls. It is rumoured there were two endings of the screenplay, one where the relationship was consummated and one where it wasn't.

The chief redeeming feature of this posturing movie is its physical beauty – the splendour of the valleys and mountains, the sense of America's awesome size, the texture of wood and saddle leather, the sheen of the horses' flanks, the weathered faces of the ranchers, all superbly photographed by Robert Richardson. That the audience might think the film looks a trifle like a commercial is anticipated when Annie's husband asks her over the phone: 'How are you doing out in Marlboro country?' One of the film's most striking dramatic moments occurs on the New Yorkers' drive to Redford's ranch as they stop to contemplate the monument at Little Big Horn commemorating Custer's Last Stand.

Unquestionably, however, the most significant movie where the West of the present is linked to that of the past is John Sayles' *Lone Star* (1996), one of his series of panoramic films on different areas of America that began with *City of Hope* (1991) on a rust-belt town in New Jersey, and has continued with *Limbo* (1999) about Alaska, and *Sunshine State* (1902) on the progress of a city in Florida. The interconnectedness of the citizens in *City of Hope* was shown by starting a shot on one person and then switching to another as they pass in the street. In *Lone Star*, which takes place in a small Texas community near the Mexican border, the seamless connection between past and present is demonstrated by the camera panning from 1995 to 1957 without a cut or a dissolve, a technique brought to a fine art by Theodor Angelopoulos in *The Travelling Players* (1975). It's a film about history, as well as a thriller, and all the violence is in the past. It begins with two men in the arid countryside on a disused army rifle range; it ends with a man and a woman looking at the blank screen of an abandoned drive-in cinema.

Between these striking images of nature being allowed to reclaim land on which its despoilers have left strange clues of their presence, Sayles subtly examines the interrelated lives of three families over forty years, and the way they embody the experience of Texas since the first settlers arrived. One family is Anglo, one African-American, one Hispanic. Each group is competing to claim their own place in the area's history and Sayles's aim – to some extent didactic – is to suggest that they have a shared culture.

The two men in the opening scene discover a skull, a corroded sheriff's star and a masonic ring that belonged to Charlie Wade (Kris Kristofferson) a corrupt, racist sheriff hated by the blacks and Hispanics, who vanished in 1957. Wade was succeeded by his deputy, Buddy Deeds (Matthew McConaughey), a racist lawman, who thanks to his political acumen was regularly re-elected until his death in 1991, surviving through a period of unprecedented social change. The .45 slug found beside Wade's body may have come from Buddy's Colt. Investigating the murder is the present sheriff, who happens to be Buddy's son, Sam Deeds (Chris Cooper). He'd left town to escape his oppressive father and recently returned after his marriage broke up. Also involved are the Hispanic schoolteacher Pilar (Elizabeth Pena) who was Sam's childhood sweetheart, and Colonel Del Payne (Joe Morton), the black commandant of a nearby fort, shortly to be closed. Wade had murdered Pilar's father and persecuted Payne's bar-owner father.

Substantial performances and the patient way Sayles develops his detective story keep *Lone Star* from becoming overly schematic, and the film is both a dissertation on history and a clever spin on the Oedipus myth. The great pleasure the film gives us comes as much from the issues that are left unresolved as from the overall symmetry.

Over the years there has developed a new genre that might be called 'The Las Vegas Movie' in which one might see a continuation of the western and frontier history. In what is generally accepted as the first great western of the sound era, John Ford's *Stagecoach* (1939), the representative cross section of nineteenth-century Americans making their journey across Arizona from Tonto to Lordsburg are seen off from their point of departure by smug, censorious members of the Ladies of the Law and Order League who are there to drive Dallas, the prostitute, out of town. Who, Ford and his screenwriter Dudley Nichols imply, would wish to live in a place run by them? But they can be seen, historically at least, to have won the contest.

The chief male recreations of the West – drinking, gambling, consorting with whores – were to be banned in most parts of the United States. They continued to exist in the western (the whore usually disguised as a saloon queen) as part of the male-dominated communal centre of every movie cow town, contrasted with the countervailing female-dominated institution, the church. The nostalgic fantasies generated by the saloon are among the genre's appeal, and they were eventually to be realised in real life in the casinos of Las Vegas. In 1910 it had a population of under a thousand, in 1945 it had grown to 24,000, and today to over a million.

The whore, the gambler and the provider of liquor from *Stagecoach* are all there in Las Vegas, as is the outlaw in the form of Bugsy Siegel and the Mafia, who helped create the modern Vegas, and the crooked banker who assisted them. In a sense Las Vegas is just the western saloon writ large, a kitschy, neon-lit cow town in Nevada, and in its demands on the land in terms of power and water it's an ecological disaster. Movies set there are therefore modern westerns. And a movie like Martin Scorsese's *Casino* (1995) which traces the development of Las Vegas from a crime-ridden place with its own frontier conventions to a centre of family entertainment run by anonymous conglomerates, recapitulates the domestication of the frontier that is the central thrust of the western.

8 Transpositions and Displacements

Copies and echoes of westerns and commentaries on them continue to turn up everywhere. Some are very straight-forward. Peter Hyams's sci-fi *Outland* (1981) is a more or less direct transposition of *High Noon* to a nasty little titanium mining town on Io, one of the moons of Jupiter in the late twenty-first century. Grizzled lawman Sean Connery stumbles across a conspiracy between the mine's conglomerate owners and the galactic underworld to increase production by supplying the workers with drugs. They despatch a pair of hit men to kill Connery, and like Marshal Kane's wife in *High Noon*, his spouse deserts him, taking their son back to earth, leaving only a hard-bitten, middle-aged doctor (the splendid Frances Sternhagen in the Walter Brennan role) to support him. The killers are coming on the next space shuttle and the countdown starts – though here it is by digital clock over several days, rather than by pocket watch over ninety minutes. By fascinating synchronicity, *Outland* opened in Britain in a week of major political crisis, when President Reagan struck back at President Gaddafi after the Libyan airforce had foolishly invited massive retaliation from the American Mediterranean fleet off the North African coast. Science fiction and the western were conjoined, as high technology and what the critical European press called 'cowboy diplomacy' were brought to bear on Libya.

Some instances are quite bizarre. Wisit Sasanatieng's *Tears of the Black Tiger*, for instance, among the first Thai movies to get a proper release in Britain. The film brings together the western, the all-stops-out Bollywood action movie, and the popular Thai movie genre of fifty years ago known as *Raberd poa, Khaow pao kratom*, which apparently translates as 'Bomb the mountains, Burn the huts'. The setting is the now distant mid-twentieth century, though like many Hollywood B-westerns of the 30s and 40s featuring Gene Autry and Roy Rogers where cars and horses co-existed, there's no distinction between the present and a mythical past. The film's heroes, bandits recruited from the peasant class, dress in fancy clothes as if working on a dude ranch or playing in a blue grass band. Their enemies – chiefly the police – carry machine guns, fire bazookas, drive jeeps and wear uniforms that resemble those of Mexican Federales. The hero, a bandit known as Black Tiger, courts the gorgeous daughter of a rich landowner, who prefers her to go out with a police captain who drives an MG. There are references to *Once Upon a Time in the West*, and pastiche Morricone in the eclectic score that includes part of Dvorak's *New World Symphony* and Thai love songs. The violence is deliberately excessive, clearly influenced by Sam Raimi's *The Quick and the Dead*, and a deal of the action is set against outlandishly painted backdrops and shot in garish acid colours, recalling old Asian movie posters, The overall effect is hallu-cinatory for European audiences, as if we're experiencing someone else's druggy dream.

Then there's the British comedy, directed by Richard Eyre from a screenplay by the actor Brian Glover, *Laughterhouse* (1984), the unpromising title of which ('Slaughterhouse' without the 'S') is as laboured as the film itself. Eyre had previously directed *The Ploughman's Lunch* (1983), one of the best 'Thatcher's Britain movies', brilliantly criticising the social and moral ethos of the 1980s. If she ever saw it, Thatcher would have loved *Laughterhouse*, a union-bashing film that opened during the miners' strike of the mid-80s. Its hero is a prosperous East Anglian farmer called Singleton (Ian Holm), who decides to drive his Christmas geese from Norfolk to Smithfield market in London on foot when the Transport and General Workers Union boycott him after an employee has been injured by a plucking machine. The movie's tone is Ealingesque, and in fact a comic re-working of Howard Hawks' *Red River* with the maverick Singleton replacing John Wayne's Texas rancher Tom Dunson. At the beginning of the journey Wayne's famous line to Montgomery Clift's Matthew Garth, 'Take them to Kansas, Matt', becomes 'Take them to London, Hubert', addressed to his chief farm hand (Richard Hope), who has donned a Stetson for the journey. The comparison with *Red River* that Eyre and Glover invite results in the realisation that taking Wayne out of the West and replacing him with a diminutive English farmer makes for a sad commentary on the small, unheroic nature of present-day British life. If the film had managed to put a smile on our faces, this would take it off.

Before going to Hollywood to direct *Young Guns II*, Geoff Murphy made an impressive if uneven film in his native New Zealand, *Utu* (1983), which draws closely on the western with clear thematic and stylistic debts to John Ford, as well as to Robert

Aldrich's *Apache* and *Ulzana's Raid*. But it is well rooted in his own country's history and tells, through vigorously staged action sequences, the story of a disgusted Maori sergeant (Anzac Wallace) breaking away from a vindictive British army to lead a ferocious insurrectionist movement after his family have been slaughtered in 1870. The title is Maori for 'retribution'.

After he'd directed *Lonesome Dove* in the States, Simon Wincer returned to Australia to make *Quigley Down Under* (1990), which like a number of Australian films before it – from *The Overlanders* to *The Chant of Jimmy Blacksmith* – consciously draws on the western. This is altogether more thoroughgoing than its predecessors and stars Tom Selleck, sporting a Buffalo Bill-like goatee, as gunslinger Matt Quigley coming from 1880 Wyoming to the Australian outback in response to an advertisement for the world's best long-distance rifleman. But the evil rancher Marston (a black-coated patrician played by Alan Rickman with the same relish he brought that year to the Sheriff of Nottingham in *Robin Hood: Prince of Thieves*) has hired him to exterminate Aborigines, not to keep down dingoes. Matt immediately throws his employer through the window and casts in his lot with the threatened natives.

Quigley Down Under eschews subtlety, but the action set-pieces are handled with some flair and the awesome landscape of the Northern Territories is powerfully utilised. The American screenwriter John Hall puts the Australians in the clear by making the genocidal villains British, and Quigley's attitude towards the Aborigines is so impeccable that the movie might well have been called 'Waltzes with Wallabies'.

A good many traditional Bombay movies borrow the techniques of Hollywood westerns and thrillers. But by some way the most impressive Indian film to apply lessons learnt from the western to local subject matter is Shekhar Kapur's *Bandit Queen* (1964). The film tells the true story of Phoolan Devi, the village girl from the impoverished state of Uttar Pradesh, who rebelled against her humiliating treatment as a low caste woman and became a dacoit or bandit. During the four years before her surrender to the authorities in 1983, she rose to command an outlaw band and exacted terrible revenge on those who used rape as a political weapon to degrade her, and she brought hope and pride to the exploited and downtrodden. The movie in its ferocity and its sharp, sympathetic observation of rural folkways is like a collaboration between Sam Peckinpah and Satyajit Ray, and the landscape is a lot like the

Mexico of *The Wild Bunch*. It's also about the creation of an outlaw hero along the lines of Robin Hood and Jesse James, and Kapur and his screenwriter, Mala Sen, use Phoolan's career to anatomise a whole society, the way Francesco Rosi did with the life of a comparable Sicilian social bandit in the Marxist classic, *Salvatore Giuliano* (1961).

In this new century's crop of westerns, two pick up their Western heroes and take them in different directions, Edward Zwick's *The Last Samurai* (2003) and Joe Johnston's *Hidalgo* (2004). Both manage simultaneously to express disgust at the treatment of Native Americans on the frontier, and yet demonstrate Yankee know-how to their hosts in respectively Asia and the Middle East. These past thirty years young American directors – most recently Jim Jarmusch with *Ghost Dog: The Way of the Samurai*, the Wachowski Brothers with *The Matrix*, and Quentin Tarantino with *Kill Bill* – have been more attracted to Asian martial arts movies than to the western, and Zwick, who directed the excellent Civil War picture *Glory*, is very consciously taking the western in an easterly direction.

His movie opens in San Francisco in the centennial year of 1876, a few weeks after the Indians obliterated Custer's cavalry at Little Big Horn and twenty-five years after Commodore Perry steamed into Tokyo Harbour to open up a major trading area and end centuries of Japanese isolation. Captain Nathan Algren (Tom Cruise), a gallant Civil War veteran disgusted by the racist manner in which the US is destroying the culture of the American Indian, works as an arms salesman and finds relief in liquor. To escape America he accepts a lucrative invitation to teach modern methods of warfare to the Japanese imperial army. But arriving there, he discovers that his task is to defeat the traditional warlords opposed to the Emperor's determination to disarm the samurai and turn Japan into a modern industrial society. His new enemies are in effect the local equivalent of the Indians being destroyed back home. A magnificently staged pitched battle ensues in which Algren's ill-trained troops with their muzzle-loading rifles are routed by a much smaller force of samurai cavalry. Armed with bows and swords, wearing traditional armour and horned helmets, the victors come roaring out of the woods like warriors in a Kurosawa movie. Algren's life is spared by Katsumoto, most feared of warlords (Ken Wanatabe), and in captivity he is converted to the samurais' sacred code of honour and discipline. In return he teaches baseball to the village kids.

The film is in effect a version of those westerns like *A Man Called Horse, Run of the Arrow* and *Dances With Wolves*, where the hero turns against what he comes to see as the shallow, materialistic society in which he is reared, and embraces a supposedly primitive but in fact much richer culture. Zwick brings a grand epic style to this somewhat simplistic material, and as in *Glory* and *Legends of the Fall* is attracted to the notion of victory-in-defeat and the romantic purity of self-sacrifice.

Hidalgo, also vaguely based on a true story, follows a similar dramatic trajectory but in another direction. A cavalry scout and crack horseman, Frank Hopkins (Viggo Mortensen), witnesses the massacre of the Sioux at Wounded Knee in 1890 and, as he delivered the message that helped trigger it off, is plagued by guilt. He takes to drink and becomes a self-disgusted performer in Buffalo Bill's Wild West Show, which has become in the western a symbol of the misrepresentation and degradation of the frontier experience. Hopkins then finds redemption in participating in a gruelling 3,000-mile horse race across the desert from Aden to Damascus. Hopkins is half-Indian and his mustang Hidalgo is a 'wild horse of the plains' up against great Arab thoroughbreds.

Hidalgo is an odd cross between a traditional western, a racetrack movie like *Seabiscuit, Lawrence of Arabia* (inevitably evoked by the presence of Omar Sharif as a grand sheikh) and those old Hollywood Arabian Nights movies starring Valentino and Maria Montez, in which Arabs begin every sentence with the fateful phrase, 'It is written...'. This adventure yarn virtually ignores the politics of its time with not a hint of the Turkish presence in the Middle East, though there are references to British involvement in local intrigues. In fact it would be easy to present the film as a double-edged allegory about America today and its relationship to Europe, the Arab world and its own ethnic minorities. In a picture that deals largely in clichés, myths and stereotypes, we are invited to find amusing the fact that Omar Sharif's sheikh is in thrall to the legends of the Earps, Wild Bill Hickok and the heroes of the West. While he talks like something out of a stilted translation of the *Arabian Nights*, his favourite reading is Beadle's Dime Novels.

9 Native Americans

On the whole recent movies about contemporary life among American Indians have been disappointing. Potentially fascinating, Franc Roddam's *War Party* (1989) turns on the re-staging at a small town Labor Day rally in Montana of a massacre that occurred a hundred years ago when the US Cavalry confronted the Blackfoot Indians, with local Indians re-enacting their forefathers' roles. Once again violence ensues as racial tensions explode, there are killings and some young braves take to the hills and are pursued by the police. The subject is marvellous, more pertinent than *Dances With Wolves*, one of whose Native American actors, Rodney Grant, appears here, but the writing, acting and direction fall short of the mark.

Of equal interest but just as disappointing is John Woo's *Windtalkers* (2002), based on the true story, long buried in military archives for reasons of national security, of Navajo Indians used by the US army during World War II as front-line wireless communicators or 'codetalkers' because the Japanese couldn't decipher messages in their tribal language. The movie opens splendidly with a montage of the buttes and mesas of Monument Valley, a rare occasion that this unique corner of the West is seen as the home and possession of the Indians rather than their subjugators. But the star roles in the film go not to Native American actors but to a pair of Marine Corps sergeants – a cheerful extrovert and a traumatised hero played by Christian Slater and Nicolas Cage – who are assigned as minders of the front-line Navajo messengers, charged with killing them should they come near to capture. Woo presumably set out to up the World War II ante on the realism of *Saving Private Ryan* and *The Thin Red Line*. But the film deals crudely with the relationship between the xenophobic marines and the stoical Indians thrust into their midst, and is as cliché-ridden as any Errol Flynn picture made during World War II.

Both these movies were made by non-Americans, and the same is true of a pair of movies of a more accomplished kind by the British filmmaker Michael Apted, the fiction film *Thunderheart* and the feature-length documentary, *Incident at Oglala*, which appeared together in 1992. Like his slightly older French contemporary Louis Malle, Apted (famous for his on-going TV series *7 Up*) has profitably alternated between documentaries and features. *Incident at Oglala* focuses on the conflict in the 70s between political activists and corrupt tribal leaders on the Oglala Sioux reservation, South Dakota, and the murky role played out there by the federal agencies. His outstanding 90-minute documentary is gripping, lucid, disturbing, though perhaps slightly marred by unnecessarily dramatised moments.

Apted's commercial movie, *Thunderheart*, is merely the latest of numerous well-meaning entertainments seeking a text, or pretext, through which to look at contemporary reservation life and the injustices experienced by Native Americans. The central character is a gung-ho FBI agent, Ray Levoi (Val Kilmer), chosen because he is part-Sioux to investigate the murder of an Indian at Pine Ridge in the 1970s. He finds himself in the middle of a civil war between venal Indian politicians and the Aboriginal Rights movement and uncovers a federal plot to divide and rule the Indians.

John Fusco's screenplay is perfunctory in its plotting and overloaded with information, most of which is unfamiliar to a popular audience. But the film is sustained by solid performances, especially from Sam Shepard as an experienced FBI field officer determined to lead the naive Ray astray, and from Graham Greene, now ubiquitous in westerns, as a Sioux tribal policeman who puts Ray on the right track. (Even Greene, however, can't get away with such sententious lines as 'There ain't no word in Sioux for goodbye.') The movie also has an authoritative look (the cinematographer is Britain's Roger Deakins), and the visual contrast between the stark beauty of the Badlands and the squalor of the Indian communities needs no verbal underlining.

It was of course a movie dealing with Native Americans, Kevin Costner's *Dances With Wolves* (1990), that announced the modest revival of the western in the early 1990s, though during its production, when it over-ran its budget and shooting schedule, show-business writers with their predilection for *schadenfreude* prematurely dubbed it 'Kevinsgate'. Costner has said that he fell in love with the genre at the age of seven when he saw James Stewart as the mountain man at the beginning of *How the West Was Won*, perhaps the last western that could be regarded as an unqualified celebration of the making of America, the fulfilment of Manifest Destiny. The trace of this in *Dances With Wolves* is found in the hero's initial aspirations. The film partakes of the negativity of the countercultural westerns of twenty years earlier that turned a jaundiced eye on corrupt white civilisation and embraced the superior life of the Indians that it was destroying. But through Costner's performance as Lieutenant Dunbar (a sturdily named Wasp of Scottish extraction) and his sympathetic treatment of the Sioux, he turned his film into a wholly positive experience that brings to mind an earlier James Stewart movie, the optimistically liberal *Broken Arrow* which launched the 1950s pro-Indian cycle.

In the opening scene, the badly wounded Dunbar performs a suicidal act of heroism that inspires a demoralised company of Union soldiers to take a Confederate position in 1863 Tennessee. His reward is to choose his next posting, and he elects to go West 'to see the frontier before it goes'. His journey resembles those physically and psychologically wounded Hemingway heroes seeking therapy in the wilderness after World War I. As the fastidious, puritanical Dunbar leaves the last dismal remnants of civilisation, its commandant commits suicide from the self-disgust produced by a debilitating war wound, and he proceeds on his journey into Indian country accompanied by a noisome, foul-mouthed trader.

His new post is mysteriously deserted, so with Cisco, his wonder horse, and a neighbourhood wolf for company, Dunbar settles into a disciplined Crusoe-like routine before contacting the Native Americans. They turn out to be as sharply divided as the Brazilians in John Boorman's *The Emerald Forest*. On the one hand, there are the violent, predatory Pawnees, their heads half-shaven, their faces hideously painted, their bodies nearly naked. On the other hand there are the Sioux – long-haired, dignified, eloquent, peaceful, generous, democratic, in touch with their inner selves, the environment and the universe. The film traces the moral journey by which the hero sheds his hollow identity as Lieutenant Dunbar and becomes the honorary Sioux named 'Dances With Wolves'. One of the agents of this change is the forceful widow, Stands With a Fist, a white woman raised by the Sioux after the Pawnees massacred her pioneer family when she was seven. She's played by Mary McDonnell, whose strong jaw, deep voice and large liquid eyes bring to mind Jane Fonda.

Dances With Wolves is long, simplistic, and lacking in irony, though not in generous humour. The action set-pieces (two ambushes, two pitched battles, a grand buffalo hunt) are dynamically handled. The picture lacks the visual authority of the best westerns of, say, Ford, Mann and Peckinpah. But the sincerity of Costner's performance, Dean Semler's handsome photography, John Barry's lush score, and the striking faces of the Indian actors give the film a rich romantic aura that sweeps it along. At first viewing I loved *Dances With Wolves*. The second time around, when I reviewed it, the film seemed sentimental, simple-minded, too easily dismissive of the modern world. Later that same year my enthusiasm was rekindled by the release of a special edition director's cut which restored nearly an hour of material. All of the additional footage was interesting for the way it expanded and clarified character and plot. The important new sequences were the slaughter by the Sioux of the white buffalo hunters, which leads Dunbar to the melancholy conclusion that 'the gap between myself and my new friends was greater than I imagined'. There is also a long trip that Dunbar makes with Kicking Bird, the medicine man, that deepens his understanding of Sioux culture. The sheer length of the special edition contributes to our appreciation of Dunbar's isolation from the European world and his absorption into the indigenous culture.

Quite as good as *Dances With Wolves* is *Geronimo: An American Legend* (1994), the second and best of Walter Hill's three westerns. In the 1939 *Geronimo*, the title role was relatively minor but played by the full-blooded Cherokee actor Victor Daniels, who worked under the name of Chief Thundercloud. In the 1962 picture of the same name, *Geronimo* was played by the Irish-American Chuck Connors, a former baseball star from Brooklyn, with the impassivity of a cigar-store Indian. Hill's film was among the first to give a major role as an Indian chief to a Native American – Wes Studi – though like *Dances With Wolves* (in which Studi also appeared), the film is narrated by a US cavalry officer. Hill and his screenwriters, Larry Gross and John Milius, have the advantage of a well-documented military campaign as well as the autobiography that, through the intervention of President Theodore Roosevelt, Geronimo was able to dictate to a white sympathiser. From this material they have fashioned a tragic story that does justice to the complexities of the central character and his situation. The film is about the confrontation of apparently incompatible societies, and how the government used officers of the US cavalry, the very people most understanding of the Indians, to destroy them.

The writers have taken certain liberties with the facts, all of them justified except for the decision to have the legendary cavalry scout

Al Sieber (well played by Robert Duvall) killed during an 1886 expedition into Mexico rather than in a 1907 quarrying accident. Making palpable the shimmering heat, blinding light and stifling dust of the Southwest, the picture focuses on a climactic period in the mid-1880s between Geromino's flight from the claustrophobic reservation to which he had been assigned by the honourable General Crook (Gene Hackman), and his final surrender to Crook's devious, self-serving successor, General Miles (Kevin Tighe). In an act of racist vindictiveness, Miles fires all his Apache scouts, sending those from Geronimo's tribe to the same Florida concentration camp as the great warrior. 'We won, that's all that matters,' says Miles, a chilling line that evokes many military occasions of more recent times.

Geronimo is neither sentimentalised nor demonised. He's portrayed as a ruthless, embittered man, a guerrilla leader of genius, determined to live a free life roaming a land that has been appropriated by his enemies. He is feared and respected by foes and followers alike, and Wes Studi has a presence that makes convincing the awe with which he is regarded by the young cavalry officers, Lt. Gatewood (Jason Patric) and Lt. David (Matt Damon), who acts as narrator.

Walter Hill is the director of his generation closest to the great filmmakers of Hollywood's Golden Age such as Walsh, Ford and Hawks, and *Geronimo* is probably his finest picture. Certainly it is his most humane. As in most of his movies, the hero is an enigmatic loner living according to the dictates of his conscience and a personal code. The final image is of Geronimo and his followers being deported in a cattle truck. Belching black smoke, the train crosses the desert into the far distance, and we think of other rail journeys in similarly cramped conditions, of ominous smoking chimneys, and a later attempt to exterminate a race of people.

One of the greatest movies ever made, John Ford's *The Searchers*, has cast a long shadow, continuing to influence movies, and not just westerns, from the late 1950s to the present. Wherever there is a story of abduction, of someone, male or female, in need of rescue from the hands of 'the other', whether it be hostile Indians (as in the case of *The Searchers*), kidnappers, bad influences, hostage takers or some other hostile force, there you'll find echoes of Ford's resonantly compelling picture.

In John Milius's *Hardcore* (aka *The Hardcore Life*, 1978), a Midwestern Calvinist father goes in search of his daughter in the porn movie underworld of Los Angeles. In Milius's *The Wind and the Lion* (1975), an American woman and her children are kidnapped in North Africa by an Arab outlaw; in a later film, *Uncommon Valor* (1983), scripted by Milius and directed by Ted Kotcheff, a father spends years searching for his soldier son reported missing in action in Vietnam and discovered to be held in a prison camp in Laos. Martin Scorsese's *Taxi Driver* (1976) stars Robert De Niro as a Vietnam veteran seeking to rescue a teenage prostitute from her Manhattan pimp. George Lucas's first *Star Wars* (1977) begins by recapitulating the opening of *The Searchers* with Luke Skywalker returning to find his adoptive parents killed and their house reduced to ashes. That same year in Spielberg's *Close Encounters of the Third Kind*, there's a search for a child taken by aliens. More recently in Taylor Hackford's *Proof of Life* (2000), the wife of an engineer captured by guerrillas in Latin America hires a professional hostage negotiator to rescue him, and in the animated movie *Finding Nemo* (2003) two adult fish go in search of a baby clownfish, caught by an Australian dentist to exhibit in the tank in his surgery. Both *Uncommon Valor* and *Proof of Life* end by echoing the line that has now entered the language, 'We're going home, Debbie', spoken by John Wayne to his abducted niece Natalie Wood in *The Searchers*. This line also concludes the latest movie that openly acknowledges its debt to Ford's film, Ron Howard's *The Missing*, but here the line is given to a woman. Most recently *The Searchers* has been drawn on for moral support in David Mamet's *Spartan* (2003), where an honourable secret service agent, betrayed by his Washington employers, sacrifices his life and redeems his honour by bringing back to America the President's daughter, who has fallen into the hands of Middle-Eastern white slave traders. 'I'm taking you home,' he says, echoing Wayne's Ethan Edwards, and he does so, though the implications are not that simple.

Shortly before giving up acting for direction, Howard appeared in a couple of westerns as a wide-eyed adolescent, hero-worshipping gunfighters – the bad guy Lee Marvin in *The Spikes Gang*, the good guy John Wayne in *The Shootist*; the two had earlier been on different sides of the traditional moral conflict in *The Comancheros* and *The Man Who Shot Liberty Valance*. Howard must have remembered these roles because *The Missing* pursues these earlier movies and is in the classic tradition. Set in New Mexico in 1885, the year before the final surrender of Geronimo, the film introduces its heroine Maggie (Cate Blanchett) with a close-up of her sitting in half-darkness. It is in fact a privy, a significant situation in westerns since the early 1960s. In the opening scenes a mysterious stranger called Jones (Tommy Lee Jones) turns up at the small ranch where Maggie, a widow with two daughters, ekes out a living with her hired hand lover (Aaron Eckhart) by working as an unqualified doctor and pharmacist.

Initially taken for a Native American, Jones turns out to be Maggie's father, a laconic drifter of mystical bent who deserted his family to live among the Apaches. The presence of her new-found grandfather thrills Maggie's younger daughter Dot (Jenna Bond), who's very much at home on the range. The older daughter, Lilly (Evan Rachel Ward), however, wants to quit the frontier for elegant city life back east of the Mississippi. She loathes this uncouth ancestor. Besides, she's in a bad mood because she's having a difficult period – the first time, I believe, that this condition has been mentioned in a mainstream western.

Suddenly the film's romantic interest is snuffed out as brutally as Janet Leigh is despatched in Hitchcock's *Psycho*. (Leigh, incidentally, appeared in only one western, Anthony Mann's classic *The Naked Spur*, and was nearly killed by James Stewart before she got to speak a word. As the villainous Robert Ryan's crop-haired moll, she was spared when Stewart realised she was a woman.) The handsome Eckhart is atrociously murdered by a ruthless band of renegade Apaches, who abduct Lilly with the intention of taking her across the border and selling her into prostitution in Mexico. Maggie, her trail-wise father and spunky little Dot set out in pursuit. Their journey begins in the snowy north of New Mexico and finishes in the deserts and mountains of the south. It's a familiar moral terrain. There's a terrifying flash flood that nearly sweeps them away, and a succession of violent encounters as the tables are turned and the pursuers become the hunted. Every incident is a test; the journey is an occasion for redemption and reconciliation. This is very much a post 9/11 western.

The film's West, its social detail vividly presented, its awesome landscape memorably captured by the cinematographer Salvatore Totino, is a strange, confused place. An itinerant photographer is among the captives, and the Apache marauders' leader, a witch doctor of ferocious mien with a deep hatred of white men, has a necklace of framed photographs around his neck like a fetish. It is difficult not to identify him with Osama bin Laden. A gramophone salesman enchants the children of the local town with his toy, and a recently installed telegraph brings misinformation about the Apaches' movements. The town's marshal won't help the rescue mission because he's too busy with the visiting fair. A cavalry company is of no assistance because it's going in the wrong direction. Moreover, its commander (a brief appearance by Val Kilmer, advertised as one of the film's stars) has no control over his racist rabble who are more interested in looting abandoned ranches than chasing Apaches.

At the centre of the movie is a clash of cultures – of Christianity and Indian beliefs, of European medicine and tribal healing. But the politically correct sanctimoniousness found in the treatment of Native Americans in liberal westerns of the 1950s is not present here. We are shown the good and bad aspects of both cultures and it is Maggie's father who mediates between the two worlds. Blanchett and Jones are both admirable. His face speaks of inner experience, his scarred body of desperate encounters. She looks as if she's endured freezing winters and scorching summers; her hands bear witness to a life of toil. Jenna Boyd is impressively tough as Dot, but she's not sentimentalised, and both she and her abducted elder sister make mistakes that have disastrous consequences. *The Missing* illuminates and allegorises the America of the new century.

Two important movies of the 1990s dealing centrally with Native Americans belong in the category I have called the pre-western – Bruce Beresford's *Black Robe* (1991) and Michael Mann's *Last of the Mohicans* (1992). When winter comes in *Dances With Wolves*, we do not shiver. The beauty of the snow-covered West seduces us; we know that Costner has his buffalo cloak and his love to keep him warm. In *Black Robe*, a film on the identical theme of an outsider confronting the Native American culture, the winter landscape chills the bone and the spirit, compelling us to share the privations and moral challenges of the protagonist's life in the wilderness. This excellent film, adapted by the Irish-Canadian novelist Brian Moore from his own novel, is set in early seventeenth-century Quebec and concerns a hazardous journey undertaken by a young French Jesuit, Father Laforgue (Lothaire Bluteau), to a remote mission in the tribal territory of the Huron.

Samuel de Champlain, the formidable French explorer and colonial governor, has charged the Algonquin chief, Chomina (August Schellenberg) with guiding this 'black robe' (the American Indian name for a Jesuit priest) to his destination, and the party heads off in seven canoes. From a distance the fragile flotilla resembles iron filings being drawn along by some unseen magnetic force. As a story the film is as engrossing as a Fenimore Cooper adventure. The Algonquins and Laforgue wearily size each other up. The main body of the escort party deserts to winter quarters and the remaining are captured by the merciless Iroquois, then escape to renew their journey. There is even a romance between a French artisan, the only European accompanying Laforgue, and the chief's daughter. But the open sexuality and the ferocious cruelty of the American Indians are treated with relentless realism, while the hope of heaven that the aristocratic Laforgue seeks to bring to them seems increasingly absurd.

The writers *Black Robe* brings to mind are Graham Greene and Joseph Conrad, and the film pursues two major themes that ran through Moore's work since his 1955 debut with *Judith Hearne* – coming to terms with failure, and the acknowledgement of an ebbing Catholic faith, both involving an existence without illusions. Sharply photographed by Peter James (like Dean Semler, who lit *Dances With Wolves*, an Australian), Laforgue's journey takes him into the dark, cold heart of a harsh continent, whose savage inhabitants he aims to convert, and into his tortured conscience, which he has sought to pacify through martyrdom. The Native Americans are encouraged to view the 'black robe' as an evil spirit; Laforgue struggles with the torments of the flesh and terrible theological doubts. Merely to entertain the idea that the integrated American Indian system of belief and behaviour (at once brutal, playful, spartan, magical and poetic) might be a better code for survival and transcendence in this godforsaken terrain would undermine Laforgue's mission.

Bluteau as the lean conscience-stricken Laforgue facing Schellenberg as the confidently totemic Chomina is something to behold, and *Black Robe* creates a convincing historical context for a forceful debate on culture and religion between flesh-and-blood characters. And the end is as remorselessly honest as anything by Samuel Beckett, affirming the social bond that unites all humanity and confirming our existential fate – that each of us is alone in this world.

After starting his literary career with a pastiche of Jane Austen, Fenimore Cooper went on to create the espionage novel with *The Spy* (1821) and the modern sea story with *The Pilot* (1923). More importantly, he launched the western with the five Leatherstocking novels that cover the life, from the 1740s to the early nineteeth century of Natty Bumpo, also known as Hawkeye. This intrepid frontiersman, the orphaned child of Anglo-Scottish immigrants, is raised by the Mohawk chief, Chingachgook, alongside his own son. Cooper's Leatherstocking saga would make a splendid multi-part TV epic, but Michael Mann has settled on the most famous of the novels, *The Last of the Mohicans*, a title that has entered the language. Moreover he has approached the 1826 text by way of Philip Dunne's screenplay for the 1936 Hollywood version, directed by George B. Seitz and starring Randolph Scott as Hawkeye.

The characters remain – Hawkeye (Daniel Day-Lewis); the upright British officer Major Heyward (Steven Waddington); Colonel Monroe's daughters Cora (Madeleine Stowe) and Alice (Jodhi May), fresh from England; Chingachgook (played by the leading Indian activist Russell Means); Uncas (Eric Schweig); and the fiercely vengeful Huron brave, Magua (Wes Studi, later to play the title role in Hill's *Geronimo*), who seeks to destroy Monroe and his family. The time and place are still Upper New York State in the summer of 1757 during the Seven Years War between England and France. As in the novel there are exciting ambushes, battles, chases and rescues; the crucial siege of Fort Henry is brilliantly realised, and there is an appropriately high body count. But most of the book's incidents are re-ordered and the relationships between the characters are considerably changed. Hawkeye and Heyward are now sworn enemies and rivals for the hand of Cora.

Like Ford's *Drums Along the Mohawk*, De Mille's *Unconquered* and other pre-westerns, *The Last of the Mohicans* and *Black Robe* take place in a more remote world historically than the western proper, and because they lack recognisable conventions, considerable thought must be given to matters of speech and period detail. In this respect both films are pretty successful in the presentation of strangers in a strange new world. Moore adopts a formal language for the colonists that contrasts with the breezy vernacular for the Indians, whose speech is rendered in sub-titles and is far less obscene than the dialogue in his novel. Mann's particular success comes through the creation of a a surreal world where a European war is imposed on the American wilderness, the colonial combatants exploiting the natives and the settlers in a conflict to which they have no real commitment. Beyond, or beneath, the official imperial incomprehension, there is a fine sense of the friendly contact between the Indians and the working-class pioneers (a primitive game of lacrosse is an especially nice touch). Hawkeye (his intelligence, vigour and charismatic presence superbly registered by Day-Lewis), the new man who confidently straddles both worlds, speaks an idiomatic modern American; Cora (looking like one of the proud military daughters painted by Gainsborough) speaks in a stylised period idiom.

The weaknesses of *The Last of the Mohicans* are an occasional narrative incoherence and a lack of variety in its hectic pacing. The undifferentiated tone is emphasised by an unusual score (by Randy Edelman and Trevor Jones) that incorporates what sounds like eighteenth-century fiddle music into a modern electronic buzz that numbs as it hums.

10 Eastwood Ho!

Clint Eastwood waited nine years after *The Outlaw Josey Wales*, to direct his next western, *Pale Rider* (1985), and he was only to make one more, *Unforgiven* (1992), before the next century. Nevertheless he has remained the dominant figure in the genre, one of the Mount Rushmore faces of the western, in part because he's been constantly active, and in part because his earlier films – most especially Sergio Leone's 'Dollar Trilogy'- have been re-valued upwards and become classics. When George W. Bush, Vladimir Putin and other leaders of Pacific Rim countries attended the Apec (Asia–Pacific Economic Cooperation) summit in Chile in November, 2004, they were photographed wearing ponchos presented to them by the Chilean prime minister. The newspapers immediately recognised their resemblance to Clint Eastwood in the Leone films and one sub-editor came up with the caption, 'The Bad, the Bad and the Ugly'. It is quite natural that the young hero of *Back to the Future III*, when suddenly transported to the Old West and forced to adopt a *nom de guerre*, should choose the first name that comes into his head – Clint Eastwood. When *Pale Rider* appeared it was as welcome in those western-starved days as the rain at the end of *3.10 to Yuma*, another hopeful movie that likewise partook of the mystical. *3.10 to Yuma*, the story of a redemptive journey, is underpinned by references to the Grail legend. *Pale Rider* takes its title from the Book of Revelations (Ch. 6, v. 8): 'And I looked, and behold a pale horse: and his name that sat on him was Death and Hell followed with him.'

Eastwood himself plays this ethereal eponymous cavalier, another man without a name, known simply as 'Preacher', who rides down from the Sierras as the literal answer to a maiden's prayer. The supplicant teenager is Megan Wheeler (Sydney Penny). Her widowed mother Sarah (Carrie Snodgress, her lined face reflecting a hard-won probity) and the mother's dour lover, Hull Barret (Michael Moriarty), are the leaders of a small Californian gold-mining community threatened by the local land baron Lahood (Richard Dysart), whose inefficient thugs menace the newcomers and whose proficient, ecologically barbarous, hydraulic mining system is destroying the land. Preacher's presence, resolution and populist rhetoric ('only by standing together are you going to be able to break the Lahoods of this world') unites and incites the miners. So Lahood calls in a notorious gunfighter, Marshal Stockburn (John Russell), who arrives with six deputies in tow, all identically dressed in ankle-length dusters and Stetsons. Stockburn (a name richly suggestive of cattle, capital and destruction) recognises Preacher as a man he once knew and, we infer, killed. Eastwood has a pattern of bullet wounds on his back and ends up killing Stockburn, leaving a similar pattern.

Pale Rider consciously brings together Eastwood's own cynical, sanguinary post-Leone western, *High Plains Drifter*, and George Stevens' affirmative, sanguine *Shane*, and he clearly expects his audience to notice this. In *High Plains Drifter* an avenging angel returns to destroy a town that had betrayed its sheriff, but his behaviour is more satanic than angelic. In *Pale Rider* this revenant comes as a protector to play the role Shane did in the lives of the sodbusters and is generally benign until provoked. There are in fact numerous large and small references to *Shane*. The heroic tree-stump chopping sequence is recapitulated with a breaking of a boulder in a creek; the shooting of the drunken Southerner Torrey in *Shane* is re-worked here with a firing squad of seven killers and snow replacing mud. The miner Barret, his mistress and daughter correspond to the farmer Starrett and his family in the earlier film. More importantly, Eastwood takes up the idea of a western operating simultaneously at a mythic level between the legendary gunfighters coming from elsewhere and at a realistic one between the pioneer families and their organised oppressors. Eastwood heightens the mythic conflict by casting the ageing Russell (most famous as the Texas cattle king who sends waves of gunmen after John Wayne in *Rio Bravo*) as the ruthless killer, and by making explicit the unworldliness of a hero who appears and disappears as mysteriously as (though less disconcertingly than) the snow does on the wintry landscape. And he gives a different emphasis to the rivalry for possession of the land by making neither side settled tillers of the soil, and having the bad guys be the representatives of a corporation as well as environmental and sexual rapists. The film's qualified optimism spoke to the contradictory mood of America at the confident beginning of President Reagan's second term in the White House and on the eve of Eastwood's own brief and enthusiastic entry into electoral politics as mayor of Carmel, California.

Pale Rider was the last Eastwood film to be lit by Bruce Surtees, who had been director of photography on most of his pictures since his debut, *Play Misty for Me*, and is notable for its dark exteriors and stygian interiors. From Eastwood's next movie, *Heartbreak Ridge*, a post-Vietnam Marine Corps movie that could as easily have been a Fordian cavalry picture, his cameraman would be Jack N. Green, the camera operator on *Pale Rider*. Green would continue the tradition of low-key lighting that would bring him one of the nine Academy Award nominations attracted by *Unforgiven* (1992). *Unforgiven*, with an eloquent, elegantly constructed script by David Webb Peoples, is a magisterial film, lean, moral, immaculately acted. The story of bounty hunting and revenge is set in motion by a mockery of machismo and a denial of proper justice. On a stormy night in the isolated, half-built Wyoming township of Big Whisky, a cowboy carves up a prostitute's face as his buddy holds her. The emasculating offence of this woman, appropriately called Delilah, was to giggle at the diminutive size of his penis. 'She didn't know no better,' explains Alice, the chief whore in the squalid saloon-cum-brothel owned by the repulsive Skinny.

The pragmatic sheriff, Little Bill Daggett (Gene Hackman), who's both lawman and judge, settles the matter in appropriate fashion by demanding that come the spring the cowboys should give six horses to Skinny, to compensate him for the loss of Delilah's services. The infuriated whores put a price of $1,000 on the malefactors' heads, and they prove remorseless, even when the lesser offender offers an especially valuable horse as a present to the scarred Delilah. Big Whisky is a raw, awesomely beautiful and cruelly inhospitable place where the Old Testament lies in wait to ambush the ethical compromises of an encroaching civilisation.

Meanwhile among those attracted by the widely publicised reward are a myopic would-be gunfighter styling himself 'The Schofield Kid' (Jaimz Woolvett), and a notorious former outlaw, William Munny (Eastwood). Now an impoverished Kansas pig farmer with two young children to raise, the prematurely aged Munny is attempting to live up to the high standards of his pious late wife, who weaned him away from crime, whoring and hard liquor. Like Gary Cooper in Mann's *Man of the West*, Munny finds himself back in a world he had foresworn. He's a combination of the charismatic gunfighter and the earthy sodbuster in *Shane*. His fair-haired son and the callow Schofield Kid are versions of the hero-worshipping Joey through whose eyes the events of *Shane* are seen. But Munny is out of shape and at the start he can't hit a tin can at ten yards and has difficulty mounting a horse.

To join him on the mission, Munny recruits his old partner in crime, Ned Logan (Morgan Freeman), smiling for almost the only time in the movie when Logan agrees to come along. It is possibly a true reflection of frontier history and certainly of current atittudes that no mention is made in the film's initial stages of Logan being black. They are preceded to Big Whisky by a larger-than-life, gun-toting dandy called English Bob (Richard Harris), acompanied by the bespectacled dime novelist W.W. Beauchamp (Saul Rubinek), who is recording Bob's memoirs for posterity. Surrounded by a posse of nervous young deputies, the middle-aged Daggett disarms Bob and with sadistic glee destroys him physically and mentally as an example to others. Reversing the old Marxist formula, the cruel farce of Daggett's encounter with English Bob is repeated in the tragedy of his final meeting with Munny.

There is no confrontation in *Unforgiven* between good and evil. The meaning of right and wrong changes as the tale unfolds. And there are no villains. The film questions the very notion of heroism. English Bob tries to live up to his legendary reputation. Munny tries to live down his legendary notoriety. The Schofield Kid tries to invent a legend. Sheriff Daggett is a brutal demystifier, but happy to have Beauchamp, the mercenary recorder of frontier myth, cross over to become his Boswell.

Munney and Logan find redemption by different routes. When the chips are down, Logan refuses to return to his old ways, and is brutally killed by Daggett. Munny, having pursued the cowboys to collect the whores' reward, comes to recognise that he is a cursed transgressor and makes the existential decision to challenge the false values of Big Whisky and the sanctioned official violence embodied by Daggett. In a shoot-out on a doom-laden rainy night inside the town's saloon, the full weight of Munny the avenger is brought to bear on Daggett and his followers. *Unforgiven* is realistic rather than cynical, and although the script had apparently been around for some years, the film comes over as a comment on the state of the Union in the early 1990s. Watching the movie at the time, audiences inevitably thought of Rodney King's public beating by the Los Angeles police, of the invasion of Panama, and the 'turkey shoots' in the Gulf War, so far removed from the sense of a fair fight as exemplified by the traditional western. At times Sheriff Daggett has a striking resemblance to President George Bush Sr., who was soon to be defeated after a single term in office. Invariably Daggett is away from his office, working on his emblematic jerry-built house when trouble is brewing, then over-reacting with excessive violence when threatened from outside, and putting on his broadest grin to suggest that it isn't all that serious.

11 Two New Western Stars

Though some star actors have appeared in westerns since I completed the first revision of this book in early 1977, only two new figures of star status have emerged whom we identify with the genre. Both born in Los Angeles but thirty-five years apart, they're Richard Farnsworth (1920–2000) and Kevin Costner (b. 1955), and they represent two enduring figures in the western. Costner is the handsome hero, an all-American type, steadfast, undomesticated, a questor, an upholder of the law. Farnsworth is the dependable older man, the seasoned ranch hand, the wise, pawky humorist, the eternal sidekick. Sadly, the pair never worked together, but as a symbiotic team they would resemble John Wayne and Walter Brennan in Hawks's *Red River* and *Rio Bravo*, or James Stewart and Millard Mitchell in Anthony Mann's *Winchester '73* and *The Naked Spur*, or at a much lower level any number of B-movie heroes coupled with George 'Gabby' Hayes. I suppose the tradition can be traced back to Don Quixote and Sancho Panza.

Farnsworth began his Hollywood career as a teenage stuntman, appearing in endless westerns and action pictures that called for fine horsemanship and sensible courage. As late as *Rambo: First Blood Part II* (1985) he was credited as stunt co-ordinator at the age of 65, but for some years he'd been making odd small character appearances, often uncredited. Then, in 1978, as a grizzled 58-year-old, he was cast in *Comes a Horseman* as the elderly ranch hand helping Jane Fonda run her spread until war veteran James Caan comes along to assist. No one could seem more at home on the range, more weathered and reliable than this white-haired veteran with his glittering, slightly rheumy eyes. It is a magnificent performance that rightly brought him an Academy Award nomination as best supporting actor (in the event he lost out to Christopher Walken for *The Deer Hunter*). When he's thrown from a horse and badly injured while chasing stray cattle through wooded land, he has one of the greatest, most heartbreaking lines in the western, or maybe it's just the stoical manner in which he delivers it – 'I guess my ridin' and ropin' days is over.'

Of course, his ridin' and ropin' days weren't over. In his next film, *Tom Horn* (1980), Farnsworth was billed third after Steve McQueen and Linda Evans in a movie that can be seen as a companion piece to *Heaven's Gate* of the same year. He plays Coble, a sympathetic rancher in 1901 Wyoming, who draws the eponymous cowboy into the fraught situation that will end in his death on the gallows. Horn has become a legendary figure as lawman, rodeo performer, Indian tracker, Pinkerton agent, and mule packer for Roosevelt's Rough Riders in Cuba. At the turn of the century, however, he was an unemployed drifter when Coble, representing the local Cattlemen's Association, hired him to combat rustlers and illegal sheep farmers by whatever means necessary. But as represented in the film, his job as 'stock detective' was executed with too great a thoroughness for his hypocritical employers, and the Association leaders, with the help of a politically ambitious marshal, framed him for the murder of a sheep farmer's 12-year-old son.

Though flawed and unnecessarily elliptical, this thoughtful, impressive picture was a project initiated by McQueen himself. He was already terminally ill, and it turned out to be his penultimate screen appearance. His Tom Horn is a major figure in the Old West who has become an anachronistic survivor and has to be sacrificed in the name of progress, prosperity and social order. He's a loner, a man with his own code of honour and too much pride to plead for his life, and preserves his dignity by going nobly to the gallows, operating them himself through a hydraulic process because no one is prepared to act as hangman. The film can be seen as a personal testament of the fiercely independent McQueen, and he is greatly aided by a deeply sympathetic performance from Farnsworth as the troubled man of probity trapped between the lethal duplicity of his fellow cattlemen and his friendship for Tom Horn. In a sense he represents the tradition of decency continuing from the frontier into the New World.

Two years after this, Farnsworth got his name above the title as the star of Phillip Borsos's *The Grey Fox*, a western made in Canada and set in the Pacific Northwest of America. Based on a real-life character, Farnsworth's Bill Miner is an elderly stagecoach robber, who according to the film coined (or popularised) the command 'Hands up', and emerges in 1901 from thirty-two years in San Quentin to find himself a stranger in the world of the early twentieth century. He doesn't much care for the company of his sister and her conventional husband in Washington State, or for regular work as an oyster gatherer on the beaches of the Pacific. Then he

sees *The Great Train Robbery* and discovers his new vocation as a
train robber. In a lovely scene he buys his first revolver for three
decades, choosing a rather larger one than the prissy gunsmith
suggests, balancing the weapon in his hands and knowledgeably
explaining, 'I like the heft.' He becomes not merely an outlaw, but
a defender of those oppressed by the railways and big business. But
he isn't particularly successful in the choice of fellow criminals or in
planning crimes. In fact he ends up in Canada, trapped by his
Pinkerton Agency nemesis, and given a 25-year sentence. Along the
way he's become the lover of the feisty middle-aged photographer
Kate Flynn (Jackie Burroughs), who, the film suggests, helps spring
him from jail to join her in a new life in old Europe. *The Grey Fox*
is an optimistic, low-key re-run of *Butch Cassidy and the Sundance Kid*,
in love with life rather than with death. It's a warm, funny, deeply
moving picture that should have brought Farnsworth an Oscar.

Seventeen years later, at the age of 79, he got his second Oscar
nomination for his final movie, David Lynch's *The Straight Story*
(1999), one of the most highly regarded pictures at Cannes that year.
He played a determined old codger, a widower and World War II
combat veteran, who makes a heroic 200-mile journey across the
American Midwest on a motor mower to visit the sick brother from
whom he has been long estranged. It's a mystical act of contrition,
a road movie that also echoes the idea of a cattle drive. Farnsworth
brings to the role of old man Straight a quietness, dignity, depth and
total lack of sentimentality that appeals to the best in everyone he
meets in the film, and to the best instincts of the audience. To see
him after the first screening at Cannes, sitting beside Harry Dean
Stanton (the great character actor who plays his brother) at a press
conference wearing a smart Western suit and boots, his white
Stetson on the table before him, his eyes twinkling, his large white
moustache catching the TV camera lights, is a vision that no one
present that day is likely to forget. As with McQueen in *Tom Horn*,
Farnsworth was terminally ill when he made *The Straight Story*. On
6 October 2000, he committed suicide.

In 1985 there were two determined attempts to revive the classic
western. The first was Clint Eastwood's *Pale Rider*. The second film,
in which for the first time in a major picture Kevin Costner received
important billing, is *Silverado*, the first western by Lawrence Kasdan,
whose mastery of genre cinema as writer or director had been
demonstrated in *The Empire Strikes Back*, *Raiders of the Lost Ark* and
Body Heat.

It's essentially a compendium of western themes and situations – an outlaw in search of redemption running into old associates, a corrupt sheriff working for a ruthless landowner, a tough female saloon manager, a wagon train of pioneers, a band of outlaws operating from a hidden canyon, a pair of brothers caught up in a war between settlers and brutish cattlemen, two jail escapes on the night before a hanging, several chases, a cattle stampede, a black cowboy (Danny Glover) out to revenge the death of his father at the hands of racists (only the Indians are missing, though there is a peaceful cluster of wigwams in the background of a settlement in an early scene). For all the knowing calculation, however, the film is unpretentious, affectionate, made without condescension or irony. In this it differs from the archness of *Butch Cassidy and the Sundance Kid*, and it is serious about familiar material in a way that *Raiders of the Lost Ark* isn't. Like Kasdan's earlier *The Big Chill* (1983) and later *Grand Canyon* (1991), *Silverado* is an ensemble piece with no one dominant figure like Eastwood in *Pale Rider*. The action is constant and the body count is as spectacular as that of any Italian western, but as in a B-western of the 30s and 40s you don't really notice it. The characters have no psychological problems or serious doubts, and the depth they're given derives from the iconic aura of the actors, which is considerable. The dialogue is sharp and there are some good exchanges, but there are no weighty speeches or folksy talk. The score by Bruce Broughton seems to have come from a textbook of orthodox film music to enhance the lyrical, the exciting and the elegiac.

There are only two actors in the large cast who had previously appeared in a western – Sheb Wooley, the country singer who was one of the gunmen waiting at the station for Frank Miller in *High Noon* and here appears briefly as a cavalry sergeant, and Scott Glenn, who had a role in Lamont Johnson's likeable minor western *Cattle Annie and Little Britches* (1980) and has a major part here. The movie has only two oddities as far as casting is concerned. First, there's John Cleese playing the relatively small role of the authoritarian sheriff John Langston, who immediately proclaims his obvious foreignness by saying: 'As you may have guessed I don't come from these parts.' There were of course a good many English people in the West, often employed as lawmen. His nastiness, racism, and emphasis on the preservation of order above the disinterested rule of law is concealed behind a mask of English gentlemanliness, just as the same attitudes of an even more brutal marshal later in the movie (played by Brian Dennehy) are hidden beneath a surface of easy bonhomie. Cleese was perhaps too widely known as a comedian to bring off this role, but he gets a deserved laugh that many another comic actor wouldn't have obtained when some sharp-shooting fugitives turn against the posse he's leading and a bullet removes his smart town hat. 'Today my jurisdiction ends here,' he says, ordering an underling to pick up his hat as he turns to ride back home.

The second curious piece of casting is both daring and effective. The diminutive (4 foot 10 inches) character actress Linda Hunt plays Stella, a seasoned saloon keeper who needs a ramp to reach a concealed platform so she can get her head above the bar to do her job. She's a strong, impish, highly intelligent presence and there is an immediate rapport struck between her and the handsome, humorous ex-outlaw Paden (Kevin Kline), when they discover a mutual love of saloons. A discreetly handled romance follows of an affecting kind and unlike any other in the western.

In this attractive group, Kevin Costner's Jake Swann is the loose cannon, the younger brother of Emmett (Scott Glenn), who's just been released from a Kansas penitentiary after serving seven years for killing in self-defence. Unlike the hirsute figures around them, both are clean-shaven but are otherwise very different. Emmett is a dour, determined man, set on riding out to California with Jake and visiting their sister in Silverado along the way. Jake is Emmett's opposite, a dashing horseman and gunfighter, ususally firing both his revolvers simultaneously. He's a hot-headed, fast-talking womaniser, reckless but kindly and generous, a kinetic near-psychopath of great charm. He stands apart from the quartet of decent cautious men he joins in opposing the crooked sheriff and his employer, the cattle baron. In a more solemn movie than this, Jack would undergo some character change or be killed, but here he and all the good men survive, though it may be they were preserved for a sequel that, as a result of the picture's failure at the box-office, was not to come.

Costner was to co-produce the next westerns, and to direct two of them, and before the first of these, *Dances With Wolves* (1990), his screen persona was to undergo a significant change. The hyper-activity of his performance in *Silverado* disappeared, to be replaced by an earnestness and a relaxed exterior that suggested inner tensions. In a series of films – most notably *The Untouchables* and *Field of Dreams* – he became a contained, quietly spoken all-American hero, a man of obvious probity, distinguished by his modest determination rather than his flamboyance. This led many observers to compare him with Gary Cooper and Henry Fonda, and in retrospect it seems obvious that he would be drawn to making another western.

In all his subsequent westerns, beginning as Lieutenant Dunbar, the Union cavalry officer in *Dances With Wolves* (which I've writen about in the chapter on Native Americans), Costner is heavily moustachioed. This contributes to his new gravitas. In terms of Costner's career development, *Dances With Wolves* revealingly reverses the dramatic arc of *Sergeant York*, the Howard Hawks film that brought Gary Cooper an Oscar in 1940. In *Sergeant York*, Cooper starts out as an innocent son of the primitive backwoods frontier world, a pacifist cut off from the mainstream of American life. He ends up an accidental hero of World War I with a brilliant coup against the Germans on the Western front and embraces and is embraced by the triumphalist ethos of twentieth-century America. In *Dances With Wolves*, Costner becomes by accident a legendary hero of the Civil War through a suicidal act that leads to a Union victory. He subsequently rejects so-called civilisation and embraces the alternative culture of the Native Americans.

With his third western, *Wyatt Earp*, another collaboration with Lawrence Kasdan, he moved from the interface between the developing modern world and the traditional culture of the Native Americans it was eroding, to the internal disorders and conflicts of this new capitalist society. Here the problems are internalised in terms of the family values discussed earlier in this book, in the section on Tombstone movies. Costner's Earp is faced with reconciling his responsibilities to his clan as a brother with those towards the burgeoning Tombstone community, and this leads to what is probably his most complex performance.

Costner's fourth western, *Open Range* (2003), emerged during that surprising revival of the western in this new century. It's a slow, carefully paced movie that pares down *Silverado* to a single strand of its plot – the conflict between two independent cowboys running their cattle across the open range in the early 1880s and a ruthless Irish-American rancher who controls a small town and is forcibly laying claim to the surrounding territory. It is in style a classic movie with only six significantly developed roles, and until the final extended shoot-out the action is spasmodic, with a couple of the most violent encounters happening off-screen. *Open Range* begins by evoking the opening of Ford's *My Darling Clementine* where the

Earp brothers drive their cattle towards Tombstone. Here a long line of cattle is strung out across the rolling prairie with mountains towering above. Two middle-aged horsemen, moving with authority, survey their herd. A younger man is down among the cattle; a cheerful fat man drives the accompanying wagon. A rich melodic theme by Michael Kamen, both epic and elegiac, plays on the soundtrack. In the distance storm clouds gather, as a warning of dangers ahead and a token of the hard lives these men have chosen to live in this picturesque, unforgiving country. It is a beautiful start to a visually expressive movie, and only later do we learn – inevitably from the marker on a primitive, newly dug grave – that the year is 1882.

The older men are Charley Waite (Kevin Costner), a reformed gunfighter who became a hardened killer in the Civil War, and Boss Spearman (Robert Duvall), head of the outfit. They've been riding together for a decade without divulging much about their past lives. The two younger men are a Mexican-American known as Button (Diego Luna), a good-looking 16-year-old who's like an adopted son, and Mose, cheerful, portly, Jewish (Abraham Benrubi), who has gained respect through being trusted by Boss and Charley. They're like a family and they want to live a simple nomadic existence, driving their cattle on the range. But the days of this way of life are numbered. Farmers are staking out smallholdings, and big ranchers with corporate backing from the East Coast are fencing in the land and making war on the free grazers. There is a magnificent image in the movie when Charley and Boss ride out to confront four menacing horsemen, white flour-bags masking their faces as if they were in the Ku Klux Klan. In the foreground of the shot are a couple of strands of barbed wire, the ugly invention of little more than a decade before that stands for exclusion, possession and pain.

These men are the hired guns of the Irish immigrant cattle baron, Baxter (Michael Gambon), who runs the local town through his control of the sheriff, and he intends to make an example of Boss and Charley. They are prepared to ride on in peace, but Baxter, all brutality and bluster, provokes them into making a stand. This they do out of respect for their friends who are brutally treated by Baxter's men, and as a moral duty. There is, however, nothing pious about them. They are stern but not humourless, fierce but controlled, hard yet capable of risking themselves to save a dog endangered by a flood. They recall the central duo of *Lonesome Dove*, and not only because one of them is Robert Duvall. They dislike towns and the settled life, but they meet and are attracted by the acceptable face of civilisation in the shape of Sue (Annette Bening), the sister and assistant of the town's doctor. Her features look like those on a Victorian cameo brooch, and she serves them tea in her mother's china cups, the handles of which are too small for the cowboys to hold.

Sue draws out Spearman to the extent of making him reveal that he's a longtime widower whose wife and child died of cholera. In Charley she finds a kindred troubled spirit, and a sweet, chaste romance develops of a kind one might associate with a movie star-ring Gary Cooper, James Stewart or Henry Fonda. She also tends the wounds that both Mose and Button have received at the hands of Baxter's thugs, thus creating a special bond with the two older men. As with most women in the traditional western, Sue is the voice of reason, but she's untypical in her recognition that there are times when compromise doesn't work and men must resort to violence. This reflects a widely shared feeling in the United States following the events of 11 September 2001, that the responsible use of violence is morally justified and politically necessary. Significantly, there is in *Open Range* no alternative woman, no Magdalene to the pure heroine's Madonna. Instead, when after the final showdown Sue comes into town from her white picket-fenced house some half-mile outside, her meeting with the wounded Charley and her declaration of love take place in the deserted saloon. The implication is that she transcends the customary polarisation or at least embodies and commands the two worlds of the stereotyped western women – the settled home and the licentious places where men gather to drink, gamble and have sex. The showdown itself comes in the muddy streets of the raw, unfinished Harmonsville, formerly Fort Harmon, but deserted by the cavalry now the Indian wars are over in this part of the country. Before the fighting breaks out there's a slow, humorous build-up as Boss buys the best cigars and most expensive European chocolate the local store stocks, and reveals his real Christian name to Charley. The superbly staged, prolonged gunfight begins at the town's corral, and only briefly, for less than a minute, goes into slow motion, a climactic montage accompanied by a quasi-Wagnerian theme. A long, reflective coda of great warmth and charm ends the picture.

12 Some Left-field Entries

S am Shepard is one of a number of recent American writers closely associated with life in the contemporary American West and its small, dusty, isolated communities where trucks, cars and buses only occasionally stop, its itinerant population, its saloons, motels and ghost towns and its drugstore cowboys. In Shepard's *Motel Chronicles*,[35] his charming book of jottings, reflections and poems made as he drifted round the West, there is a particularly attractive item dated '4/28/80, Santa Rosa, Ca':

> I keep praying
> for a double bill
> of
> BAD DAY AT BLACK ROCK
> and
> VERA CRUZ

That would make any western fan's night out at the drive-in. Unfortunately Shepard's own ventures into the genre have been mixed. He's acted in a number of movies with western settings – most notably Michael Apted's *Thunderheart*, as an FBI agent investigating a homicide on an Indian reservation, and more recently as a lawyer in *All the Pretty Horses* – and scripted Wim Wenders' excellent *Paris, Texas* (1984), a movie about the drifting, irresponsible Western life. One of his best stage plays, *Fool for Love* (1986), was brought uneasily to the screen by Robert Altman. The play, a four-character chamber piece set in a seedy motel room, carries the stage direction, 'To be performed relentlessly without a break', and has been unwisely opened up by Shepard himself. The result is less like the contents of Pandora's Box escaping excitedly into the atmosphere than the bodies of a sealed sarcophagus dissolving when exposed to fresh air.

Fool for Love is a sort of country-and-western *Who's Afraid of Virginia Woolf?*, another play opened up for the screen and also about a couple locked in a hopeless relationship who parade their dark

---

35 City Lights Books, San Francisco, 1982; Faber, London, 1984.

secrets and attempt to exorcise family ghosts in the presence of a horrified outsider. Here it's a rodeo performer, Eddie (Sam Shepard), and his washed-out half-sister, May (Kim Basinger), who rehearse the circumstances of their incestuous past for May's small-town boyfriend (Randy Quaid). Instead of a New England campus, the setting is the bleak Mojave desert. Opening the play out involves taking the action to other parts of the motel and introducing flash-backs of a literal kind to the couple's childhoods. It forces Altman to show the vengeful 'Countess' who comes gunning for Eddie, and makes painfully awkward the role of the omnipresent 'Old Man' (Harry Dean Stanton), a character unseen by the others, who turns out to be the couple's dead father. The piece gains little from this, and in the process loses dramatic intensity, ambiguity and the sense of driven people living in a private hell that is an anteroom of the real world. The flashbacks serve to make the film seem like a sad case history, sociology rather than myth. The movie is, however, well acted, even if Shepard is too charming, handsome and intelli-gent as the head-banging misfit Eddie. The part is better suited to Ed Harris, who created the role on stage in San Francisco, or Will Patton who played it off-Broadway.

Shepard went on to direct two movies located in the West, both extremely disappointing. His debut, *Far North* (1988), set in contemporary Minnesota, stars Jessica Lange as a young woman returning to the family farm to discover that her irascible hospitalised father (Charles Durning) has chosen her to kill the horse he holds responsible for his injuries. William Faulkner might have got away with this story in his private corner of the Deep South. But here there is no social context and Shepard goes all out for high-decibel eccentricity. His second picture as writer-director, *Silent Tongue* (1993), is nearer to the traditional western in setting and dramatis personae, but in tone reflects the influence on Shepard of classical tragedy. Alan Bates and Richard Harris co-star as Eamon McCree and Prescott Roe, wild Irishmen in 1893 New Mexico, who pay a properly high price for their transgressions against Native Americans. Bates is the drunken owner of a travelling medicine show, luring customers with clowns, animals and dramatic sketches, and selling them worthless elixirs. He has raped a Kiowa squaw, called 'Silent Tongue' because her people have cut out her tongue for lying, and she has borne him two daughters. One of them has been bought by the horse trader Roe for his son, and when she dies he attempts to buy her sister. In the climactic scene the ghost of the boy's dead half-Indian wife is released to attack Roe and seek her freedom. Wholly lacking in humour, the drama is as bleak as the surrounding countryside and the performances are overwrought.

Silent Tongue is much inferior to Wayne Coe's all-out super-natural western, which fulfils the promise of its punning title, *Grim Prairie Tales* (1990). There have been numerous attempts, mostly unsuccessful, to link the western to the horror and occult genres, ranging from such schlock products as *Billy the Kid vs. Dracula* (1966) to Jan Kounen's absurd, pretentious *Blueberry* (2003), based on a French comic strip. *Blueberry* stars Vincent Cassel as a Cajun in 1880s Arizona, torn between a nasty frontier world of venal settlers, whom he has served as sheriff, and the mystical world of the Apaches, one of whose shamans saved his life. As a token of his divided allegiance he wears both a crucifix and an Indian charm around his neck. An extraordinary international cast, ranging from Ernest Borgnine (a crippled sheriff) and Eddie Izzard (a Prussian geologist) to the Maori Temuera Morrison and the West African Djimon Hounsou go for nothing, or very little.

Made on a modest budget, *Grim Prairie Tales* features four gothic stories of frontier life, and is in a post-modernist vein. The tales feature a trapper buried alive by his Indian captors, a naïve cowhand seduced by a malevolent ghost, a southern couple moving to unspoiled frontier life only to find the evil spirit of the Ku Klux Klan pursuing them, and the conflict between two gunslingers continued from the grave. What makes the picture interesting and raises it above the ruck, as with a good many portmanteau movies, is the narrative framework. This takes the form of a dialogue between two mutually suspicious strangers who share a campfire one night in the West and keep dangerous sleep at bay by telling tall stories. They're the slight, prissy, small-town businessman Farley (Brad Dourif), dressed in a three-piece suit, and the gigantic, noisome bounty hunter Morrison (James Early Jones), clad in a buffalo coat, who carries with him the corpse of his latest quarry. Both actors are in fine form. Farley, a rational city boy, and Morrison, a romantic, self-mythicising force of nature, engage in a sophisticated debate and interrogate the nature and purpose of the narrative they're appearing in. Their stories are designed to test each other, and to lay claim to their contrasting but complementary interpretations of social expe-rience and the myth of the West.

Like *Silent Tongue* and *Grim Prairie Tales*, Jim Jarmusch's fasci-nating venture into the western, *Dead Man* (1995), had the shortest of theatrical runs in Britain. The film is exquisitely shot in black-and-white by Robby Müller to look like photographs of the 1870s, or horse operas of the 1930s. Its hero, a young accountant called William Blake played by a graceful, almost angelic Johnny Depp, is a sad young man. He's first seen heading West by train across the plains, the mountains and the desert in the 1870s to take up a job at a metal works in a soulless town with the emblematic name of Machine. His flat hat, pallor and earnestness suggest a deadly serious version of Buster Keaton (a similarly put upon pioneer in several silent comedies).

Another possible point of departure is Kafka's unfinished *Amerika*, which breaks off as its innocent hero heads out West. When Blake is buttonholed by the train's fireman, one recalls that Kafka's protagonist, Karl Rossmann, had an encounter with a ship's stoker while crossing the Atlantic. Machine, with its depressed workers and conspiring clerks, is a Dickensian, Kafkaesque hell deposited on the virgin West and ruled over by an arbitrary sadist, played by Robert Mitchum in the manner of his demented preacher from *The Night of the Hunter*. Refused a job, the hapless Blake comes to the help of a young woman, an act of natural goodness that leads to him accidentally killing Mitchum's son and fleeing further West, mortally wounded and with a price on his head. An outcast Indian who calls himself 'Nobody' and has the tribal name 'He Who Talks Loud And Says Nothing', takes the wounded white man under his wing. The pawkily humourous Nobody believes that Blake is the incarnation of the great English writer and escorts him on a bleak, meandering journey to the sea to receive the proper Viking-like funeral that will return his spirit to its rightful home.

'That weapon will replace your tongue,' Nobody says of Blake's six-shooter. 'Your poetry shall be written in blood.' And along the way killing becomes a habit, a reflex for the dying accountant as he despatches everyone in his path – missionaries, lawmen, bounty hunters. *Dead Man* is a grimly comic movie about preparing to face death, and it creates its own poetic world.

Latest Books

There has been a proliferation of books on the western since 1976, more of them than westerns in fact. One book above all others should be on the shelf of anyone interested in the West and the western – *The New Encyclopedia of the American West* (Yale University Press, New Haven and London, 1998) edited by Howard R. Lamar, the outstanding living historian of the West. Much expanded from his *Reader's Encyclopedia of the American West* (Crowell, New York, 1977), this magnificent work features 2,400 entries by more than 300 writers, virtually all academics, and is indispensable. Another valuable book, also by a variety of hands, is *The Oxford History of the American West*, edited by Clyde A. Milner II, Carol A. O'Connor and Martha A. Sandweiss (Oxford University Press, New York and Oxford, 1994).

Specifically on the genre, there are two admirable reference works. Edited by Phil Hardy, *The Western: The Aurum Encyclopedia of the Western* (Aurum, London, 1988, rev. 1991) is one of a series of outsize books (others deal with horror, crime and science fiction) on a year by year basis. *The BFI Companion to the Western*, edited by Edward Buscombe (British Film Institute, London, 1988), is a handsomely illustrated book arranged alphabetically and covering key movies, filmmakers, and relevant aspects of frontier history and folkways.

Buscombe helped initiate the splendid series of monographs BFI Film Classics and BFI Modern Classics while he was at the BFI, and has himself written three of them – on *Stagecoach* (1992), *The Searchers* (2002) and *Unforgiven* (2004). Other books on westerns in these series include Phillip Drummond's *High Noon* (1997), Edward Countryman and Evonne von Heussen-Countryman's *Shane* (1999), Suzanne Liandrat-Guigues's *Red River* (2000, trans. Nick Coates), *Rio Bravo* (2003) by Robin Wood (his BFI monograph on Howard Hawks in the Cinema One series was published in a revised edition in 1983), and Jonathan Rosenbaum's *Dead Man* (2002).

Among the most notable studies of directors are three on Sam Peckinpah – *Peckinpah: The Western Films* (University of Illinois Press, Urbana and London, 1980, rev. 1997) by Paul Seydor, an academic and film editor; *Bloody Sam* by Marshall Fine (Donald I. Fine, New York, 1991); and *'If They Move… Kill Em': The Life and Times of Sam Peckinpah* by David Weddle (Grove Press, New York; Faber, London, 1994). Of several books on John Ford, the most significant are the definitive biography, *Searching for John Ford: A Life* by Joseph McBride (Faber, London, 2003) and *John Ford and the American West* by Peter Cowie (Harry N. Abrams, New York, 2004). But there is as well the superb, long-awaited monograph by his most illustrious student and admirer, *About John Ford* by Lindsay Anderson (Plexus, London, 1981). We also have another definitive biography, *Howard Hawks: The Grey Fox of Hollywood* by Todd McCarthy (Grove Press, New York, 1997).

The most original thinking on the genre in general is to be found in Michael Coyne's *The Crowded Prairie: American National Identity in the Hollywood Western* (I.B. Tauris, London and New York, 1997), which takes a socio-political approach, and *Westerns: Making the Man in Fiction and Film* (The University of Chicago Press, Chicago and London, 1996), by Lee Clark Mitchell, Professor of Belles-Lettres at Princeton, a wide-ranging work of cultural history. Both are well written by critical enthusiasts on different sides of the Atlantic seeking to address a wide audience from the groves of academe while maintaining scholarly standards. *West of Everything: The Inner Life of Westerns* (Oxford University Press, New York and Oxford, 1992) by Jane Tompkins, also an academic, is a feminist work by someone who has problems with a genre she has but lately turned her attention to; as a vegetarian and supporter of animal rights she views cattle drives as near-criminal activities. Writing from outside the campus, there is the combative, passionate, not to say dogmatic, *Western Films: A Complete Guide* (De Capo Press, New York, 1982) by Brian Garfield, an informed insider as author of westerns and thrillers, *Death Wish* among them. A better book, both lively and thoughtful, is the British critic and novelist Kim Newman's *Wild West Movies: Or How the West Was Found, Won, Lost, Lied About, Filmed and Forgotten* (Bloomsbury, London, 1990), the sub-title of which suggests a less serious book than in fact it is.

Two outstanding books have recently appeared in new versions, both among my favourite studies of the genre. Jim Kitses's *Horizons West: Anthony Mann, Budd Boetticher, Sam Peckinpah: Studies of Authorship Within the Western*, published in 1969 in the BFI Cinema One series (a couple of years before my *Westerns*) has re-appeared as *Horizons West: Directing the Western from John Ford to Clint Eastwood*

(BFI Publishing, London, 2004). It's well over twice the length of the original book.

Christopher Frayling's *Spaghetti Westerns: Cowboys and Europeans from Karl May to Sergio Leone* (1981) is back under the same title with some additions (I.B. Tauris, London, 1998). Frayling has since written *Sergio Leone: Something to Do With Death* (Faber, London, 2000), a first-rate biography, and has rightly commended *Once Upon a Time in the Italian West: The Filmgoers' Guide to the Spaghetti Westerns* by Howard Hughes (I.B. Tauris, London, 2004), a study of twenty Italian westerns.

There are some excellent essays in *The Movie Book of the Western*, edited by Ian Cameron and Douglas Pye (Studio Vista, London, 1996), ranging from Robin Wood on *Drums Along the Mohawk* to Brian Woolland's fine essay on *Heaven's Gate*. One of its contributors, Peter Stanfield, who writes on country music and the 1939 western, has written a valuable book on the coming of sound and the era that precedes the principal concern of my book, *Hollywood, Westerns and the 1930s: The Lost Trail* (University of Exeter Press, Exeter, 2001).

Filmography

For the sake of convenience this selection of westerns, most of them made since the end of World War II, is listed by directors. This does not mean that in all cases their importance or interest derives from their directors. Indeed, in many instances I would regard the contributions of screenwriters, actors, cinematographers and maybe even producers, as of greater significance.

Robert Aldrich: *Apache* (1954); *Vera Cruz* (1954); *The Last Sunset* (1961); *Four for Texas* (1963); *Ulzana's Raid* (1972); *The Frisco Kid* (1979); *Fool For Love* (1986)

Robert Altman: *McCabe and Mrs Miller* (1971); *Buffalo Bill and the Indians* (1976); *Fool for Love* (1986)

Robert Benton: *Bad Company* (1972)

Bruce Beresford: *Black Robe* (1991)

Antonia Bird: *Ravenous* (1999)

Budd Boetticher: *The Cimarron Kid* (1951); *Horizons West* (1952); *Bronco Buster* (1952); *Seminole* (1953); *The Man from the Alamo* (1953); *Wings of the Hawk* (1953); *Seven Men from Now* (1956); *The Tall T* (1957); *Decision at Sundown* (1957); *Buchanan Rides Alone* (1958); *Ride Lonesome* (1959); *Westbound* (1959); *Comanche Station* (1960); *A Time for Dying* (1969)

Philip Borsos: *The Grey Fox* (1982)

Marlon Brando: *One-Eyed Jacks* (1961)

Mel Brooks: *Blazing Saddles* (1974)

Richard Brooks: *The Last Hunt* (1955); *The Professionals* (1966); *Bite the Bullet* (1975)

Christopher Cain: *Young Guns* (1988)

Michael Cimino: *Heaven's Gate* (1980); *Sunchaser* (1996)

James B. Clark: *One Foot in Hell* (1960)

Fielder Cook: *A Big Hand for the Little Lady* (1966; UK title, *Big Deal at Dodge City*)

George P. Cosmatos: *Tombstone* (1993)

Kevin Costner: *Dances With Wolves* (1990); *Open Range* (2003)

George Cukor: *Heller in Pink Tights* (1960)

Michael Curtiz: *Dodge City* (1939); *Virginia City* (1940); *Santa Fe*

Trail (1940); *Jim Thorpe – All American* (1951; UK title *Man of Bronze*); *The Hangman* (1959); *The Comancheros* (1961)

Delmer Daves: *Broken Arrow* (1950); *Return of the Texan* (1952); *Drumbeat* (1954); *Jubal* (1956); *The Last Wagon* (1956); *3.10 to Yuma* (1957); *Cowboy* (1958); *The Badlanders* (1958); *The Hanging Tree* (1959)

Cecil B. De Mille: *The Plainsman* (1937); *Union Pacific* (1939); *North West Mounted Police* (1940); *Unconquered* (1947)

Andre de Toth: *The Man in the Saddle* (1951); *Springfield Rifle* (1952); *Carson City* (1952); *The Stranger Wore a Gun* (1953); *Bounty Hunter* (1954); *The Indian Fighter* (1955); *Riding Shotgun* (1955); *Day of the Outlaw* (1959)

Edward Dmytryk: *Broken Lance* (1954); *Warlock* (1959); *Alvarez Kelly* (1966); *Shalako* (1969)

Richard Donner: *Maverick* (1994)

Gordon Douglas: *The Great Missouri Raid* (1952); *Only the Valiant* (1952); *The Charge at Feather River* (1953); *The Fiend that Walked the West* (1958); *Yellowstone Kelly* (1959); *Rio Conchos* (1964); *Stagecoach* (1966); *Chuka* (1967); *Barquero* (1970)

Kirk Douglas: *Posse* (1975)

Allan Dwan: *The Woman They Almost Lynched* (1953); *Cattle Queen of Montana* (1954); *The Silver Lode* (1954); *Tennessee's Partner* (1955); *The Restless Breed* (1957)

Clint Eastwood: *High Plains Drifter* (1972); *The Outlaw Josey Wales* (1976); *Bronco Billy* (1980); *Pale Rider* (1985); *Unforgiven* (1992)

Blake Edwards: *The Wild Rovers* (1971); *Sunset* (1988)

John Farrow: *California* (1947); *Copper Canyon* (1950); *Ride, Vaquero* (1953); *Hondo* (1954)

Richard Fleischer: *These Thousand Hills* (1959); *The Spikes Gang* (1974)

Peter Fonda: *The Hired Hand* (1971)

John Ford: *Stagecoach* (1939); *My Darling Clementine* (1946); *Fort Apache* (1948); *Three Godfathers* (1948); *She Wore a Yellow Ribbon* (1949); *Wagonmaster* (1950); *Rio Grande* (1950); *The Searchers* (1956); *The Horse Soldiers* (1959); *Sergeant Rutledge* (1970); *Two Rode Together* (1961); *The Man Who Shot Liberty Valance* (1961); *How the West Was Won* (1962, co-director); *Cheyenne Autumn* (1964)

William Fraker: *Monte Walsh* (1970); *Legend of the Lone Ranger* (1981)

Melvin Frank: *The Jayhawkers* (1959)

Stephen Frears: *The Hi-Lo Country* (1998)

Hugo Fregonese: *Apache Drums* (1950); *The Raid* (1954)

Samuel Fuller: *I Shot Jesse James* (1948); *The Baron of Arizona* (1949); *Run of the Arrow* (1956); *Forty Guns* (1957)

Sidney J. Furie: *The Appaloosa* (1966; UK title, *Southwest to Sonora*)

Tay Garnett: *Cattle King* (1963; UK title, *Guns of Wyoming*)

Maggie Greenwald: *The Ballad of Little Jo* (1993)

Tom Gries: *Will Penny* (1967); *100 Rifles* (1968); *Breakheart Pass* (1976)

Charles Haas: *Star in the Dust* (1956)

John Lee Hancock: *The Alamo* (2004)

Henry Hathaway: *Rawhide* (1951); *Garden of Evil* (1954); *From Hell to Texas* (1958; UK title, *Manhunt*); *North to Alaska* (1960); *How the West Was Won* (1962, co-director); *The Sons of Katie Elder* (1965); *Nevada Smith* (1966); *5 Card Stud* (1968); *True Grit* (1969); *Shoot Out* (1972)

Howard Hawks: *Red River* (1948); *The Big Sky* (1952); *Rio Bravo* (1959); *El Dorado* (1967); *Rio Lobo* (1970)

Monte Hellman: *Ride in the Whirlwind* (1966); *The Shooting* (1966); *China 9, Liberty 37* (1978)

George Roy Hill: *Butch Cassidy and the Sundance Kid* (1969)

Walter Hill: *The Long Riders* (1980); *Geronimo* (1992); *Wild Bill* (1995)

John Huston: *The Unforgiven* (1960); *The Misfits* (1960); *The Life and Times of Judge Roy Bean* (1972)

Ron Howard: *Far and Away* (1992); *The Missing* (2003)

Hugh Hudson: *Revolution* (1985)

Jim Jarmusch: *Dead Man* (1995)

Lamont Johnson: *Cattle Annie and Little Britches* (1980)

Joe Johnston: *Hidalgo* (2004)

Jonathan Kaplan: *Bad Girls* (1994)

Phil Karlson: *Gunman's Walk* (1958); *A Time for Killing* (1968; UK title, *The Long Ride Home*)

Lawrence Kasdan: *Silverado* (1985); *Wyatt Earp* (1994)

Philip Kaufman: *The Great Northfield Minnesota Raid* (1971)

Burt Kennedy: *Mail Order Bride* (1964; UK title, *West of Montana*); *The Rounders* (1965); *Return of the Seven* (1966); *Welcome to Hard Times* (1966; UK title, *Killer on a Horse*); *The War Wagon* (1967); *Support Your Local Sheriff* (1968); *Young Billy Young* (1969); *The Good Guys and the Bad Guys* (1969); *Dirty Dingus Magee* (1970); *The Deserter* (1970); *Hannie Caulder* (1971); *Support Your Local*

Gunfighter (1971); *The Train Robbers* (1973)

Jan Kounen: *Blueberry* (2003);

Henry King: *Jesse James* (1939); *The Gunfighter* (1950); *The Bravados* (1958)

John Landis: *Three Amigos!* (1986)

Fritz Lang: *The Return of Frank James* (1940); *Western Union* (1941); *Rancho Notorious* (1952)

Ang Lee: *Ride With the Devil* (1999)

J. Lee Thompson: *Mackenna's Gold* (1969); *The White Buffalo* (1977)

Sergio Leone: *A Fistful of Dollars* (1964); *For a Few Dollars More* (1965); *The Good, the Bad and the Ugly* (1967); *Once Upon a Time in the West* (1969); *A Fistful of Dynamite* [aka *Duck, You Sucker!*] (1971)

Richard Lester: *Butch and Sundance: The Early Years* (1979)

Henry Levin: *The Man from Colorado* (1948); *The Lonely Man* (1957)

Joseph H. Lewis: *The Halliday Brand* (1957); *Terror in a Texas Town* (1957)

Joseph L. Mankiewicz: *There Was a Crooked Man* (1970)

Anthony Mann: *Devil's Doorway* (1950); *Winchester '73* (1950); *The Furies* (1950); *Bend of the River* (1952; UK title, *Where the River Bends*); *The Naked Spur* (1953); *The Far Country* (1955); *The Man from Laramie* (1955); *The Last Frontier* (1956); *The Tin Star* (1957); *Man of the West* (1958); *Cimarron* (1960)

Michael Mann: *Last of the Mohicans* (1992)

George Marshall: *Destry Rides Again* (1939); *The Savage* (1952); *Red Garters* (1954); *The Sheepman* (1958); *How the West Was Won* (1962, co-director); *Advance to the Rear* (1964; UK title, *Company of Cowards*)

Vincent McEveety: *Firecreek* (1968)

Don McGuire: *Johnny Concho* (1956)

Andrew V. McLaglen: *Gun the Man Down* (1956); *McLintock!* (1963); *Shenandoah* (1965); *The Rare Breed* (1966); *The Way West* (1967); *Bandolero!* (1968); *The Undefeated* (1969); *Chisum* (1970); *One More Train to Rob* (1971); *Something Big* (1971)

Michael Mann: *Last of the Mohicans* (1992)

John Milius: *The Rough Riders* (1997)

Ray Milland: *A Man Alone* (1955)

Stuart Millar: *When the Legends Die* (1972); *Rooster Cogburn* (1975)

David Miller: *Lonely Are the Brave* (1962)

Allen H. Miner: *Black Patch* (1957); *The Ride Back* (1957)

Anthony Minghella: *Cold Mountain* (2003)
Robert Mulligan: *The Stalking Moon* (1968)
Geoff Murphy: *Young Guns II* (1990)
Silvio Narizzano: *Blue* (1968)
James Neilson: *Night Passage* (1957); *Return of the Gunfighter* (1966)
Ralph Nelson: *Duel at Diablo* (1965); *Soldier Blue* (1970)
Joseph M. Newman: *The Outcasts of Poker Flat* (1952); *The Gunfight at Dodge City* (1959); *A Thunder of Drums* (1961)
Jack Nicholson: *Goin' South* (1978)
Gerd Oswald: *The Brass Legend* (1955); *Fury at Showdown* (1956)
Alan Pakula: *Comes a Horseman* (1978)
Robert Parrish: *Saddle the Wind* (1958); *The Wonderful Country* (1959)
Richard Pearce: *Heartland* (1979)
Sam Peckinpah: *The Deadly Companions* (1961); *Ride the High Country* (1962; UK title, *Guns in the Afternoon*); *Major Dundee* (1965); *The Wild Bunch* (1969); *The Ballad of Cable Hogue* (1970); *Junior Bonner* (1972); *Pat Garrett and Billy the Kid* (1973)
Arthur Penn: *The Left Handed Gun* (1958); *Little Big Man* (1970); *The Missouri Breaks* (1976)
Frank Perry: *Doc* (1971)
Sydney Pollack: *The Scalphunters* (1968); *Jeremiah Johnson* (1972); *The Electric Horseman* (1979)
Abraham Polonsky: *Tell Them Willie Boy Is Here* (1969)
Ted Post: *The Legend of Tom Dooley* (1959); *Hang 'Em High* (1968)
Otto Preminger: *River of No Return* (1954)
Luis Puenzo: *Old Gringo* (1989)
Sam Raimi: *The Quick and the Dead* (1995)
Nicholas Ray: *The Lusty Men* (1952); *Johnny Guitar* (1953); *Run for Cover* (1954); *The True Story of Jesse James* (1956; UK title, *The James Brothers*)
Robert Redford: *The Horse Whisperer* (1998)
Carol Reed: *Flap* (1970; UK title, *The Last Warrior*)
Dick Richards: *The Culpepper Cattle Company* (1972)
Martin Ritt: *Hud* (1963); *The Outrage* (1964); *Hombre* (1967)
Cliff Robertson: *J.W. Coop* (1971)
Frank Roddam: *War Party* (1988)
Russell Rouse: *The Fastest Gun Alive* (1956); *Thunder in the Sun* (1959)
Mark Rydell: *The Cowboys* (1972)
Sidney Salkow: *Sitting Bull* (1954)

John Sayles: *Lone Star* (1995)

Fred Schepisi: *Barbarosa* (1982)

Harold Schuster: *The Dragoon Wells Massacre* (1957)

Sam Shepard: *Silent Tongue* (1993)

George Sidney: *The Harvey Girls* (1946)

Don Siegel: *Duel at Silver Creek* (1952); *Flaming Star* (1960); *Coogan's Bluff* (1968); *Death of a Gunfighter* (1969, credited to 'Allen Smithee' but directed by Robert Totten and Don Siegel); *Two Mules for Sister Sara* (1969); *The Shootist* (1976)

Elliot Silverstein: *Cat Ballou* (1965); *A Man Called Horse* (1970)

Robert Siodmak: *Custer of the West* (1967)

Douglas Sirk: *Taza, Son of Cochise* (1954)

Barry Sonnenfeld: *Wild Wild West* (1999)

George Stevens: *Shane* (1953); *Giant* (1956)

John Sturges: *The Walking Hills* (1949); *Escape from Fort Bravo* (1953); *Bad Day at Black Rock* (1954); *Backlash* (1955); *Gunfight at the OK Corral* (1957); *The Law and Jake Wade* (1958); *Last Train from Gun Hill* (1959); *The Magnificent Seven* (1960); *Sergeants Three* (1961); *The Hallelujah Trail* (1965); *Joe Kidd* (1972); *The Valdez Horses* (1973)

Billy Bob Thornton: *All the Pretty Horses* (2000)

Jerry Thorpe: *Day of the Evil Gun* (1968)

Jacques Tourneur: *Stranger on Horseback* (1955); *Wichita* (1955); *Great Day in the Morning* (1956)

Edward G. Ulmer: *The Naked Dawn* (1954)

Ron Underwood: *City Slickers* (1991)

Melvyn Van Peebles: *Posse* (1993)

King Vidor: *Billy the Kid* (1930); *The Texas Rangers* (1936); *North West Passage* (1939); *Duel in the Sun* (1946); *Man Without a Star* (1955)

Raoul Walsh: *The Big Trail* (1930); *They Died With Their Boots On* (1941); *Pursued* (1947); *Silver River* (1948); *Colorado Territory* (1949); *Along the Great Divide* (1950); *Distant Drums* (1951); *The Lawless Breed* (1952); *Gun Fury* (1953); *The Tall Men* (1955); *The King and Four Queens* (1956); *The Sheriff of Fractured Jaw* (1959); *A Distant Trumpet* (1963)

Charles Marquis Warren: *Hellgate* (1952); *Arrowhead* (1953); *Tension at Table Rock* (1956); *Trooper Hook* (1957)

John Wayne: *The Alamo* (1960)

Robert D. Webb: *The Proud Ones* (1956)

William A. Wellman: *The Ox-Bow Incident* (1942; UK title, *Strange*

Incident); *Yellow Sky* (1948); *Across the Wide Missouri* (1951); *Westward the Women* (1952)

Paul Wendkos: *Face of a Fugitive* (1959)

William Wiard: *Tom Horn* (1980)

Hugh Wilson: *Rustler's Rhapsody* (1985)

Richard Wilson: *The Man With a Gun* (1955; UK title, *The Trouble Shooter*); *Invitation to a Gunfighter* (1964)

Simon Wincer: *Lonesome Dove* (1988); *Quigley Down Under* (1990)

Michael Winner: *Lawman* (1971); *Chato's Land* (1972)

Robert Wise: *Blood on the Moon* (1948); *Two Flags West* (1950); *Tribute to a Bad Man* (1956)

William Wyler: *The Westerner* (1940); *Friendly Persuasion* (1956); *The Big Country* (1958)

Robert Young: *The Ballad of Gregorio Cortez* (1982)

Robert Zemeckis: *Back to the Future III* (1990)

Fred Zinnemann: *High Noon* (1952)

Edward Zwick: *Glory* (1989); *Legends of the Fall* (1994); *The Last Samurai* (2003)

Index of Films

Index of Names